NEW DEAL ART
★★★ *in* ★★★
ARIZONA

NEW DEAL ART
★ ★ ★ *in* ★ ★ ★
ARIZONA

BETSY FAHLMAN

THE UNIVERSITY OF ARIZONA PRESS
Tucson

THE UNIVERSITY OF ARIZONA PRESS
© 2009 The Arizona Board of Regents
All rights reserved

www.uapress.arizona.edu

Library of Congress Cataloging-in-Publication Data
Fahlman, Betsy.
New Deal art in Arizona / Betsy Fahlman.
p. cm.
Includes bibliographical references and index.
ISBN 978-0-8165-2292-7 (hard cover)
1. Art, American—Arizona—20th century. 2. New Deal art. 3. Federal Art Project.
I. Title.
N6530.A6F34 2009
709.791'09043—dc22
2009018531

♻

Manufactured in the United States of America on acid-free, archival-quality paper containing
a minimum of 30% post-consumer waste and processed chlorine free.

14   13   12   11   10   09   6   5   4   3   2   1

Frontispiece: Lon Megargee, *Agriculture,* 1934, oil on canvas, 83" × 48½".

For Dan,
The Coolidge Dam and Jerome,
Where the journey began

★ ★ ★

CONTENTS

List of Figures   ix

Acknowledgments   xiii

1. The Government as Patron: Federal Support for the Arts in Arizona   1

2. Arizona Welcomes You: Entering the New Deal   8

3. The Cultural Desert: New Deal Arts Agencies in Arizona   23

4. Art in Public Places: New Deal Murals and Sculpture in Arizona   41

5. The Government Lens: Documentary Photography in Arizona   71

6. The Landscape of Arizona: The Natural and Unnatural Sublime   109

7. The Depression Ends: The World War II Years   128

8. Conclusion: The Legacy of the New Deal in Arizona   149

Notes   155

Selected Bibliography   167

Figure Credits   189

Index   197

FIGURES

1.1   Chart of major New Deal Agencies operating in Arizona, and map of Arizona with locations of major New Deal art activity.   xvi

2.1   Arthur Rothstein, Arizona-New Mexico State Line, March 1940.   9

2.2   Dorothea Lange, Sign near Saint David, May 1937.   10

2.3   Russell Lee, Lineman on telephone pole at Casa Grande Valley Farms, April 1940.   11

2.4   Russell Lee, Tourist court, Phoenix, April 1940.   13

2.5   Hoover Dam, *Arizona Highways,* June 1939.   15

2.6   Lon Megargee and Charles Percy Austin, Mural in the Arizona display at the Century of Progress International Exposition, Chicago, 1933–34.   17

2.7   Russell Lee, Roadside tourist attraction, Maricopa County, April 1940.   18

2.8   Russell Lee, Zoo and Museum, Apache Junction, April 1940.   19

2.9   Russell Lee, Cactus light standard in front of Hotel Westward Ho, Phoenix, May 1940.   19

3.1   Exterior, Phoenix Federal Art Center, 710 East Adams Street.   25

3.2   Interior, Phoenix Federal Art Center.   27

3.3   Creston Baumgartner, Kathleen Wilson, Burdell Tenney, Lew Davis, Raymond Phillips Sanderson, and Sim Bruce Richards, Federal Art Project artists.   28

3.4   Lew Davis, *Underground,* oil painting executed for the Federal Art Project, unlocated.   30

3.5   Cover, *Arizona: A State Guide.*   34

3.6   Ross Santee, 1940.   35

3.7   Elizabeth Johnson, 1942, Brand from the Lazy B Ranch, watercolor.   37

3.8   Russell Lee, Shells of old buildings on the main street, Tombstone, May 1940.   39

4.1   Joseph Morgan Henninger, *Spanish Influence in Arizona,* 1934, oil on canvas, 7' × 16'.   42

4.2   Joseph Morgan Henninger, *Industrial Development in Arizona,* 1934, oil on canvas, 7' × 16'.   43

4.3   Emry Kopta, *Kachina Fountain,* 1934.   44

4.4   Lon Megargee, *Agriculture,* 1934, oil on canvas, 83" × 48½".   46

4.5   Raymond Phillips Sanderson, *Miners' Monument,* 1935, Bisbee.   47

4.6   Raymond Phillips Sanderson, *Miner,* 1939.   48

4.7   Sim Bruce Richards, *Desert Mining Community,* 1937, Pencil and ink on paper, 29" × 11".   49

4.8   Lon Megargee, Phoenix Post Office competition entry, 1937.   50–51

4.9   Lew Davis, Phoenix Post Office competition entry, 1937.   52–53

4.10   Lew Davis, Phoenix Post Office competition entry, 1937.   52–53

4.11   Lew Davis, Phoenix Post Office competition entry, 1937.   54–55

4.12   Lew Davis, Phoenix Post Office competition entry, 1937.   54–55

4.13   Oscar Berninghaus, *Communication during the Period of Exploration,* 1937–38, oil on canvas, 19' wide × 4' 6" high, Post Office, Phoenix.   56

4.14   Oscar Berninghaus, *Pioneer Communication,* 1937–38, oil on canvas, 19' wide × 4' 6" high, Post Office, Phoenix.   56

4.15   Laverne Nelson Black, *Historical Background,* 1937–38, oil on canvas, 19' wide × 4' 6" high, Post Office, Phoenix.   57

4.16   Laverne Nelson Black, *The Progress of the Pioneer,* 1937–1938, oil on canvas, 19' wide × 4' 6" high, Post Office, Phoenix.   57

4.17   Seymour Fogel, 48 States Competition entry for Safford Post Office, 1939.   59

4.18   Seymour Fogel, *The History of the Gila Valley: Migration,* 1939–42, tempera on gesso and plaster, 8' wide × 3' high, Post Office, Safford.   61

4.19   Sim Bruce Richards, Modern dance murals, 1939, 20' high × 70' long, Women's Activity Building (now the Moeur Building), Arizona State University.   63

4.20   John Porter Leeper, *Women in Sports and the Arts,* 1939, oil on canvas, 9' × 24', Women's Activity Building (now the Moeur Building), Arizona State University.   63

4.21   Robert Kittredge, *Apache Chiefs Geronimo and Vittorio,* 1939, plaster relief, 4' diameter, Post Office, Springerville.   64

4.22   Robert Kittredge, *Arizona Logging,* 1940, plaster relief, 6' long × 4½' high, Post Office, Flagstaff (unlocated).   65

4.23   Jay Datus, *Arizona Pageant of Progress,* 1937–38, oil on canvas.   66

4.24   Gerald Nailor at work on *The History and Progress of the Navajo Nation,* Navajo Nation Council Chamber, Window Rock, 1943.   69

5.1   Russell Lee, Municipal golf course, Phoenix, May 1940.   74

5.2   Russell Lee, Salesman demonstrating an electric refrigerator to members of the United Producers' and Consumers' Cooperative of Phoenix, May 1940.   75

5.3   Russell Lee, Agua Fria Farm Security Administration Camp for migratory workers, chart showing occupants of shelters, May 1940.   76

5.4   Russell Lee, Agua Fria Farm Security Administration Camp for migratory workers, view from the water tower, May 1940.   76

5.5   Russell Lee, Migratory laborer and his wife at the Agua Fria FSA Camp, May 1940.   78

5.6   Russell Lee, Migrant agricultural worker planting flowers in front of his metal shelter, Agua Fria FSA Camp, May 1940.   78

5.7 Russell Lee, Operation at Cairns General Hospital, Eleven Mile Corner, February 1942.   79

5.8 Russell Lee, Jitterbug contest, Second Annual Field Day, FSA Camp, Yuma, March 1942.   81

5.9 Russell Lee, Casa Grande Valley Farms, wife of a member displaying canned goods with which she won prizes at the state fair, May 1940.   82

5.10 Russell Lee, Chandler Farms, trench silo, May 1940.   83

5.11 Russell Lee, Chandler Farms, apartment house, May 1940.   84

5.12 Russell Lee, Bisbee, May 1940.   85

5.13 Russell Lee, Sacramento Pit, Bisbee, May 1940.   86

5.14 Russell Lee, Home of a merchant, Concho, September 1940.   86

5.15 Russell Lee, Members of the last remaining Mormon family, Concho, October 1940.   87

5.16 Russell Lee, Taliesin, May 1940.   88

5.17 Russell Lee, WPA work, as visualized by Homer Tate, Safford, May 1940.   89

5.18 Russell Lee, Madonna of the Trail, Springerville, April 1940.   90

5.19 Russell Lee, Marriage mill, Salome, February 1942.   91

5.20 Dorothea Lange, Highway 87 near Coolidge, migratory cotton picker stopped by engine trouble alongside the road, November 1940.   95

5.21 Dorothea Lange, Cortaro Farms, Pinal County, November 1940.   97

5.22 Dorothea Lange, Truckload of cotton pickers from Arkansas, Pinal County, November 1940.   98

5.23 Dorothea Lange, Cotton picker coming down the row, Maricopa County, November 1940.   99

5.24 Dorothea Lange, *Migratory Cotton Picker, Eloy, Arizona,* 1940, gelatin silver print, 10⅜" × 13⅜".   100

5.25 Dorothea Lange, On Highway 87, south of Chandler, November 1940.   101

5.26 Dorothea Lange, Near Coolidge, young girl works in cotton field on Saturday morning, November 1940.   102

5.27 Dorothea Lange, Children in a democracy. Bus carries migratory cotton pickers' children from FSA mobile camp for migratory laborers to the Eloy district school, Pinal County, November 1940.   103

5.28 Dorothea Lange, Children of drought refugee family, Chandler, May 1937.   104

5.29 Dorothea Lange, *Zanjero,* Eloy District, Pinal County, November 1940.   105

5.30 Dorothea Lange, Weighing cotton at the truck, Cortaro Farms, Pinal County, November 1940.   106

5.31 Dorothea Lange, Yaqui Indian cotton picker, Cortaro Farms, Pinal County, November 1940.   107

5.32 Dorothea Lange, Yaqui Indian Jacal, Cortaro Farms, Pinal County, November 1940.   107

6.1 Russell Lee, Copper smelter, Douglas, May 1940.   110

6.2 Ansel Adams, Grand Canyon National Park, 1941.   113

6.3 Russell Lee, Grand Canyon of the Colorado River, October 1940.   114

6.4 Ansel Adams, White House Ruins, Canyon de Chelly, 1941.   115

6.5 Ansel Adams, Navajo woman and infant, Canyon de Chelly, 1941.   116

6.6 Ansel Adams, Walpi, 1941.   117

6.7 Russell Lee, Roosevelt Dam, Gila County, May 1940.   118

6.8 Ansel Adams, Hoover Dam, 1941.   119

6.9 Ben Glaha, Workman with water bag, 1934.   121

6.10 Maynard Dixon, *Tired Men,* 1934, oil on canvas, 25" × 30".   122

6.11 Maynard Dixon, *High Scalers,* 1934, oil on board, 19½" × 15½".   123

6.12 William Gropper, *Construction of the Dam,* 1938–39, oil on canvas, 27¼" × 87¼".   124–125

7.1 Jack Delano, Train load of military tanks on the Atchison, Topeka and Santa Fe Railway, March 1943.   131

7.2 Jack Delano, Young Indian laborer working in the Atchison, Topeka and Santa Fe Railway yard, Winslow, March 1943.   132

7.3 Fritz Henle, Open-pit copper mine of the Phelps Dodge Mining Corporation, Morenci, December 1942.   133

7.4 Fritz Henle, Electric shovel, open-pit copper mine, Morenci, December 1942.   134

7.5 Fritz Henle, Phelps Dodge Mining Corporation workers, Morenci, December 1942.   135

7.6 Russell Lee, Morenci copper mine mill, May 1940.   136

7.7 Toyo Miyatake, *Garden of Native Cactus,* Gila River, c. 1944–45.   140

7.8 Isamu Noguchi, Plans for Poston Cemetery, 1942, blueprint.   142

7.9 Lew Davis, *The Founding of Fort Huachuca,* 1943, oil on board, 8' high × 12' wide.   144

7.10 Lew Davis, *The Negro in America's Wars,* 1944, oil on board, 60" × 144".   144–145

7.11 Art Workshop, Fort Huachuca, Sergeants Dillard and Shearer assist Sergeant Lew Davis in finishing *The Surrender of Geronimo.*   146

7.12 Lew Davis, *History Will Judge Us by Our Deeds,* c. 1943, silkscreen poster, 21" × 15".   147

8.1 Dorothea Lange, Saturday afternoon, Eloy, November 1940.   150

8.2 Fritz Henle, Guard, Phelps Dodge copper mine, Morenci, December 1942.   151

8.3 Russell Lee, A member of the Chandler Farms FSA part-time farming and cooperative project, with his wife and child, May 1940.   152

ACKNOWLEDGMENTS

I came to Arizona State University in 1988, and several years later commenced the research that became this book. As a New Hampshire native who had lived on the Chesapeake Bay for eight years, moving west proved a great adventure. I encountered a region totally new to me, and extensive travel throughout the state as a member of the Speakers Bureau of the Arizona Humanities Council enabled me to get under the skin of the large desert state that had become my home. Personal and state artistic identity thus became intertwined.

At the University of Arizona Press, I want to thank Chris Szuter, former director of the press, who enthusiastically encouraged this project as it began. Patti Hartmann was patiently supportive throughout the process of completing the manuscript. It has been a pleasure to work with Kristen Buckles, who took over the process of shepherding the book to publication. Thanks also to other staff members who assisted me, especially Al Schroder. It was a pleasure to work with my copyeditor, Ken Plax, whose careful attention to detail strengthened the text considerably. I am also grateful for the close readings given the manuscript by my four anonymous readers. Their suggestions have strengthened it immensely, and I appreciate the time they took on my behalf.

A researcher owes many debts of gratitude, and while I cannot acknowledge all those who have aided me, I would like to thank especially Cristin O'Keefe Aptowicz, Ana Archuleta, Lynne Aspnes, Scott Baker, Jim Ballinger, Evelyn Barnes, LaRee Bates, the late Peter Bermingham, Beverly Brannon, Susan Bryan, Sarah Burt, Cecilia Chin, Heidi Coleman, Andrew Connors, Dianne Cripe, Keith and Kathryn Cunningham, Donnelyn Curtis, the late Philip C. Curtis, Pete Daniel, the late Jack Delano, Bruce Dinges, Robin Doolin, Lonnie Dunbier, Fran Elliott, Peter Ensenberger, Ed Evans, James A. Findlay, Lois Fink, Eric Firestone, Kathryn A. Flynn, Roy Fluckinger, Merry Forresta, Susan Fukushima, Leslie Green, Steve Gregory, Donald Hagerty, Lise Hawkos, Abe and Gregory Hays, the late Fritz Henle, the late Therese Thau Heyman, Peter Huestis, Peter Iverson, Naomi Jackson, Bill Jay, Kirsten Jensen, Drew Johnson, Eileen Johnston, Stephanie Jones, Eunice Kahn, Mario Klimiades, Helen Langa, the late Jean Lee, David Lembeck, Tricia Loscher, Barbara Buhler Lynes, Christine Marin, James McBride, Edward McCarter, Brenda McClain, Ron McCoy, Archie and Alan Miyatake, Katherine Morrissey, Nick Natanson, Barbara Ohrbach, Sarah O'Mahen, Richard Pearce-Moses, Gerald Peters, Sandy Phillips, Holly Reed, Robert Reid, Donna Reiner, Janet Richards, Jeremy Rowe, Richard Rudisill, Adrienne Schiffner,

Pamela Scott, Tom Sheridan, Earle G. Shettleworth, Jr., Pamela Simpson, Ashley M. Smith, Thomas B. Smith, Richard Sorensen, Robert P. Spindler, David Tatum, Sharyn Udall, Emily Umberger, Amy Verheide, Manuelito Weaver, Catherine Whitney, Richard Guy Wilson, Nancy Kirkpatrick Wright, Mandy York, and Marian Yoshiki-Kovinick.

I offer a special thanks to Anne Gully, who cast a sharp editorial eye over several drafts of this manuscript, as well as to Susan Selkirk, who designed my map and chart. I am grateful also to Rachel Leibowitz, who generously shared unpublished material on Gerald Nailor from her dissertation.

I would also like to thank the staffs of several research institutions: Archives of American Art; Arizona Historical Society; Arizona State Archives, Department of Library, Archives, and Public Records; Arizona State University Archives; Center for Creative Photography, University of Arizona; Fort Huachuca Museum; Harry Ransom Research Center, University of Texas at Austin; Howard University Art Gallery; Library of Congress; National Archives and Records Administration; Photographic Archives, Northern Arizona University; Japanese National Museum; Northern Arizona University, Special Collections, Cline Library; Photographic Archives, University of Louisville; Smithsonian American Art Museum; Southwest Art History Council; and the Southwestern Writers Collection, Southwest Texas State University, San Marcos.

Most of all I thank my husband, Daniel H. Ball, who happily entered the orbit of my life and research and has cheerfully undertaken many unsought tasks, large and small. This book is dedicated to him.

Grants from Arizona State University, the Herberger College of the Arts, the Arizona Humanities Council, and the Smithsonian Institution have supported this research. A publication grant from the Society for the Preservation of American Modernists defrayed the costs of acquiring illustrations, and I am most grateful for their support.

NEW DEAL ART
★ ★ ★ *in* ★ ★ ★
ARIZONA

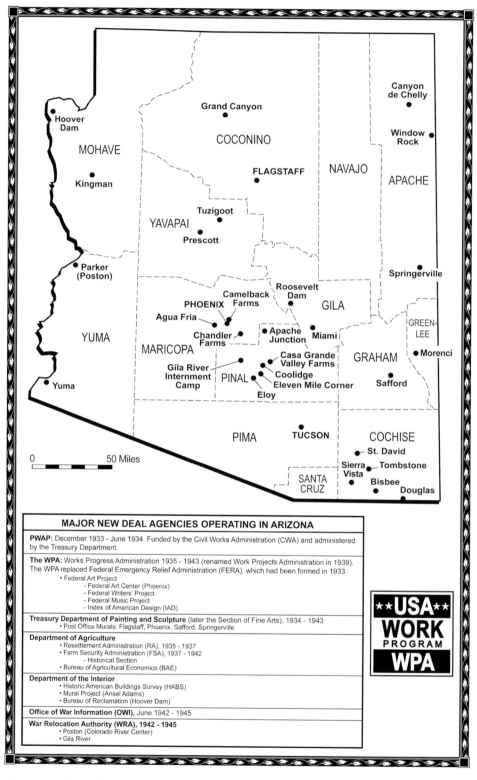

FIGURE 1.1. Chart of major New Deal agencies operating in Arizona, and a map of Arizona with locations of major New Deal art activity.

CHAPTER 1

THE GOVERNMENT AS PATRON
Federal Support for the Arts in Arizona

This book explores the federal cultural initiatives implemented in Arizona during the New Deal era, which spans the twelve years between 1933, when Franklin Delano Roosevelt became president, and 1945, when World War II ended. Despite the immense social and economic upheaval that rocked the nation, significant new opportunities emerged for artists in every state during the Depression; Arizona was no exception. While this is a study of the arts in Arizona, of the artists discussed, only one was a native of the state, though several others spent substantial portions of their careers here.

In 1935, Roosevelt's administration commenced a major effort of governmental cultural support by implementing a series of relief programs (known as "alphabet agencies" for their many acronyms), and Arizona was a beneficiary of these efforts. The photographers, painters, writers, musicians, and arts administrators who were employed by government agencies were the impetus for a broad range of artistic production during the thirties and forties, and their art served a distinctly public purpose. Because agencies established programs in every state, the overarching umbrella of federal art patronage meant that those American artists who received government support participated in an implicit national cultural agenda, linked by a remarkable consistency of representational styles and coherent themes, albeit with considerable regional variation. For a relatively modest investment, the country got a great deal of fine art that was distributed nationwide in post offices and other federal buildings.

Many New Deal cultural agencies operated in Arizona during this period (fig. 1.1). Some were specifically mandated to support the arts, while others employed artists to document government activities or to record significant artifacts of cultural heritage. The view of the state acquired from a consideration of artistic production depends on the agency that sponsored it. A state map plotted with the sites of government patronage is a decidedly skewed one. Except for a photograph Dorothea Lange took for the Farm Security Administration of the Labor Temple (whose arena was the site of professional wrestling and boxing matches), Tucson is largely absent from the Farm Security Administration photographs, yet the nearby mission church of San Xavier del Bac dominates the efforts of the Historic American Buildings Survey. Flagstaff was the site of a post office mural, but mostly it was a busy place through which many freight trains passed. Muralists and photographers seldom worked in the same places, and when they did, the images they portrayed diverge sharply in content. A mural installed in a government building is permanent, whereas a documentary photograph is unpredictably viewed in shifting contexts.

People as well as places are missing from the map. Despite the vast acreage of reservation land, Native Americans have little presence in the works sponsored by the agencies considered in this study, though photographers occasionally documented Native Americans when they worked off-reservation, and painters celebrated their idealized counterparts in murals. The Hispanic community is similarly invisible, except as economically vulnerable migratory labor. Only in a series of photographs of Concho do they have a substantial presence.[1] The African Americans who picked cotton and lived in segregated camps are similarly marginalized but surprisingly are celebrated during World War II at Fort Huachuca. The internment camps were the site of Asian American artistic activity.

The government as the patron negotiates the perspective of all federally sponsored works, and I consider the photographs, sculptures, and paintings created in Arizona during this period against a broad cultural backdrop of thirties art in a single state. In the case of the Farm Security Administration/Office of War Information (FSA/OWI), photographers were artists and skilled professionals first, and documentarians employed by the federal government second. That point of view was not necessarily their employers', but it was fundamental to the artists' identity.[2] The stark black and white of the photographs conveys a strong impression of fact whose truth appears convincingly grounded in the particularity of time and place. Taken together with their contemporaries, the muralists who also produced work in a public context and with government support, the photographers made equally artful images, yet as viewers we recognize the obvious artifice in a painting more readily than in a "documentary" photograph. But whether it was produced with a camera or a paintbrush, the art was all propaganda in the most fundamental sense, and its purpose was to convey official information as part of an intensive program of governmentally sponsored artistic production.

This book is about New Deal artists working in Arizona—makers of images—whose photographs, paintings, and sculpture are seen through a lens that is dually broad and narrow. Histories are inevitably selective and constructed endeavors, and the chronicle as written and pictured is not the same. My intention has not been to write a history of the New Deal in Arizona, but rather to consider what the chronicle of the visual arts can reveal about this era that histories not grounded in works of art cannot. For instance, the Taylor Grazing Act of 1934 had a significant impact on Arizona and other large western ranching states, but it is hard to find its effects in FSA photographs or WPA murals. Works of art reconstruct history in fascinating ways, and the "facts" of history may be read with different emphasis in a painting or photograph than on the page.

The literature on the art of the New Deal era is extensive, and a series of imaginative studies have explored this topic from a national perspective.[3] At the state level, publication in the area of photography has been particularly active, and my approach to the Arizona chronicle has been shaped by these previous studies.[4] While this story is emphatically state-based, my aim has been to avoid the pitfalls inherent in these other studies. The many volumes that have derived from the readily accessible FSA/OWI collections of the Library of Congress are a case in point. Available online, an impressive body of fascinating images may be efficiently assembled into a well-illustrated album. But the formulaic nature of many such publications has meant that the similarities of content and presentation have had the unintentional effect of flattening the regional vibrancy of art from a period that constitutes one of the most remarkable in the entire history of American art. Horizontal in format, and preceded by a historical introduction, they are organized thematically, echoing the taxonomy of the thesaurus that governed the original organization of the file when it became part of the collections of the Library of Congress during the 1940s. Such historical studies generally emphasize the imagery, rather than the artists who made them, thus submerging their fundamental identity as works of art, as well as the intentionality of those who made them. Rephotographic projects, enriched by interviews with thirties survivors, match up historical images with contemporary scenes, some of which have been altered beyond recognition, while others retain a palimpsest of the Depression. But the history as nostalgia approach that is the trap of such studies can deflect the resonant visual evidence these images as works of art can provide.

Oddly disengaged from the broader history of art, rarely do these state-focused photographic studies consider the painters and sculptors who were the cultural contemporaries of the FSA/OWI photographers. Publications on New Deal murals often fail as well to reference photographers. There are relatively few state-based mural studies, but that they have been grounded within the broader history of American art has meant that their cultural analysis of the paintings has generally been more sophisticated than the photographic studies, in large part because the authors are conscious of their subjects as practicing artists.[5]

In integrating works in several media and considering them from a state-based perspective, this book is therefore an intellectual hybrid. By foregrounding the artists and their photographs, paintings, and sculpture, I am asserting that they were active participants in a broad governmental effort of cultural production, as opposed to being illustrative adjuncts to historical analysis, so that their roles may be better understood. Further, taking an intermedia, an interdisciplinary, and an interagency approach to the study of New Deal art in Arizona, and explicating the larger art historical and cultural context in which these images were produced, permits a richer understanding of this work and the period during which it was made.

My study of New Deal art in Arizona is supported by a wealth of previously unpublished material, yet I acknowledge that it is only a partial history. Because the holdings in federal archives are so extensive, it was necessary to leave some parts of the story out, mainly in the area of documentary photography. Other significant bodies of Arizona photographic work sponsored by government agencies include images produced for the Bureau of Reclamation, the Bureau of Indian Affairs (until 1947 the Office of Indian Affairs), and the War Relocation Authority, all of which are deserving of separate study. These agencies are discussed but not in the depth given other art patronage.

I have organized this book thematically, and each chapter considers a particular aspect of federal art patronage in Arizona under the New Deal, a period during which the government emerged as a significant cultural patron. In "The Cultural Desert: New Deal Arts Agencies in Arizona," I discuss a range of government cultural initiatives. The Arizona Federal Art Center that opened in Phoenix in 1937, headed by painter Philip C. Curtis, presented exhibitions, and local artists taught classes to adults and children. Ross Santee, a noted Western writer and illustrator, headed the Federal Writers' Project in the state, whose most important effort was the publication of the *Arizona Guide* in 1940. Other cultural initiatives included the Index of American Design, which recorded objects of everyday use, and the Historic American Buildings Survey, which employed architects, draftsmen, and photographers to record historic structures. The Civil Works Administration assisted in the restoration of archaeological sites and the construction of museums to exhibit the artifacts that were unearthed. The Federal Music Project provided work for unemployed musicians and entertainment for the general public.

Painting and sculpture were important areas of New Deal support, and their chronicle, the subject of "Art in Public Places: New Deal Murals and Sculpture in Arizona," provides telling parallels and contrasts to work produced by government-sponsored documentary photographers. The FSA/OWI photographs were taken of the state and distributed nationwide from agencies in Washington, D.C., whereas murals were installed within the state, though administered from the capital. Arizona artists entered national competitions. While works were executed in every state, there was no guarantee that commissions would go to resident artists as the blind judging that made the large national competitions more democratic prevented selection committees from deliberately choosing artists who lived in the states where the murals were to be installed. However, smaller commissions could be awarded on the basis of the artistic merit of submissions to larger competitions.

The most notable works funded by this agency remain the post office murals. Executed in every state, they celebrated local and regional history, or historical events related to communication and mail delivery. Budgets did not permit on-site research, and therefore, artists depended on secondary sources for information, which necessarily meant they dealt with broad themes and archetypes. One artist relied on children's books for handy summaries of history. The result for commissions in Arizona was often generic Southwestern imagery. Artists worked at a distance, most showing up only to install their murals that were painted on canvas, making transportation straightforward. Those murals portraying modern scenes are especially interesting as they present a contemporary perspective on current events, even as they construct new state symbols.

Murals and sculpture commissioned for public buildings throughout the state were embellishments that enjoyed great visibility. The Public Works of Art Project (PWAP) provided the first government support for the visual arts in the state, and funded works were installed at the Arizona State Teacher's College, the State Capitol, and in Bisbee. Post office murals were connected with new construction or renovation, and as a result relatively few were executed in Arizona, though the number was typical for a large western state with few urban centers and a sparse rural population. A national competition was held for the Phoenix Post Office in 1937, and from the thirty entries submitted, Oscar Berninghaus and Laverne Nelson Black were selected. Robert Kittredge produced sculpted reliefs for post offices in Springerville (1939) and Flagstaff (1940). The 48 States Competition, held in 1939, was won by New York artist Seymour Fogel, and the controversy his Safford mural generated in that community is an interesting one. Federal funds supported murals by Jay Datus in the State Library and Archives in Phoenix (1937–38). Working for the Civil Works Administration, Gerald Nailor executed a series of murals in the new Navajo Nation Council Chamber in Window Rock (1942–43).

Photography was a significant area of government artistic patronage and is explored in "The Government Lens: Documentary Photography in Arizona." The most famous body of work was created by the FSA, an agency whose mandate was to alleviate rural poverty and the effects of the dislocation of agricultural workers caused by farm mechanization. To document and promote its programs and to highlight where aid was needed, the FSA established a Historical Section to make a visual record of its activities. While most large Washington agencies also did this, only the FSA transcended bureaucratic mandates in compiling a national archive created by America's leading photographers. Although they were officially tasked to provide documentation of federally sponsored programs rather than to create works of fine art, that these photographers were skilled artists makes their images resonant beyond mere snapshots of record.

Two agencies, the Farm Security Administration and the Bureau of Agricultural Economics, sponsored extensive coverage of Arizona. Russell Lee and Dorothea Lange—two of America's most notable documentary photographers—both worked for the FSA, though Lee's work in the state was far more extensive than hers. Lange's most important Arizona photography was done for the Bureau of Agricultural Economics. In several series, Lee conveyed the multiple ways in which people constructed a sense of community, however temporary. Impelled by a strong sense of social justice, Lange exposed the unsettled plight of the migratory laborer.

No subject offered such stunning visual possibilities as did the landscape of the American West, and the conventions of its portrayal were deeply rooted in the nineteenth century. Arizona's geologically impressive features inspired many artists, most notably Thomas Moran, whose huge canvases captured the immense scale and rich color of the Grand Canyon. His magisterial renditions are thoroughly grounded in the ideologies of westward expansion. This subject is explored in "The Landscape of Arizona: The Natural and Unnatural Sublime."

Federal patronage and landscape had been inextricably linked since the nineteenth century. In 1871, Moran made his first journey west, as part of F. V. Hayden's Yellowstone expedition. His panoramic canvas *The Grand Canyon of the Yellowstone* (1872), was seen by John Wesley Powell, famed explorer of the Grand Canyon, who invited Moran to Arizona in 1873. The painting that resulted, *The Chasm of the Colorado* (1873–74), was purchased by Congress as a pendant to his earlier one of Yellowstone and both were hung in the Senate lobby of the United States Capitol.[6] Congress paid the artist $10,000 for each. Government-sponsored surveys such as Hayden's and Powell's included painters and photographers, and although Moran was not an official member of the second survey, that his work was purchased by the government for such an impressive price and installed in the nation's most important federal building gave them ample official sanction.

The Department of the Interior and the Bureau of Reclamation (administratively part of Interior) were the sources of extensive art patronage. Some artists were hired to document the massive public works projects of this era, and in Arizona efforts were focused on the Hoover Dam. Ben Glaha photographed the entire construction process, and painter Maynard Dixon made canvases of similar scenes. William Gropper was commissioned to do a mural inspired in part by the dam for the Department of the Interior's Washington headquarters.

No modern photographer is more identified with imaging the American West than Ansel Adams, and his Arizona work is strongly linked with the nineteenth-century landscape traditions exemplifying the Manifest Destiny that was regarded as the foundation of democratic institutions, as well as with twentieth-century environmental activism spurred by his long involvement with the Sierra Club. A California native, he began his professional career in the 1920s with a series of handsome views of Yosemite National Park. Commercial work brought him extensive commissions, and his role in the marketplace, which included the Yosemite concession operated by his wife's family, reflects the strong role of tourism in establishing his reputation.

There was an ongoing tension between the implicit activism for change in the work made by the FSA photographers and that done by those, like Ansel Adams, whose content was grounded in rigorous formal terms, though both groups received government patronage. For Adams, social purpose found its outlet in the vastness of the American landscape, in which political and aesthetic aims were intertwined. Preferring wilderness to people, he contemplated the human relationship within the vast spaces of the American western landscape. The region resonated deeply with him, representing a profound spiritual and moral truth. But despite his near mystical photographic paeans to undeveloped regions, human intervention was usually never far away. Much of what he portrayed was a landscape well intersected with human activity, though his photographs represent it as disconnected from civilization. Rarely able to document actual wilderness, he created it in his prints.

His work for the Department of the Interior on the Mural Project exemplifies the complexities with which he had to negotiate his professional career and personal image, balancing his need for patronage, his deep belief in American democratic institutions, and his love of the natural wonders of the West. The Department of the Interior had oversight of several departments critically influential on the region, including the Bureau of Reclamation, the Office of Indian Affairs, and the National Park Service. Because it generated many of the big public works projects undertaken during this period, Interior, of all federal agencies, had the greatest impact on the modern West through its policies. Although on the surface, Adams's gorgeous black-and-white prints of awe-inspiring nature contrast with the quotidian pathos recorded by the FSA photographers and the obvious artfulness of the mural painters, his perspective was as officially sanctioned as theirs.

"The Depression Ends: The World War II Years," chronicles art production in Arizona during the war years. Two photographers—Jack Delano and Fritz Henle—worked for the OWI, the agency that succeeded the FSA. The internment of Japanese Americans is an important part of the chronicle, and the experiences of photographer Toyo Miyatake and sculptor Isamu Noguchi with the War Relocation Authority are instructive. I end with a series of remarkable paintings and work-incentive posters portraying African Americans executed by Lew Davis under Army sponsorship at Fort Huachuca.

As this chronicle will reveal, Arizona's New Deal legacy is a significant one and represents an important chapter in the state's art history. This volume therefore reclaims a richly textured story of Arizona between statehood and the post–World War II boom.

CHAPTER 2

ARIZONA WELCOMES YOU
Entering the New Deal

In March 1940 Arthur Rothstein, traveling between New Mexico and
California, stopped to photograph the sign welcoming visitors at the
Arizona-New Mexico border on the eastern edge of the state (fig. 2.1). His
image could be regarded as an ordinary tourist snapshot; one might think he was
merely gauging a journey's progress by recording a milestone en route, while taking the opportunity to break the tedium of travel on long western highways by
getting out of the car to look around and stretch his legs.

But what Rothstein, who was then employed by one of the many New Deal
agencies established during the Depression, recorded was also a cultural marker
as well, one demarcating more than a geographical boundary between two states.
Historical borders, simultaneously artificial and real, have long defined Arizona's
cultural history. At the north, the Grand Canyon—the state's signature emblem—
provides an emphatic edge, separating Arizona from Utah. The Colorado River
that made the canyon flows between California and Nevada to the west and has
been the site of massive federal works projects, like the Hoover Dam, providing
flood control, electricity, and irrigation. From the south, migratory laborers still
journey north from Mexico in search of work, legally and illegally. That border
remains highly permeable, both physically and politically.

Rothstein, traveling west on Route 66, one of America's most famous
roads, entered the realm of New Deal Arizona, then in the midst of the Great
Depression. What would he and other artists find when they got here? What they
saw and how they portrayed it would vary depending on which agency sponsored them.

For those seeking employment within the state (whether resident or transient), the sign photographed by Dorothea Lange in May 1937, "For Sale, This
Place And Cow" (fig. 2.2) conveyed a more local reality than the welcoming landmark that Rothstein recorded. Portrayed is about the lowest economic common
denominator possible in an unpromising landscape. Communication is basic, the
desired transaction simple, and the situation urgent.

Figure 2.1. Arthur Rothstein, Arizona-New Mexico State Line, March 1940.

FIGURE 2.2. Dorothea Lange, Sign near Saint David, May 1937.

Transients and travelers known as "automobile gypsies"[1] and bindlestiffs were familiar sights along the road. While the tourists who were welcomed by Rothstein's sign must have seen the caravans of migratory laborers traveling through Arizona in search of work, their social spheres did not significantly intersect. Recognizing the tension of hope and hopelessness implicit in the nature of the two signs photographed by Rothstein and Lange is fundamental to understanding the Depression in Arizona. Tourists, residents, and migratory laborers all had different perspectives, and in describing the historical and cultural context of Depression-era Arizona, I set the foundation in this chapter for those that follow.

FIGURE 2.3. Russell Lee, Lineman on telephone pole at Casa Grande Valley Farms, April 1940.

The Depression Begins in Arizona

If the Depression began dramatically on the East Coast with the great stock market crash on October 24, 1929, triggering a series of "black" days of financial panic, its commencement in Arizona was quiet, and neither the Tucson nor the Phoenix newspapers gave any sign of what would soon be recognized as a national economic disaster. A headline appearing in Arizona the day before the crash declared with bullish pride: "Business Good in Arizona." Sharp swings had long been characteristic of the state's economy, and the events unfolding on Wall Street must have seemed as remote to Arizonans as their ordinary concerns were to Manhattanites. Only once during the first week of the growing panic did the situation even merit a headline on the front page.

The editorial stance of the *Arizona Republican,* the major newspaper in the state's capital and largest city, was attuned to the concerns of their readership and emphatically local in focus. Reporters expressed a cautious optimism that the economic shifts occurring in the East would prove to be only temporary. At a far remove from major eastern financial centers, a state like Arizona barely flickered on the mental radar of the country's leading capitalists. That the state had scant direct connection with financial powers on either coast is referenced in Robert Emmet Sherwood's 1935 play, *The Petrified Forest,* when a character in this Arizona desert melodrama identified only as "First Lineman" comments: "What do we do—day after day? We climb up poles, and fix the wires, so that some broker in New York can telegraph in a split second to some guy in Los Angeles to tell him he's ruined."[2] Farm Security Administration photographer Russell Lee captured the essence of these words in his photograph of a telephone lineman at Casa Grande Valley Farms in Pinal County (fig. 2.3). The arrival of modern communication amenities increased the efficiency with which some learned of their economic collapse.

The devastation experienced in the West generally, and in Arizona specifically, was not defined by state borders. Citizens on the move further blurred the economics of boundaries, as did the sparse population base and the geographical expanses characteristic of the large western states. By the time Franklin Delano Roosevelt became president in 1933 at the nadir of the Depression, the situation in the state was desperate. While Arizona's chronicle parallels the national story, distinctive challenges included an economy dominated by the copper industry, a large Native American population, the presence of the federal government as the state's largest landowner, and the steady consolidation of economic power in the hands of an increasingly small number of people. The federal government intersected more and more with many areas of daily life, and local concerns reflected broad trends nationwide, as issues of regional identity defined themselves within a national context.

Some of the standard Arizona histories have minimized the Depression's severity in this state, and typical is the optimistic tone of C. Leland Sonnichsen's declaration in his boosterish history of Tucson, "No city in the nation handled the Depression better,"[3] a statement improbably balanced with the observation that Arizona's poorest residents felt the impact of thirties economic devastation less than others: "Probably the Yaquis suffered less than their American neighbors during the Depression. They were used to doing without and living from day to day."[4] Other accounts have blandly asserted: "The Great Depression slowed progress and brought some problems"[5] to Phoenix. Such views are not supported by the visual evidence, and Sonnichsen's conclusion that "by 1935 the worst times were over"[6] would have been news to the subjects of photographs taken by Lange and Lee. Nor would members of the Hispanic, Asian, and Indian communities in Tucson have believed that the city's charities "rose above political issues and racial prejudice."[7] The existence of shantytowns known as Hoovervilles, populated by the homeless and the unemployed not far from the city center of Phoenix, reveals people at the end of their resources. Documentary photographs in the files of the Farm Security Administration and the Bureau of Agricultural Economics starkly show the ongoing effects of the Depression. Cotton and copper prices fell, unemployment was up, tax revenues were down, and banks failed.

The Landscape of Tourism

Tourism, recognized even then as a significant economic engine for the state, is an important thematic thread in this chronicle. How an individual experienced the Depression in Arizona depended on whether one came to the state for work or for leisure. The image portrayed outside the state to entice visitors did not reveal economic crisis. For those able to afford it, tourism had expanded throughout the twenties and thirties, as evidenced by the construction of luxury accommodations

FIGURE 2.4. Russell Lee, Tourist court, Phoenix, April 1940.

in the Phoenix area, and dude ranches were popular in outlying communities. At the Grand Canyon National Park, Mary Jane Colter continued to design "parkitecture" on the South Rim throughout the thirties, including the Desert View Watch Tower (1933) and the Bright Angel Lodge (1936). Civic leaders in the "Valley of the Sun," as the Phoenix area came to be known, realizing that "sunshine is one of Arizona's greatest assets,"[8] began promoting the state as an attractive winter destination and health mecca during this period.

That the tourist industry statewide experienced downturns during this period is documented in Russell Lee's photograph of the cabins at a "Cottage Court" in Phoenix in 1940 (fig. 2.4). The sparse vegetation surrounded by stones, some of which have been painted white, is not especially welcoming. Shot in April, the dusty expanses of dirt that comprise its landscaping reminds visitors that the summer heat will soon come, contrasting with the scenes of lakes, snow-capped mountains, and cool woods that have been painted on the sign over the entrance. The economics of small operations like this one were shaky, as the sign "Auto Court For Sale" indicates. Motel owners who could not sustain a living from vacationers, as a last resort rented out rooms to migratory laborers and their families.

Tourism was aided by road improvements. The federal government continued to expand the national highway system, and automobile travel throughout the state was encouraged by a range of attractive promotional materials designed to lure visitors west. A key player in this effort was the highly pictorial magazine *Arizona Highways*.[9] Published by the state's Highway Commission, its motto was "Civilization Follows the Improved Highway," reinforcing that its underlying purpose was connected to the continued expansion of the federal highway system nationwide, which in turn was directly linked to the tourist economy. *Arizona Highways* was founded in 1921 as a newsletter and transformed into a magazine in 1925; it was under the editorship of Raymond Carlson beginning in 1938 that the matrix for the scenic travel magazine was established. Its goals would be reinforced by the WPA guide to the state, published in 1940.

Arizona Highways began to emphasize its signature staples of tourism, travel, and scenery during the New Deal years. Carlson began to include more photographs and articles on places to visit in order to promote the romantic West of landscape and Native peoples. The Depression was scarcely evident on its pages, as one of its writers declared in 1934: "Arizona has forked the 'New Deal' bronc and is riding high, wide and handsome; . . . Prosperity in Arizona is *not* around the corner—we've got it out in the open and are running it down."[10] From the start, photography was central to its mission.

The agendas of government agencies and tourism intersected in the areas of recreation and flood control. In June 1939, a photograph of a group of young women on the rocks below the Hoover Dam waving at a TWA airplane flying above was published on the inside front cover of *Arizona Highways* (fig. 2.5). In its optimistic tone, the image represents a harbinger of the end of the Depression in this state. It also references the modes of transportation that would spur the tourist industry that had lagged over the previous decade—the automobile and the airplane gradually supplanted the railroad as the preferred means of American leisure travel. It was "Motoring America" speeding over the dam on U.S. Highway 93, passengers comfortably seated inside consulting their guidebooks as to points of interest, that realized the magazine's fundamental purpose.

The Grand Canyon remains the state's most famous landscape feature, inspiring painters and photographers alike and, as a result of assiduous marketing by the Santa Fe Railroad in partnership with the Fred Harvey Company, was a mecca for tourists eager to experience the ethnic and scenic richness of northern Arizona.[11] Its apparent timeless grandeur might appear impervious to something so earthbound as the Depression. But the tourist industry suffered economic fluctuations during the thirties, and gas rationing during World War II further cut the number of visitors.

Arizona and Popular Culture

The popular view of Arizona was crafted by writers, painters, photographers, and filmmakers, whose chief symbols have been, as Lawrence Clark Powell noted in his Bicentennial history: "cavalry soldiers and cowboys, the Grand Canyon and the Painted Desert, Saguaros at sunset, Indian dances and anglo rodeos, bad men, sheriffs, and shoot-outs."[12] An iconography of state identity was established

FIGURE 2.5. Hoover Dam, *Arizona Highways,* June 1939.

at statehood when Lon Megargee was commissioned to paint a series of fifteen large canvases for the State Capitol building whose subjects broadly summarize Arizona, encompassing its spectacular landscape and natural wonders, the structures and customs of its indigenous Native American peoples, artifacts of Spanish colonial settlement, and the agriculture, mining, and ranching that sustained its early settlers.[13] These themes paralleled the imagery of the state seal and infused the work of New Deal artists.

Interest in the American West as spectacle and entertainment had long been developed by novelists. Their conventions were continued in the Hollywood Western, which, rooted in Buffalo Bill Cody's Wild West shows, reinforced popular ideas of the romance of good cowboys and bad Indians. The visual analogues of the large-scale mythmaking typical of the movies may be found in mural paintings, and both featured standard themes and stock characters such as pioneer settlers, gunfighters, outlaws, and singing cowboys.

Their elaborate artifice corresponded to popular displays of southwestern culture. The Century of Progress International Exposition opened in Chicago in 1933, and its dazzling light displays, pleasant lagoons, and impressive modernist buildings represented a symbol of hope to a nation in the depths of the Depression. The Arizona display was organized by Southwest trader, art patron, and former Phoenix City Manager Fred Wilson and celebrated Arizona's progress over two decades of statehood. Signage lauded Arizona as the "Land of Romance" and the "Land of Sunshine," presenting it as a place of possibility: "Come to Arizona, the youngest state in the Union, where opportunities are still unlimited."

A series of canvases jointly executed by Megargee and Charles Percy Austin portrayed major state symbols. Most splendid was a large mural installed at the entrance to the Arizona exhibit in "The Court of States" (fig. 2.6). Set against a backdrop of the snowy peaks of the San Francisco Mountains and set off by impressive sunlit clouds, modern Arizona is spread out in the foreground. Flanking either side, the typical structures of agribusiness and mining suggest a strong economy. At the center are several figures whose outfits imply the wealth and leisure that it made possible, including a polo player mounted on his horse (an unusual element for a state whose image is strongly shaped by the cowboy), a fisherman with gear and tackle (alluding to the state's lakes and rivers), and a photographer with his camera on a tripod, ready to record Arizona's many photogenic scenes. Recognizable modern and historic buildings include Mission San Xavier del Bac in Tucson, the Hotel Westward Ho in Phoenix, and the Arizona Temple of the Church of the Latter Day Saints in Mesa. The mural embodies the major archetypes of Arizona that were the essence of cultural tourism. The Great Depression is nowhere to be seen in this artful billboard designed to lure gainfully employed visitors to the state.

As in literature, frontier themes dominated the movies that presented stories of action and adventure worthy of a Frederic Remington painting, exemplified

FIGURE 2.6. Lon Megargee and Charles Percy Austin, Mural in the Arizona display at the Century of Progress International Exposition, Chicago, 1933–34.

by his stirring equestrian masterpiece *A Dash for the Timber* (1889, Amon Carter Museum) that had been inspired by his southwestern travels (he first came to Arizona in 1885).[14] Such imagery is echoed in the novels of Zane Grey, who visited Arizona in 1907, and who made annual trips to his lodge in Arizona's Tonto Basin between 1918 and 1929. The mythological and formulaic epic masculine Western movie and novel held strong throughout the first half of the twentieth century, their conventional plots providing a welcome escape from the economic distress of the Depression. Their popularity bolstered by widely distributed Western pulp magazines, the images that flickered on the silver screen were comfortably predictable.

As a result of the energetic growth of the big Hollywood studios, Arizona was used extensively by moviemakers beginning in the 1920s, and the movie industry continued to grow in the state during the thirties. The public flocked to films, enjoying entertainments that were both popular and populist. Constructed in 1939 for the filming of *Arizona,* the sets of Old Tucson were regularly used by California casts and crews. But the production that made the state famous in terms of movie making was John Ford's classic 1939 film *Stagecoach,* starring John Wayne. The film was set against the spectacular landscape of Monument Valley, and the director knew his art history: "I tried to copy the Frederic Remington style."[15]

FIGURE 2.7. Russell Lee, Roadside tourist attraction, Maricopa County, April 1940.

The fictional portrayals of literature, movies, and expositions helped attract tourists to the state, and visitor expectations created a lively industry that catered to their needs. Russell Lee's photograph of a roadside attraction on the main road into Phoenix (fig. 2.7) prominently features Arizona stereotypes. On either side of the path leading to the building where souvenirs may be purchased are cacti and century plants in an arid desert setting. The cactus nurseries promise an ample supply of typical state plants (which will not thrive in the visitors' home states). The sign advertising "Reptile Gardens" is entwined with the rattlesnakes associated with the region.

Tourist traps abounded throughout the state, and they presented a broad array of artifacts of popular visual culture. In Apache Junction, Lee stopped at the "Zoo and Museum" there, which featured wildlife, including monkeys, rattlesnakes, Gila monsters, mountain lions, lynx, bears, and deer (fig. 2.8). He took pictures of papier-mâché figures of a prehistoric man (the WPA Guide noted the "hairy aborigines"[16] who were the state's first residents), an Indian, and a prospector, each of which represented the three stages of the state's development.

The saguaro cactus, which grows only in the Sonoran desert of Arizona and northern Mexico, remains a state symbol. An unusual adaptation may be seen in the streetlight Lee recorded in front of the Grill of the Hotel Westward Ho (fig. 2.9). The real thing abounded not far away, but the fanciful artifice it represented reinforced a sense of region for those vacationing in Phoenix.

FIGURE 2.8. Russell Lee, Zoo and Museum, Apache Junction, April 1940.

FIGURE 2.9. Russell Lee, Cactus light standard in front of Hotel Westward Ho, Phoenix, May 1940.

The Cultural Landscape of Arizona

Except for Lon Megargee's murals in the state capitol, Arizona had done little to nurture the arts before the thirties. George W. P. Hunt, the state's enthusiastic first governor, had to admit in 1918: "Arizona, like all other young States and most of the old ones, is woefully behind the age in encouraging the arts."[17] His assessment was confirmed by the artists themselves. Writing in 1942, painter Maynard Dixon recollected of artistic conditions at the turn of the twentieth century: "In those days in Arizona being an artist was something you just had to endure—or be smart enough to explain why."[18] Dixon knew whereof he spoke; his regular visits to Arizona began in 1900, and in 1940 he built a studio in Tucson. Lew Davis, one of the state's few native-born artists, agreed with Dixon: "[W]hen I was young, an artist was not only a minority, he was a sissy. It was a disgrace to be an artist and I couldn't even admit in those days I was an artist. I used to say until I was about twenty-five that I was a sign painter, because being a sign painter was a respectable trade."[19] Declaring that one was an artist took fortitude in Arizona.

The cultural differences between New Mexico and California serve to highlight Arizona's distinct character during this period. A thriving tourist industry had developed in New Mexico (which, like Arizona, had become a state in 1912), and a major stop on the tourist route was Mary Jane Colter's Indian Building at the Hotel Alvarado, along the train tracks in Albuquerque. The writers who created a national image of the Southwest with their evocative literary portrayals were comfortably situated in the art colonies of Santa Fe and Taos, places with many amenities for visitors. Santa Fe civic leaders consciously chose to develop the city as a Mission Revival stage set derived from southwestern architectural traditions. These efforts were reinforced by the Museum of Fine Arts (1915–16), where the work of regional artists was regularly shown. Groups like the Taos Society of Artists (founded 1915) further reinforced a sense of cultural identity. The early Spanish land-grant families retained a powerful presence in that state, and the intertwined ambience of Indian and Spanish culture was irresistible to tourists. New Mexico was also home to a large community of Hispanic artists. Under the leadership of Dorothy Dunn, who directed its art programs between 1932 and 1937, the Indian School in Santa Fe became famous for training an influential generation of Native American artists.[20]

That the New Mexico pueblos are relatively close together made them readily accessible to both tourists and artists; the latter also made art about tourists. The string of pueblos on the route from Albuquerque to Taos was a prominent feature of the Indian Detours organized by the Fred Harvey Company. In contrast, the Navajo settlements in Arizona were spread out over a broad geography; and the Hopi mesas were hard to get to, and once arrived, a visitor was offered few comforts. By the mid-teens, the Hopi had banned photography and sketching of its public ceremonies, which meant the artists, whose vivid paintings often lured tourists to visit specific sites, could not work there. Nothing like the concerted effort of cultural marketing that developed over time in New Mexico existed in Arizona. Only at the Grand Canyon was there a highly developed tourist industry.

The Mission Revival began in California, and the California Impressionists emerged as an influential group of painters. The cultural atmosphere of California ranged from the la-la land glitter of Hollywood and Los Angeles to what was termed the Eucalyptus school of painting in the northern tier of the state, giving it a character distinct from Arizona's. Literature and movies helped create a perception of state identity. Zorro, who made his fictional debut in 1919, was a creation of the California Mission Revival, as was Helen Hunt Jackson's portrayal of *Ramona* (1884), a tale about a half-Scottish, half-Indian orphan girl raised in a Hispanic family. These characters all predate the New Deal, but they informed the romantic flavor of the state well into the twentieth century, reinforced by popular movies made in the twenties and thirties.

Except for that of Ansel Adams, the work of artists who received federal support to work in Arizona during the New Deal era remains little known in contrast to their work in other states. Most were not resident artists. Arizona's art history generally has received little scholarly attention, while the states on either side—California and New Mexico—have dominated regional scholarship.[21] This volume on the state in between will rebalance our broader understanding of the arts of the American Southwest, while reclaiming an important portion of Arizona's cultural heritage.

The conditions that existed in Arizona during the first three decades of the twentieth century provide the foundation for what happened during the thirties and forties. Arizona had long been visited by artists who sought inspiration from the spectacular landscape of the northern part of the state and from Native American communities, and who were often sponsored by the Santa Fe Railroad, a company that formed a large art collection of paintings of western scenes along its routes. Hung in its corporate headquarters in Chicago, the images were extensively used in marketing its travel services. But Arizona's harsh summer climate meant that resident artists were few in number and scattered throughout the state, making it difficult for them to develop the sense of community that existed among their New Mexico neighbors.

There were no art schools where aspirant artists could seek training, and exhibition opportunities and collectors scarcely existed. An ambitious artist stood a far better chance of success in California or New Mexico, where there were the requisite support systems for art production—galleries, museums, patrons, and art schools.

One of the earliest public efforts in the arts was the Arizona State Fair, which had begun an annual art exhibition in 1914. Its sponsor, the Women's Club of Phoenix, purchased one work annually for the city's municipal collection. This would prove a bone of contention for the director of the Phoenix Federal Art

Center. Not until the twenties was there a flurry of civic cultural activity, mostly centered in Phoenix. Founded in 1923, the Arizona Museum of History (now the Phoenix Museum of History) opened in 1927, and Dwight and Maie Heard established the museum that bears their name in 1929. Artists' groups included the Phoenix Fine Arts Association (1925) and the Arizona Artists' Guild (1928). The Tucson Fine Arts Association had been formed in 1926 and, in Flagstaff, the Museum of Northern Arizona was established by painter Mary-Russell Ferrell Colton and her husband Harold in 1928. The stock market crash must have made the future prospects of these groups seem uncertain at best.

It was difficult to make a living as an artist anywhere in America during the Depression, but Arizona was an especially challenging place, as Raymond Phillips Sanderson recollected: "[A]rt in Phoenix in those days was dead."[22] Born in Jerome, Lew Davis had gone to New York to study art but had always intended to return to his native state: "Arizona was the only place I loved and understood."[23] New York was full of starving artists, and although he recognized that Arizona was not the most practical choice for someone wishing to avoid their ranks, he decided to return to the West: "I knew by this time that to come back to Arizona where there was absolutely nothing in art was the most risky thing a man could do with his career—ditch something and to go back to nothing."[24] Sanderson and Davis were among the Arizona artists to receive government commissions during the Depression.

CHAPTER 3

THE CULTURAL DESERT
New Deal Arts Agencies in Arizona

The start of the Depression did not help Arizona's fledgling artistic enterprises, though the federal government would eventually provide key assistance.

The Federal Art Project

Within the visual arts, the Federal Art Project (FAP), administratively part of the WPA, funded a broad range of art initiatives in the state. Its purpose was to provide support to eligible artists on the basis of economic need, and it funded the production of works of art; art education programs; and art, architectural, and archaeological research and documentation. Tucson painter Mark H. Voris was appointed state supervisor of the FAP. Born in Indiana, he had come to Arizona in 1925 and studied at the University of Arizona in Tucson. For the Public Works of Art Project (PWAP) in 1934, he painted landscapes in an expressive representational regionalist style.

The many alphabet agencies in Washington often shared mandates, and over time one artist might receive support from several sources. Funding for artists was available from multiple programs, but with government rules limiting how long they could be supported by a single agency, artists had to be resourceful in piecing together sources of income to survive. Federal monies could overlap on the same project, making it difficult to determine precisely which program employed a particular artist and for how long. Further, later in life, artists often did not recall exactly which agencies they worked for, their memories clumping all government-supported work under an overarching recollection of the WPA.

The establishment of Federal Art Centers was an important part of the FAP's mandate, and its nationwide focus was to expand what was already available in well-established cities. The FAP endeavored to correct what administrators viewed as an "unequal distribution of cultural advantage" by organizing community art centers where there were none before to "provide the public with opportunities to participate in the experience of art," and to foster "useful work for unemployed artists and art teachers."[1] The program aimed to bring culture within the reach of ordinary people in smaller communities where there were few places to view art; Arizona was typical in this regard.

One of Voris's first tasks was to determine whether the art center that had been designated for Arizona should be established in Tucson or Phoenix. The two cities had long been cultural rivals, as Ross Santee, who headed the Arizona Writers' Project, observed: "Tucson and Phoenix have about as much love for each other as Southern and Northern California."[2] Voris had hoped it would be located in Tucson, where he lived, as did members of the Tucson Fine Arts Association, who regarded their city as "the Athens of the Southwest."[3]

But several key factors were not in Tucson's favor. Its population was smaller than that of Phoenix. The membership of the Tucson Fine Arts Association were interested only in exhibitions, not the community programming that was central to the FAP's mandate. Members of the Tucson group were also concerned about maintaining their institutional independence. But with the arrival of an outside director who would have to abide by federal rules, their ability to control the new institution would necessarily lessen. Voris wrote to Washington officials that the group "balks at losing one iota of its identity," observing: "the very idea arouses immediate rebellion."[4] Because Phoenix desired the comprehensive kind of art center envisioned by federal officials and had a larger number of resident artists who could provide personnel for its programs, the capital was selected as the site of Arizona's Federal Art Center.

The endeavor was a federal-community partnership, with funding divided between local and federal sponsorship. Walter Bimson, president of the Valley National Bank, the state's largest financial institution, was a powerful supporter. A successful businessman, collector, and cultural leader who had arrived in Arizona late in 1932, Bimson was both visionary and decisive, with the combination of practicality and idealism necessary for the success of the project. Voris could report in November that "Enthusiasm was running high."[5]

Unfortunately initial excitement was frustratingly slow to translate into tangible results: "It is distressing the way things move in Phoenix. Slowly and skeptically they swing into action."[6] City Archaeologist Odd Halseth assured him that this was typical, as Voris observed in exasperation: "He knows of no other place where such an effort as we have put forth would bear so little fruit."[7] The eagerness of Phoenix arts supporters was stymied by deep-seated local "indifference to civic improvement,"[8] though Voris was confident that the cultural returns on their efforts could be significant: "The fame of Taos and Santa Fe, New Mexico, has derived mostly from their fine cultural art development."[9] His observation speaks to the ambition of early Arizona arts activists, and his notion that the arts could be a key factor in establishing the state's reputation was a progressive one.

FIGURE 3.1. Exterior, Phoenix Federal Art Center, 710 East Adams Street.

The FAP would pay staff salaries, while the city was expected to fund renovation costs and to pay for heat and electricity. Funding was secured by December 1936, and a downtown building owned by Maie Heard was selected to house the new art center (fig. 3.1).

Hiring a director was Voris's next task, and he felt that what was needed was an individual with "a fairly broad knowledge of art, so that he can aid in the selection of shows and hang them properly, an ability to preserve good harmonious relationships with the various supporting civic groups, reliable character and qualities of efficiency."[10] Painter Philip C. Curtis was selected.[11] A native of Michigan, he had earned a four-year certificate from Yale's Art School. In 1936 he moved to New York, where he found employment with the Federal Art Project as an assistant supervisor of mural painting. After studying the operations and programs of the North Carolina Federal Art Center, Curtis arrived in Arizona in late spring 1937.

He soon discovered the fledgling enterprise he was to oversee faced many challenges, as his comments regarding the local Fine Arts Association reveal:

> There is a group, the very conservative and ill advised, the Fine Arts Association which will have to be delicately handled. They have been buying a painting a year for some time—I thought it might be wise to select a few of these and show them at the same time. This would please them and at the same

time give a small note of contrast—because I imagine that these paintings represent everything that the painters today aren't doing and shouldn't do.[12]

Curtis, who dismissed the works in the city's municipal collection as "horrible," was overly harsh in his assessment, for those whose work had been purchased throughout the teens and twenties included Carl Oscar Borg, Maynard Dixon, Edgar Payne, Millard Sheets, and Jessie Benton Evans (the last-named an Arizona artist). Works by these well-respected western artists, acquired "in anticipation of establishing a municipal gallery,"[13] would have been unknown to someone coming from the East. Nor would the academically trained Curtis have seen any value in the art of the American West.

Curtis was not enthusiastic about having the municipal collection installed permanently at the art center, but he soon discovered local art politics did not always align with his plans. The issue remained a "sore spot"[14] for Curtis, who derided the taste of the members of the Fine Arts Association for what he sarcastically referred to as "'perfectly wonderful' paintings."[15] Much of his disdain for the group derived from the fact that it was comprised of women he dismissed as amateurs who sponsored "pink tea and social art events."[16] The board was largely female, and Curtis had to handle carefully the sexual politics of his female civic supporters, as well as to manage the intersection of community values and his Yale-trained East Coast art aesthetic.

When the Phoenix Federal Art Center (fig. 3.2) opened in mid-July 1937, a crowd estimated at between five and eight hundred people braved the 115-degree temperatures to attend the opening reception, an impressive number representing what was described as an "interesting cross-section of the population."[17] Maie Heard shared the disbelief of the old guard of local art enthusiasts: "People like this have never come to an art exhibition in Phoenix before."[18] The inaugural show was enthusiastically received, as one administrator commented to Holger Cahill, the head of the Federal Art Project: "We could not determine whether Phoenix was art hungry or Mr. Curtis a particularly successful publicity agent. Possibly a combination of both made the opening a success beyond our high hopes."[19]

Combining art production, education, and exhibition, the community mandate of the Phoenix Art Center was broad. Populist in nature, above all it was to be accessible, as Voris declared: "Bring living art of high quality to the man in the street, and get him to see the worth to himself and his friends. In other words, debunk it of the 'in-the-clouds-for-the-chosen-few' element it has been burdened with."[20] Those who found employment at the new art center during its first year comprised a large percentage of the local artist population. The teaching staff included Lew Davis, John Leeper, Creston Baumgartner, Burdell Tenney, R. Phillips Sanderson, and Kathleen Wilson (fig. 3.3). Architect Frank Lloyd Wright gave talks at the center in 1938 and 1939.

FIGURE 3.2. Interior, Phoenix Federal Art Center.

As government officials did not want their programs to be perceived as being in competition with private enterprise, enrollment in art classes was restricted to those who could not afford private instruction. Curtis was pleased with their success, though an account written by another administrator presents an improbably cheerful picture: "An attitude of happy industry surrounds all of the classes at the WPA Phoenix Art Center, and it is not uncommon to hear children's classes unconsciously break forth in a song during the progress of their work."[21]

Curtis was innovative in his programmatic focus on children, whose participation he hoped would lead to the involvement of their parents and other adults who had no particular interest in the arts: "I have found that I can even excite a businessman discussing a child's painting, that they will or he will unconsciously accept principles of contemporary painting in this roundabout approach."[22] A distinctive feature of the art center was "a small gallery just for children. Not to be used as a place to show necessarily the work of children but to show things designed for them and even operated by them."[23] Traveling exhibitions of young artists, including a group of paintings by children from Mexico City, were organized for installation in schools around the state.

The art center proved so successful that within two years it had outgrown its space, though Curtis reported with some irony, "on the other hand it has been severely hurt by cuts."[24] Curtis was frustrated by the lack of cooperation between various federal bureaucracies, voicing concern about what he felt was the petty

FIGURE 3.3. Creston Baumgartner, Kathleen Wilson, Burdell Tenney, Lew Davis, Raymond Phillips Sanderson, and Sim Bruce Richards, Federal Art Project artists.

enforcement of regulations by local WPA officials who were "more interested in their rules than in the success of the work project."[25] Local administrator Louise Norton complained: "One minute we are full speed ahead and the next we are in reverse."[26]

Curtis worked hard to organize exhibitions that would appeal to the Phoenix community but securing publicity proved difficult, and he railed against what he referred to as "our indifferent press."[27] Fears by local artists that their work would not be exhibited at the art center proved unfounded, for regional programming was at the heart of its mission, and traveling shows circulated from Washington were intended only to supplement local offerings.

Curtis ambitiously hoped to obtain a show of abstract work, but federal officials felt it would be too challenging for Phoenix. He also suggested a display he enthusiastically predicted would be of "tremendous news value,"[28] something that would "get the people out in droves."[29] He proposed that the Museum of Modern Art lend him a painting by Vincent Van Gogh, and with the big publicity buildup such a work would generate, he could "create the same artistic orgy that the Art Institute of Chicago did when they showed Whistler's Mother."[30] Warming to the subject, Curtis continued: "We could have the brass posts and rope the painting off, drape the wall in back of it, place a special full-time policeman in front

of it, and perhaps when I start talking this way, we might as well throw in can-
dlesticks."[31] But once again it was decided that "Phoenix is not ready for a very
advanced exhibition."[32] Although frustrated at not being able to mount more
sophisticated shows, officials reminded Curtis that the situation was not due
simply to the provinciality of Phoenix but reflected a national situation: "[T]his
particular problem is the one problem that all of the art center directors have in
common."[33] As Holger Cahill observed, "If the public were already educated to
appreciate the type of exhibition which you as a New Yorker would understand,
there would be no need for the art center."[34]

An important part of the Federal Art Project was providing work for needy
artists, though they had to negotiate with the government bureaucracy to receive
it. Artists were ineligible for support unless they were on the relief rolls, and, in
trying to qualify for inclusion, they discovered a wide gap between federal and
personal intentions.[35]

Lew Davis illustrates the plight of those in need of FAP support. It was difficult for an artist eligible for relief in one state to transfer to another, though he
was eventually able to do so. After he returned from art study in New York, he
took as his favored subject the copper mines he had known growing up, producing strong paintings of labor and mining life with FAP support (fig. 3.4).[36] One
canvas portrays the dangerous and claustrophobic work involved with underground mining. Initially supported by the Treasury Relief Art Project (TRAP),
in February 1937 Davis was notified that a reduction in easel painting staff would
necessitate his termination: "I received the assortment of colored slips today that
notified me of the fact that I will be fired at the end of the month. It was a hel-
luva trick to fix it so it got here on Washington's Birthday. How can a fellow enjoy
a holiday with a wad of death notices in his pocket!"[37] Without money, his situation was dire: "I shall save the multi colored slips in case I have to eat them."[38] But
administrators reassured him: "By all means do not devour the colored slips that
were enclosed in the letter. The slips presented to the proper WPA official will give
you a new assignment as an artist on the Federal Art Project."[39]

Resolving personal and artistic conflicts among local artists was another dip-
lomatic task that fell to Curtis. He credited Davis with much of the success of the
center's classes: "He is the one painter in Arizona on the project or otherwise who
could be called an artist, and recognized as such outside of the state."[40] However,
Curtis admitted that Davis could be a "tough guy"[41] to work with.

Balancing the personalities of his staff with the quality of art produced and
the needs of the public would be ongoing issues, requiring tact and a good sense
of public relations, as Curtis discovered with David Carrick Swing. Originally
from Cincinnati, Swing came to Arizona in 1917 after nearly a decade in Los
Angeles. In 1935, he had been employed by FERA to produce a series of panels for
the reading room of the Phoenix Junior College Library, where he taught between
1935 and 1938. He completed this project in late November 1937, but WPA officials

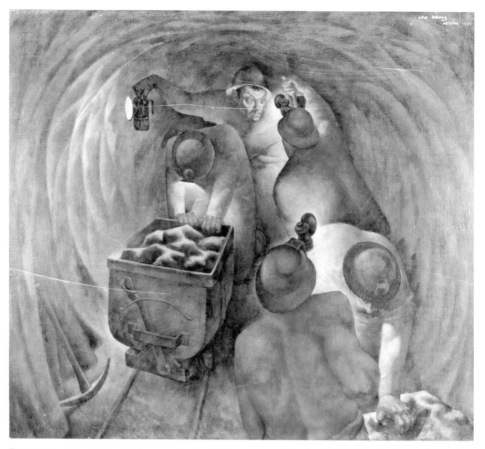

FIGURE 3.4. Lew Davis, *Underground*, oil painting executed for the Federal Art Project, unlocated.

judged it "not of the standard the Federal Art Project should maintain in works to be permanently allocated to public buildings."[42] They recommended that it not be accepted and offered to substitute a different painting in its place.

The situation was exacerbated by a number of factors, as Mark Voris noted: "Mr. Swing has a large following in the community. A part of that following is strong in feeling and quite outspoken."[43] The artist's wife had personally written both to President Roosevelt and to Arizona's venerable Senator Carl Hayden protesting what she regarded as his poor treatment.[44] Voris explained the result: "The situation, through one channel or another, became rather widely spread throughout the community carrying certain exaggerated appendages and arousing feeling on both sides of the question."[45] Wishing not to damage the reputation of the Federal Art Center through further controversy (a constant concern of FAP administrators), the dean of Phoenix College was willing to let Swing's work be hung. Although many faculty were opposed, his panels were delivered and installed.

Swing, then seventy-three, was older than most artists who received federal support, and as one administrator observed: "[H]e is a friendly, kindly old gentleman, who does not seem to understand the underlying purpose of the Federal Art Project, nor his responsibility when assigned to the project, of completing the work before undertaking other duties on other projects."[46] Nor did Swing realize that any work produced under WPA sponsorship belonged to the government, not to himself. Officials were exasperated: "He has already two wall-painting jobs half finished, which I suppose must be completed, not because there is any merit in them but simply that the rooms look a trifle worse in their present state than they will when they are finished. Mr. Swing is not a mural painter but does atmospheric easel effects."[47] If his works were often lacking in inspiration, the artist made up for it in production, as scholar Peter Bermingham later wryly observed: "for sheer acreage of painted canvas, no other Arizona artist in the thirties could rival David Swing."[48] However frustrating his work habits were for Curtis and Voris, in July 1940 an exhibition of his oil paintings was held at the art center (perhaps as a way of diffusing the situation), and the show "drew the greatest attendance ever recorded for an exhibit in the Art Center."[49]

The Federal Writers' Project

The visual arts was only one area that benefited from federal support, and the government aided a broad range of cultural enterprises in Arizona. The Federal Writers' Project aimed to do for writers what other agencies had done for painters and photographers, all of whom were, in the words of one observer: "grazing on the poverty range."[50] In providing relief to unemployed writers, the FWP aided a population not visible in the relief lines or in the caravans migrating across the country.

The Arizona Federal Writers' Project was led by Ross Santee, a cowboy author and illustrator.[51] Many FWP employees were not professional writers, and there was great variation even among those claiming to be, with only a handful of projects headed by able writers. But Santee, described as a "local colorist,"[52] was one of several published novelists who headed state projects, making Arizona's stand out. He felt he was well qualified for his new position: "Anyone who can wet-nurse a hundred and fifty saddle horses, know where they run, know all the quirks of each particular horse, ought to be able to wrangle a bunch of writers."[53] As one administrator noted: "[I]f there is any one man who knows his West and cowboy life, he is Ross Santee."[54]

Raised on an Iowa farm, Santee began art classes at the Art Institute of Chicago in 1909. Leaving for New York about 1914 with the intention of pursuing a career as a cartoonist, he was not successful as a commercial artist. After visiting relatives in Globe in 1915, he decided to move to Arizona, taking a series of jobs in mining and ranching. His experiences in cowboy culture were transformative, as Raymond Carlson wrote in an article published in *Arizona Highways:* "He learned to know Arizona the hard way: from the back of a horse. He came to love Arizona the best way possible: countless days in the sun wrangling horses, countless nights under the stars and moon around lonely campfires, in distant and isolated cow camps."[55] Listening to stories helped him develop an ear for a good tale, and the sketches he made during these years honed his visual skills. As did so many of his contemporaries, he realized that the West was changing rapidly. In making cowboy lore and imagery his trademark he aligned himself with a long tradition of preserving in word and image what he saw disappearing, though his view was more mythic than documentary.

Santee remains a notable figure of regional literature, one of a group of "rangeland writers who were also riders."[56] But although his fans emphasized the authenticity of his experience, his views were as shaped by stereotypes as those of any greenhorn easterner or romantic Hollywood movie director. In 1921, Santee began to publish his illustrations of western ranch life in prominent national magazines. He carefully cultivated his image as a westerner, and was later described as "a cowboy from Globe, Arizona, who showed up recently in New York in sombrero and red sweater, with a portfolio under his arm."[57] His work, a combination of his sketches with written accounts, first appeared in *Arizona Highways* in 1936.

The history of the West is full of personal reinvention stories, and although he was not a native, like so many who settled in Arizona, Santee "became a son of the Southwest"[58] and remained identified with the region even when he was no longer a resident. After his marriage in 1926 to a Delaware woman, they established a home in that state, but returned regularly to Arizona for visits. His *Men and Horses* was published in 1926, and a compilation of some of his *Century* stories appeared in a 1928 book entitled *Cowboy,* described in the WPA Guide as "an authentic story of life on the open range."[59] By the time he was hired as director of the Arizona Federal Writers' Project in 1936, he had published five books and numerous articles.

Santee was characterized in entirely western terms as a person who "writes straight, draws straight, talks straight,"[60] leading Raymond Carlson to advise: "If you want to read stories of the west, simple, beautiful stories of men and horses of the western range,"[61] Santee was the one to read. He portrayed the "Arizona of the open range, of lonely ranch houses and herds of cattle, of the solitary rider crossing the broad mesa—Arizona of the vast spaces and lonely nights and hot days in the sun."[62]

Santee's aesthetic paralleled that of the Western pulp magazines and regionally based novels, both of which remained popular through the thirties. Santee's was the romanticized West, with the cowboy as the central archetype. The WPA Guide characterized his writing: "Ross Santee writes of the real cowboy. His stories deal with simple and normal themes: the rodeo, the roundup, and the struggle of ranchers against drought."[63] His Arizona tales are emblematic of the West.

Arizona: A State Guide

The best-known production of the Federal Writers' Project was the American Guide Series, whose volumes aimed to create detailed portraits of individual states. They remain important documents of cultural nationalism and identity. In emphasizing the strength of the nation's cultural heritage as war loomed in Europe, they affirmed a stronger future grounded in a historical continuum of shared values.

Artifacts of modern automobile culture, the guides, detailed, populist, and affordable Baedekers, comprised a taxonomy of sites accessible by car. Those able to use the state guides for their intended purpose were privileged; as members of the middle class they owned cars and had disposable incomes for vacations and were likely white. Visiting places not well served by the railroad, these travelers represented the shift in the favored means of tourist transportation from trains to cars.

Adopting the slogan, "Take Pride in Your Country," officials stressed the "importance of acquainting the American public with the record of the American way of living."[64] President Roosevelt reinforced the view that the guides were to "illustrate our national way of life."[65] Comprised of descriptive narratives and touring suggestions, they had a view panoramic and positivist, impelled by a patriotic nationalism. Informative and readable, the guides focused on cultural heritage, rather than on the contemporary economic problems. In introducing America to Americans, by being both regionally specific and national in scope, the guides conveyed a sense of the distinctiveness of the local within an overarching view of the cultural hegemony of the United States.

Santee's "aim was to make his guide actually *smell* of Arizona,"[66] sentiments echoed in the foreword:

> The ARIZONA GUIDE seeks to tell the story of the wide-open spaces, the color that nature has generously splashed, of towns continuously inhabited prior to the coming of the white man, and of the missions. It contrasts the air-cooled-by-nature, pine clad northern area with the air-cooled-by-man desert area of central Arizona. It gives credit to the dry farmer raising beans and corn, to the farmer in the irrigated citrus, lettuce, cantaloupe, and alfalfa belt, and to the miners of gold, copper, and other minerals. The dude ranch and the cattle ranch, the modern city and the primitive Indian village, the public school, climaxing in colleges of higher learning, and the private school are portrayed. Tales of the old west are presented as mention is made of modern writers. The pictograph receives attention as does modern art. Arizona is a delightful haven for the retired, an opportunity for the ambitious young. Arizona is a study of contrasts, and this GUIDE is your guide that you may know Arizona.[67]

It neatly summarized Arizona state identity, while paralleling the goals of *Arizona Highways.*

FIGURE 3.5. Cover, *Arizona: A State Guide.*

Arizona: A State Guide was divided into several major sections. The first charts "Arizona's Background," and gives mostly historical summaries of a range of topics, presenting material on the social, cultural, economic, industrial, and artistic development of the state. Topics ranged from essays on the natural setting, the archaeology and contemporary life of its many Native American tribes, to agriculture, industry, commerce, labor, transportation, education and religion, newspapers, radio, and sports and recreation. Art and architecture were included, with

FIGURE 3.6. Ross Santee, 1940

an emphasis on Indian arts, crafts, and archeology, with the accounts being more historical than contemporary. Another section was comprised of a series of community profiles, followed by an extensive one of tours. The largest number was, not surprisingly, for the Grand Canyon, the state's most highly developed tourist site. A horse and rider, who pause at an overlook at Point Imperial on the North Rim, appeared on the cover of the first edition, combining two prominent state symbols. Neatly framed by the tall pines typical of the high country, they present an alluring introduction to the "Sunset State" (fig. 3.5).

In the *Arizona Guide* the classic western figure of the cowboy assumes a substantial presence, in part due to Santee's editorship, and the book's orientation to tourism gave emphasis to those emblematic elements that drew visitors to the state. Dude ranches, complete with swimming pools, provided safe adventures for vacationers from the East. The *Guide*'s themes parallel those of Arizona literature and Hollywood movies in this era, which remained focused on the stereotypical Old West. Illustrations emphasize "those features that have made Arizona a tourist state."[68] In doing so, Santee explored one of the most powerful western archetypes: man on his horse out in the open range, with his illustrations for the *Guide* celebrating "The Sunburnt West of Yesterday"[69] (fig. 3.6).

The Index of American Design

In a time of economic crisis and international political uncertainty, the past could provide comfort and affirmation for those confronting difficult contemporary issues. The Index of American Design (IAD) was another significant endeavor sponsored by the Federal Art Project. More than four hundred artists were employed by the Index to document national cultural traditions. During the six years of its existence, they executed drawings of American craft and folk art made in this country from the colonial era through the nineteenth century by "the peoples of European origin who created the material culture of this country as we know it today."[70] What was recorded was highly selective, and emphasis was on "the dominating Anglo-Saxon culture"[71] of the northeastern United States.

More than eighteen thousand watercolors recorded textiles, costumes, objects, and furniture. Although the Index was focused on historical artifacts, that there was a broad modernist interest in folk art and antiques during this period gave to their efforts a strong contemporary resonance. In creating a national vocabulary of design it was hoped that IAD documentation would be useful to art students, manufacturers, commercial designers, and museums.

IAD artists recorded practical objects made by anonymous artisans used by ordinary people in their daily lives. American identity was revealed in the artifacts of the past, with regional distinctiveness conveying the foundations of national character. Cultural nationalism was embedded in the interest in such utilitarian material, permitting history to be perceived as a coherent continuum both providing a touchstone during anxious times and revealing a solid base of the past that would provide a strong foundation for the future. The usable past portrayed by the IAD confirmed contemporary values, with detailed watercolor renderings of useful things revealing an American sense of design, yet separated from their cultural context.

That Native American work, an area in which the state had an exceptionally rich heritage, was the focus of a separate recording project presented Arizona IAD administrators with a dilemma. Federal officials justified this exclusion by asserting that Indian designs were "a whole field in themselves,"[72] feeling that "Indian art should be left to the ethnologists."[73] Exceptions were Indian objects that had been used by early pioneers, as was the case with several blankets in the collection of the Heard Museum in Phoenix.

At first it was not clear if an IAD project would be possible in Arizona: "We have done nothing about the Index of American Design in Arizona because the only source of original material is in Indian handicraft. If we have been wrong in believing that the Indian designs were not eligible for the Index please let me know."[74] The Arizona IAD was necessarily small, comprised of thirty-eight

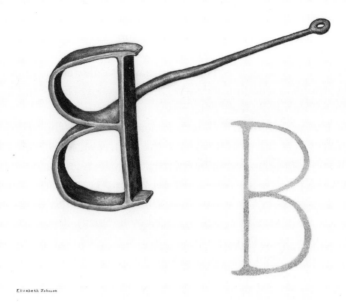

Elizabeth Johnson

FIGURE 3.7. Elizabeth Johnson, 1942, Brand from the Lazy B Ranch, watercolor.

drawings (thirty were of branding irons), all executed in 1942, and most done on-site as they were still owned by descendents of the state's early ranching families. One branding iron was sketched at the Lazy B Ranch, established by the family of former Supreme Court Justice Sandra Day O'Connor [75] (fig.3.7).

A selection of IAD work was shown at the Federal Art Center in Phoenix in 1937. The meticulous rendering of ordinary historical objects of everyday use carried a strong message to contemporary viewers, as the organizers asserted: "However the great value of this exhibition is those seeing it will perhaps realize for the first time how humble, and at the same instance, important art has been and should be today in our daily lives."[76]

The Historic American Buildings Survey

The Historic American Buildings Survey (HABS), another government-sponsored documentary project, recorded significant structures throughout the nation, including Arizona. Described as "a program designed by architects for architects,"[77] HABS was an effort that reclaimed America's built history and encouraged the protection of monuments nationwide. Established in 1933, HABS was a joint effort of several agencies. The National Park Service, part of the Department of the Interior, oversaw the recording project, the American Institute of Architects provided necessary personnel, and the Library of Congress archived the records and made them available to the public. Not only did HABS provide employment for architects, draftsmen, and photographers, it was one of several efforts to give order to our buildings heritage by means of graphic (measured drawings and photographs) and written records, using a standardized format. In affirming a rich architectural past, as with parallel New Deal projects, the documentation HABS gathered about the nation's cultural patrimony gave a steadying touchstone to a nation in distress. Because many HABS employees were architects, it was a decidedly male enterprise.

The focus was on American architecture before 1860, and for Arizona that meant Spanish colonial and structures from the pioneer era, and a few Native American sites that could be visited by tourists. Early forts and missions received the most attention, particularly San Xavier del Bac and Fort Lowell near Tucson. Tombstone, once a thriving mining boomtown, was photographed by the FSA and written up in the state guide. Half deserted by the 1930s, Tombstone was "only a ghost of the roaring camp it used to be,"[78] and while there was some small-scale mining, it was tourism that brought visitors to the town (fig. 3.8). It comprised a substantial collection of historic structures and was thoroughly recorded. Russell Lee's view of derelict buildings in the deserted town is similar in view to those taken by HABS photographers (who were not artists). The preservation of Arizona's built past has always been a fragile enterprise, and encroaching modern development was a problem even in 1937, as noted by a project architect: "Early Spanish remains in Arizona are apparently not easily saved from destruction by the fast moving commercial enterprise there."[79] Most Arizona HABS work was done in 1937, with efforts concentrated in the Tucson area.

Other New Deal Cultural Projects

Paralleling the recording efforts of HABS were archaeological projects that reconstructed and stabilized early structures, as well as worked with the Civil Works Administration to build museums to house artifacts and interpret sites. The Native American ruins at Tuzigoot, which administrators claimed was "the first archaeological research project in the United States to be done by relief workers,"[80] was the main focus in Arizona. Structures at the site underwent extensive excavation and restoration.

A number of museums were constructed during this period, including one at Tuzigoot in the style of the original pueblo ruin. All were highlighted in the *Arizona Guide* as potential stops for tourists. In Prescott, a building to house the collections of the Sharlot Hall Museum was completed. The state's first territorial historian—she was the first woman to hold salaried public office in Arizona—Hall had amassed many artifacts related to the early history of the state. The CWA assisted with the construction of the Smoki Museum (also in Prescott) in 1935. The Smoki People had been founded in 1921 to preserve Native American rituals

FIGURE 3.8. Russell Lee, Shells of old buildings on the main street, Tombstone, May 1940.

and artifacts. Under the PWAP, Prescott painter Kate Cory helped with the design and interior decoration of the rustic pueblo-inspired structure, executing paintings portraying Indian life and legends to be displayed in the Smoki and other artwork to illustrate the museum's publications.

Only larger states with a critical mass of actors could support a Federal Theatre Project (which included dance), and therefore none was established in Arizona. But the many musicians who resided in the state participated in an active Federal Music Project. Less controversial than many New Deal programs (some objected to the very fact of the government's support of the arts, as well as to specific content), nationally it "employed more people than other arts projects, reached more Americans through its artists' performances, and steered clear of political scandal."[81] However, as with other government initiatives there were concerns by union members about unfair competition, and complaints were voiced regarding WPA musicians performing at private events whose organizers would normally have hired professionals.

The Arizona Music Project had fifty employees: ten in Tucson and forty in Phoenix. Its bands and orchestras gave performances in public schools, at dances, and in parks. Russell Lee photographed the band shell in Phoenix that would have been a typical venue (it had been constructed by the Public Works Administration). Overall, 1,250 concerts were presented in Arizona, many of which were broadcast on the radio for those unable to attend in person. There were occasional musical programs at the art center. With the military buildup before America entered World War II, musicians entertained soldiers stationed at bases throughout the state.

The art and cultural programs implemented in Arizona during this period exemplify an impressive breadth. The government aimed to bring art to ordinary people and to support artists, writers, architects, and musicians, and the work of these agencies was spread throughout the state.

CHAPTER 4

ART IN PUBLIC PLACES
New Deal Murals and Sculpture in Arizona

The Depression that increased the challenges facing an artist attempting to make a living ironically led to new opportunities for Arizona artists emerging from the broad range of relief programs implemented under Roosevelt's New Deal. The many alphabet agencies in Washington often shared mandates, and over time individual artists might receive support from several sources. The biggest and best known of the arts programs, including the Federal Art Project, came under the umbrella of the WPA.

Artists eagerly sought government support, sometimes writing directly to federal officials hoping to secure commissions, as Lon Megargee did to Olin Dows, an administrator with the Treasury Section of Painting and Sculpture, in October 1935: "To date I haven't heard of any art projects for Arizona, if any are forthcoming I would like to be included as a supervisor or commissioned to do some of the work."[1] He wrote again the next month, explaining why he was suited for such support: "I am especially qualified, living in Arizona, to make a record pictorially of the Indian, the cowboy, the Grand Canyon, the desert, or any historical episode."[2] An artist desiring aid had to be flexible and willing to take on a range of assignments. By piecing together a patchwork of funding, one could manage enough money on which to live.

The Public Works of Art Project

The first federally funded New Deal arts projects in Arizona were sponsored in 1934 by the Public Works of Art Project, the agency that preceded the more famous WPA. That it was locally managed and targeted at Arizona artists gave it more flexibility than many Washington programs and permitted participation by more Arizona artists than possible in national competitions. During the six months of its existence, the Arizona PWAP sponsored sixteen artists, about half of whom were based in Phoenix. The participants produced eight murals, twenty-seven oil

FIGURE 4.1. Joseph Morgan Henninger, *Spanish Influence in Arizona*, 1934, oil on canvas, 7' × 16'.

paintings, thirty watercolors, and a fountain at Arizona State Teachers College (now Arizona State University). All but the largest works were portable, and consequently most have disappeared.

The PWAP made possible two seven-by-sixteen-foot murals portraying historical and modern Arizona by Joseph Morgan Henninger for the Arizona State Teachers College library. Both of his large canvases portray common state historical symbols. The artist had arrived in Phoenix in 1933 from Indiana, and he appreciated the extremes that struck so many first-time visitors: "I find this part of our United States severe, austere and harsh, there is no soft fusion of form and color, it is all sharp in its outline, each thing distinct from that which is next to it. Therein lies its beauty to me, there is none of the softness of the east in the rugged grandeur of this landscape. . . . In a word this country is dramatic."[3]

The artist had been trained at the Ecole des Beaux-Arts in Paris, and the strong compositional skills and facility with the human figure he learned there are evident in *Spanish Influence in Arizona* (fig. 4.1). On the left, against a backdrop of the mission church San Xavier del Bac, a padre baptizes and instructs Indian youth, while on the right Spanish conquistadors supervise the forced mining labor of Native Americans. The arrangement is strongly hierarchical, with the whites in dominant positions, though there is implicit criticism of the actions of the Spanish colonists. At the center a single Native American figure looks skyward imploringly, his gesture alluding to the long history of governmental assimilationist policies regarding the state's indigenous peoples. As Henninger wrote to his parents: "I have divided the canvas so that the bondage of the church is on the left side and the bondage of the conquistador is on the right. I have placed the figure of the Indian well forward and almost center of the composition crying to the Great Spirit for relief from the oppression of both his physical life and his spiritual life."[4]

FIGURE 4.2. Joseph Morgan Henninger, *Industrial Development in Arizona*, 1934, oil on canvas, 7' × 16'.

In portraying stock imagery referencing the Spanish colonial era—conquistadors, padres, and mission churches—Henninger conforms to the romantic archetypes of Old Spain, rather than to the "Mexican-ness" of contemporary migrant labor. Such views were reinforced by the WPA guide, which described the "swashbuckling *conquistadores,* and gentle priests who strove to impress the faith and culture of Spain upon the natives they found here."[5]

In *Industrial Development in Arizona* (fig. 4.2), the artist pictured typical state imagery, including hard rock and pan mining, sheep and cattle raising, lumbering, citrus farming, and the construction of a dam. Again the composition is dominated by a strong central figure. The view he presents of modern Arizona is much more positive, conveying the strength of labor and hard work that symbolized the progress in a young state that would eventually triumph over the Depression. When his work was finished, Henninger left Arizona and moved to California.

Emry Kopta was an Austrian sculptor who came to San Francisco with his family in 1906. Settling in Los Angeles in 1911, he met Lon Megargee, who had come to Arizona in 1896, but who was then living in southern California. They became friends, and in 1912 they visited the Hubbell Trading Post in Ganado, Arizona, a site long popular with artist-travelers. After several weeks of sketching on the Navajo reservation, the pair went to the Hopi mesas. Kopta declared: "This is where I'm going to work."[6] Remaining for the next dozen years, he immersed himself deeply in Hopi culture, sketching and sculpting portraits and taking many photographs before he moved to Phoenix in 1925.

Kopta had witnessed the Flute Ceremony, a ritual prayer for rain, and for the PWAP he designed a three-foot stone *Kachina Fountain* (fig. 4.3) that he intended to be topped by his *Hopi Flute Player,* a six-foot bronze figure clad only in a breechcloth. The plinth supporting it was comprised of four Kachinas, guardians

FIGURE 4.3. Emry Kopta, *Kachina Fountain*, 1934.

of Hopi welfare, and at the four corners of the base were metates, stones with concave tops for grinding the corn meal that the rain would make grow. The turtles on the projections also are symbolic of water. The quiet concentration of the figure absorbed in his music contrasts with the activity of the more public dances popular with tourists. Kopta's respect for the customs of the people among whom he lived is evident. Atop the pedestal was a flaring bowl on which the statue would be placed, but funding for the PWAP ended before it could be cast.

Under the PWAP, Megargee executed three large canvases for the state capitol. Each features a single, heroically scaled figure combined with well-known regional symbols to suggest the broad historical development of the state. His painting titled *The Aborigine* pictures a Native American wrapped in a red blanket, who is flanked by two large saguaros and set against a brilliant orange sky and a blue mountain. In *A Spanish Padre,* the figure is garbed in a black robe, his head covered by a wide-brimmed black hat. He holds a rolled-up paper, which may be a design for the mission under construction, visible in the distance. In the background, two Native Americans lift a log. While the largest number of extant missions were in California, whether intact or in ruins, they remained romantic symbols of the Spanish colonial era throughout the Southwest.

For *Agriculture* (fig. 4.4), Megargee created a vigorous image of a strong man, who pauses in his labors, his hands firmly folded on the handle of his shovel. He stands within a rocky canyon, and to either side of him is the farm and irrigation equipment that would enable the area's many citrus orchards to flourish. The desert metropolis of Phoenix rises behind him. Muralists, in displaying a broad summary of history, often highlighted the progress and modernity that ended the pioneer era, presenting a hopeful image of the future in the midst of the Depression.

Many people moved to Arizona for health reasons, as did Raymond Phillips Sanderson, who arrived from the Midwest in 1932. Trained at the Art Institute of Chicago and at the Kansas City Art Institute, he settled in Bisbee, where his cousin lived, remaining for five years. Opportunities for an artist in an isolated mining community in the southeastern part of the state were slender at best, and the one-industry town grappled with the slump in copper prices caused by the Depression. Sandersonstruggled to find employment, but despite his financial difficulties, his words convey the typical encounter of a newcomer with Arizona: "The West has its own unique forms of life and scene. It is a land vivid with action, romance, and adventure. The West will inevitably be pictured through an art of its own, distinctively western."[7]

Sanderson's first public commission was *Miners' Monument* (fig. 4.5), erected in 1935 on the main street directly in front of the Cochise County Courthouse. To mining Bisbee owed its existence, and Sanderson's statue could not have been more meaningful to the community. A reporter for the local paper observed: "While the empire-building role of the miner is universally recognized, his great contributions are sometimes overlooked in the routine of daily tasks. The miner statue will be a lasting tribute to the man underground and his part in the advancement of civilization."[8] For the Copper State, mining was as archetypical an endeavor as was ranching (whose emblematic figure was the cowboy), though that profession is more often denoted by a lone figure of an aging prospector who, accompanied by his burdened mule, trudges through the rugged terrain in search of the riches that will ever elude him.

Nine feet tall and weighing two thousand pounds, the cement sculpture was plated in copper and placed on a five-foot, eight-ton granite base once used for drilling contests. The artist treated the figure's strong muscles and sturdy shoulders broadly to create a monumental effect. The statue's powerful social realist

Figure 4.4. Lon Megargee, *Agriculture*, 1934, oil on canvas, 83" × 48½".

FIGURE 4.5. Raymond Phillips Sanderson, *Miners' Monument*, 1935, Bisbee. Photograph by Russell Lee.

FIGURE 4.6. Raymond Phillips Sanderson, *Miner*, 1939.

style featuring a bare-chested figure, his feet spread wide and his back erect, holding a hammer and chisel, captured the brute strength of the local miners, as expressed in the plaque: "Dedicated to those virile men the copper miners whose contribution to the wealth and lore of the State of Arizona has been magnificent." Such a hard-bodied youth conveyed the fortitude necessary to cope with the Depression.

Among his last Bisbee works was a series of eight relief panels depicting historical themes that were installed in the courthouse lobby (1936). Not long after this, Sanderson visited Phoenix to attend a meeting of WPA artists. There he met Philip Curtis and decided the city would offer him many more professional opportunities than Bisbee. He left during the summer of 1937 and began teaching at the new art center, supplementing his income with private commissions for furniture and sculpture. A 1939 relief, one of a series he made for an unknown site, portrayed a mining theme (fig. 4.6). Its powerful centralized composition of a man and his drill conveyed the strength of labor, a common element in thirties art.

The Phoenix Post Office

The most prominent murals in the state were installed in the new Phoenix Post Office, which opened in 1936. A handsome, two-story stucco Spanish colonial revival building topped with a red tile roof, it had been designed in 1935 by the

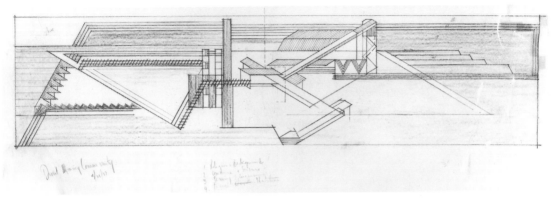

FIGURE 4.7. Sim Bruce Richards, *Desert Mining Community,* 1937, Pencil and ink on paper, 29" × 11".

Phoenix firm of Lescher and Mahoney. Four murals were planned for the lobby. As was the practice in national competitions, a regional committee made recommendations to officials in Washington, who had final approval authority. The competition attracted about thirty entries, and Laverne Nelson Black and Oscar Berninghaus were selected to do the work. Both artists had strong connections to New Mexico, though Black resided in Arizona at the time of the competition.

In their final report, the committee made special mention of a series of modern designs proposed by Sim Bruce Richards, including *Desert Mining Community* (fig. 4.7), a striking geometric abstraction showing the strong influence of Frank Lloyd Wright, under whom he had served an apprenticeship at Taliesin between 1934 and 1936. Richards, born in Oklahoma, was one quarter Cherokee. While the committee regarded his entries as constituting "a very interesting modern expression of murals,"[9] they concluded his distinctive imagery would require too much explanation for local viewers to appreciate. Megargee, lobbying his own cause, would have agreed with their view that a representational style was more suitable: "The design and subject matter should be understandable—not abstract in theme or follow out too modern a trend."[10]

Arizona's two leading artists were very disappointed not to have won. Lon Megargee, whose four entries came in third, took as his subject key historical eras of the state's history, including the Spanish conquest and the pioneer period. His final panel portrays Arizona during the New Deal years and presents a scene of modern development (fig. 4.8). The center space, flanked by two surveyors, awaits construction. Agriculture and mining are flourishing industries, and the coming prosperity that would end the Depression is clearly on the horizon.

Megargee wrote Senator Carl Hayden, whom he hoped could pressure the Washington arts administrators to give him the commission: "I feel sure you will agree that an Arizona artist should do the work—my sketches are topical and sane—depicting an understandable pictorial record of some of the most

FIGURE 4.8. Lon Megargee, Phoenix Post Office competition entry, 1937.

important events in the history of Arizona."[11] Senator Hayden, ever responsive to the expressed needs of his constituents back home, but not aware of the established protocols for such commissions, wrote the department responsible: "I shall appreciate hearing from you as to whether any encouragement can be offered to Mr. Megargee that he will be selected to do this work."[12] Edward B. Rowan, Superintendent for the Treasury's Section of Painting and Sculpture, replied, assuring the senator that the program was run on a merit basis so as to give "all the artists of America an equal chance in procuring some of the mural and sculpture decoration in the Federal buildings."[13] He explained that competition entries were submitted anonymously, and the judging blind, and concurred with the recommendation of the local committee: "[I]n spite of his reputation and experience this particular work, in our estimation, does not compare in quality or design with that of the winners."[14]

Lew Davis submitted four designs of impressive thematic scope broadly portraying the history of Arizona and the evolution of the state. His subject was "The Development of Arizona and the Growth of the Postal Service," and he was confident of winning: "Unless one of the other contestants is a genius, I think I ought to get the contract."[15] But he claimed to be prepared if things did not work out: "If by chance, I fail to win the contract, . . . you will probably have to dig me out of a copper mine, where I will be pushing a muck stick, if I can get a job. My present funds will last me a couple of months, and as this end of the state is certainly no market for paintings, my future looks none too cheerful."[16]

Chronologically organized, each panel was arranged in three sections, so that they could be easily read. The first (fig. 4.9) included scenes of the arrival of the Spaniards, a common beginning point, avoiding the Native Americans who

were here first. A trapper and a scout flank the Butterfield Stage (which carried the mail) in the center, and a fort is portrayed at right, picturing the period when early settlers were still subject to Indian attack. In this, and his other three entries, he pictured notable individuals from Arizona history, but they are also the archetypal figures used by others with no familiarity with the state for whom they were stock characters.

Another panel portrayed scenes of the growth of the Salt River Valley during the decades after the Civil War (fig. 4.10). The gaming hall to the right conveyed the rough flavor of the roaring eighties, while the settled and orderly community of Phoenix pictured at center suggests that the state has become increasingly stable. Citizens bustle in and out of the post office. On the left, the beginnings of agriculture in the Salt River Valley are shown.

The third scene, which included the surveying and construction of the Roosevelt Dam at the left, brought the visual chronicle up to statehood (fig. 4.11). In the center, a group of cowboys brand a calf in a corral, pausing to look up at a train speeding into town. At the right is the state capitol, with the inauguration of Governor Hunt.

The final panel celebrated contemporary life (fig. 4.12). Underground mining dominates the left (the artist reused the composition of *Underground*, reproduced in chapter 3), while at the right, construction projects are paired with archaeology, suggesting that Phoenix is rising on a foundation of past civilizations. An airplane flies over the center scene, where agricultural laborers are engaged in harvesting a bounty of lettuce and cotton. Davis had proposed an ambitious concept, with an energetic understanding of key events of Arizona history absent in other entries.

FIGURE 4.9. Lew Davis, Phoenix Post Office competition entry, 1937.

FIGURE 4.10. Lew Davis, Phoenix Post Office competition entry, 1937.

Berninghaus and Black were notified in late April 1937 that they had won, and their murals were completed in mid-February 1938. Berninghaus's panels dealt with the theme of Indians and early Spanish explorers, while Black portrayed scenes of cowboys, cattle, and western settlement. Their canvases were complementary and presented standard aspects of state iconography.

Oscar Berninghaus was one of the founders of the Taos art colony, and his imagery was deeply grounded in the well-established visual conventions common among southwestern artists. In the center of *Communication during the Period of Exploration* (fig. 4.13) is a large pueblo in a vast desert setting, a scene that suggests

his New Mexico residence rather than Arizona's remote Hopi mesas. A cluster of Native Americans is to the left, and to the right is a group of Spanish conquistadors with a priest. A single Indian and a single Spaniard gesture to each other across the geographical, chronological, and cultural divide. It is an image of peaceful communication rather than one of conquest. For *Pioneer Communication* (fig. 4.14), his central image was a small town nestled against a rugged, though protective, mountain. Signs advertise general merchandise, and the post office is clearly visible next door, giving material evidence of the progress of Anglo settlement. At the left, a stagecoach comes down into the valley, bringing passengers and mail. To the right, a man with a string of loaded pack mules returns from a prospecting trip.

FIGURE 4.11. Lew Davis, Phoenix Post Office competition entry, 1937.

FIGURE 4.12. Lew Davis, Phoenix Post Office competition entry, 1937.

A midwesterner, Laverne Nelson Black had moved to Taos in the late 1920s, hoping the drier environment would improve his health. In 1937, he settled in Phoenix, which was even drier than New Mexico. He died the next year at the age of fifty-one, several months after the completion of his murals, the result of a heart condition that had been exacerbated by breathing lead paint fumes in his poorly ventilated studio.[17]

Black had a lifelong interest in Indian subjects, and his work was typically done in a broad painterly style with atmospheric effects. His two murals were composed as triptychs, with six panels picturing the history of Arizona

from pioneer days to contemporary cattle and mining industries. In *Historical Background* (fig. 4.15), a cattle drive is balanced by scenes of farming, sheep raising, and mining, conveying a sense of peaceful settlement. At the center a figure on a galloping horse shoots at what is probably a Native American in pursuit. In *The Progress of the Pioneer* (fig. 4.16) settlers resolutely head west in covered wagons. The right portrays a stagecoach arriving in the town they established. The center panel pictures a Native American on horseback sending a signal, perhaps preceding an attack on the pioneers. The scenes read as movie stills, and Black presented subjects common in popular Westerns.

Figure 4.13. Oscar Berninghaus, *Communication during the Period of Exploration*, 1937–38, oil on canvas, 19' wide × 4' 6" high, Post Office, Phoenix.

Figure 4.14. Oscar Berninghaus, *Pioneer Communication,* 1937–38, oil on canvas, 19' wide × 4' 6" high, Post Office, Phoenix.

FIGURE 4.15. Laverne Nelson Black, *Historical Background,* 1937–38, oil on canvas, 19' wide × 4' 6" high, Post Office, Phoenix.

FIGURE 4.16. Laverne Nelson Black, *The Progress of the Pioneer,* 1937–1938, oil on canvas, 19' wide × 4' 6" high, Post Office, Phoenix.

The 48 States Competition

The majority of post office murals commissioned by the government were received positively by the communities in whose buildings they were installed. But a design proposed for Safford proved controversial, revealing the flash point at the intersection of art and community values. In 1939, the 48 States Competition attracted nearly 1500 entries nationwide from more than 950 artists for a mural in a rural post office in every state. Fifty-seven entries were received from all over the country for Safford. The images were varied, with some picturing specific events from Arizona's history (except for Arizona artists, none would have known any-thing about Safford), while others proposed more generic western imagery. Most celebrated the rural agricultural values fundamental to the existence of the small town where they were to be installed.

Several other entries were ultimately executed in post offices in other states. Typically, the painters, working in a representational style, favored powerful west-ern archetypes, which is why proposals produced for one site could often be exe-cuted with little alteration in another, whereas the photographers were of neces-sity grounded in the contemporaneous and conveyed a strong specificity of place.

The winning artist was Seymour Fogel, whose entry was an elegantly abstracted image of Southwest Indian ceremonial dancers (fig. 4.17). Trained in New York at the Art Students League and the National Academy of Design, Fogel had been an assistant to Diego Rivera in New York, producing his first indepen-dent murals during the mid-thirties.[18]

Indian subject matter was popular in the Southwest, and his dancers, set against a backdrop of colorful desert mesas, formed a handsome composition. A newspa-per reporter not well acquainted with contemporary art declared: "Modern art has lifted its Medusa head in Safford,"[19] and the design was described as "Futuristic in concept—or definitely modernist at any rate,"[20] reminding the writer of Picasso. Fogel's proposed celebration of Native American culture was not well received in the Mormon farming community whose original pioneer settlers had clashed with the local Apache. Art intended for public spaces raised different issues than that shown in museums and galleries. Geographical distance meant most artists had at best a rudimentary knowledge of the places where their murals would be installed, and in picturing something outside their experience, artists like Fogel failed to understand local community views. The controversy that arose was not the result of provincial aesthetic views, though racial prejudice was undoubtedly a factor.

In portraying what he thought was a peaceful symbolic scene honoring American Indian ceremonials, Fogel made no reference to a specific historical figure. But Safford residents reacted to his design with intense hostility. History remained a highly personal issue for them, and local memories of the Apache raids that killed early family members and friends remained sharp. Native Americans remained enemies, not the colorful performers at picturesque New

FIGURE 4.17. Seymour Fogel, 48 States Competition entry for Safford Post Office, 1939.

Mexico pueblos favored by tourists on Indian Detours. The artist's goals were decidedly not those of Saffordians.

H. P. Watkins, the secretary of the Graham County Chamber of Commerce, was appreciative of the new government building that had been erected in Safford, but he felt the proposed imagery was inappropriate: "The subject of the mural is obnoxious and unpleasant to the people of this community."[21] Members of this agricultural town first settled by Mormon pioneers made their living through farming and ranching: "In their early struggles so much trouble was encountered with the Indians whose chief was Geronimo, that any thought of depicting their chief enemy in their public building is distasteful to their generation, many of whose parents were either slain or cruelly treated by the Indians."[22] That their objections were grounded in recent history serves as a reminder of how young was the state of Arizona. Local history trumped New York idealism and national art values, and images of pioneer settlement offered a more reassuring history than reminders of conflict.

Watkins, always polite, yet firm in conveying the views of his fellow Saffordians, carefully explained to Rowan:

> The high regard held by the jury for the aesthetic merits found in the choice does not prevail among the people of this community because of their knowledge of the Indian. This knowledge overshadows any of the heroic, and glamour seen in him by others. His dance to us means but one thing, not peace but a sharpening of his emotions for another raid upon the lives and property of the white man whom he has always held in contempt. . . . We live too close to the Reservation—know too much about the Indian, have seen too much of his real character, know too much of his historical background, and this is too fresh in our memories to permit us to admire him. With all this we do not want to perpetuate the Indian's memory in the one building to which most of us will have to go every day.[23]

Senator Carl Hayden, in contact with his constituents, once again took an interest in art matters and concurred that the design was inappropriate: "The Safford Valley was the center of the most serious, bloody, and longest continued Indian depredations in the history of the United States, and the people who live along the Gila River do not regard the Apache Indian as a thing of beauty but as an abomination upon the face of the earth."[24]

Fogel was taken aback at the objections raised to his proposed Indian theme: "My sole purpose was to design a panel that was colorful, and which would be adaptable not only to the building, but also to the surrounding country. Indians suited all these requirements admirably."[25] He missed the point, however, for while his aesthetic purposes were met, those of Safford were not.

The artist hoped Rowan would fight for his design rather than "placate the citizens of Safford"[26] with something "they think they can digest."[27] But from a practical perspective, Rowan was not eager to engage in controversy if it could be avoided regarding a program already under sharp criticism by anti–New Dealers, and he realized that Fogel's design would have to be scrapped. When Fogel suggested making at least a small Native American reference in his new proposal (in the form of an Indian killed by pioneers defending themselves), Rowan firmly advised him to delete it. The artist appreciated the irony of being characterized as a "distinguished painter of the American Indian," while finishing a design that "would have nothing to do with the American Indian."[28]

Had it been proposed for a New Mexico site, where such themes were regularly portrayed, it is unlikely that Fogel's mural would have caused any controversy. As the praise he received when his final mural was finished indicates, local residents were obviously not opposed to art, and indeed they expressed considerable pride in the scenes he had painted. But they had strong feelings about the ownership of their history and how their community should be represented in a public building.

Originally, the Safford Post Office was scheduled to receive a large single mural fourteen feet long by five feet high, for which the artist would be paid $800. But the funds were increased to $1850, perhaps as a way of defusing the controversy, and Fogel produced six panels, each eight feet wide by three feet high. He took as his theme *The History of the Gila Valley,* and his scenes portrayed "Conquistadors," "New Lands," "Early Pioneers," "Migration" (fig. 4.18), "Home," and "Fruits of the Gila Valley." Fogel took a sweeping view of history from Spanish exploration and early settlement to the modern day, showing that the perseverance of the settlers who had faced their struggles with fortitude as their migration west resulted in a successful outcome. His scenes in which he employed "easily understood symbols"[29] of undaunted pioneers successfully overcoming a series of travails might have come straight out of a movie script or novel. The settlers' descendants reaped the rewards of their efforts in the form of flourishing ranches, their prosperity due to agriculture, cattle, and hard work.

FIGURE 4.18. Seymour Fogel, *The History of the Gila Valley: Migration*, 1939–42, tempera on gesso and plaster, 8′ wide × 3′ high, Post Office, Safford.

It would have been far simpler for Fogel to have executed the panels on canvas in his New York studio, which would require his coming to Arizona only for installation (most artists chose this option), but the artist decided to paint directly on the long lobby wall using tempera on gesso and plaster, a decision that meant he would need to be in Arizona for several months. However, for an artist on the verge of financial ruin, Safford was cheaper to live in than New York. If Fogel had any qualms about painting in front of his critics, they were quickly allayed: "[M]uch to my surprise the local townspeople are extremely enthusiastic and impressed."[30] He professed to like Safford: "The Southwest is a grand place. I've been to my first small town dance, and feel sort of bowlegged right now as I rode my first steed today. I'm afraid I'll be coming back with a drawl and a Stetson."[31]

In retrospect Fogel judged his time in Arizona "a very delightful experience,"[32] and the postmaster reported: "[H]e has given us a splendid job and the public here has praised his work very highly."[33] Once his painting tasks were completed, the artist was eager to be paid: "[E]ven the most beautiful mountains and desert pall when viewed on an empty stomach."[34] Many artists endured a financially harrowing month while waiting for their final checks to be sent from Washington, and Robert Kittredge's words, written at a similar juncture in Arizona, echo Fogel's: "May I ask as a favor that you try to get my last payment off to me with all haste as I need it badly. And will need it worse by the time it gets here."[35] Taking advantage of the low cost of living, Fogel remained in Safford several more months while he completed cartoons for a mural commission he had received for the Social Security Building in Washington, D.C.

Arizona State Teachers College

Another area of WPA mural activity was on the campus of Arizona State Teachers College. The B. B. Moeur Activity Building housed women's physical education programs, and, like the Phoenix Post Office, was designed by Lescher and Mahoney. Dedicated in 1939, the adobe building was the largest WPA structure in the state. Of the murals executed for the interior, most striking were those executed by Sim Bruce Richards (fig. 4.19). Painted on three different walls, his modernist designs showed the strong influence of Frank Lloyd Wright in their stylization and flat areas of color with little modeling. Twenty feet high and seventy feet long, they expressed the spirit of modern dance. Framed on either end by figures inspired by Native American motifs, the work represented a range of well known contemporary choreographers and dancers, for whom the artist portrayed "a movement, a gesture, or a common posture"[36] typical of their work. The names of those he depicted were part of his design and included Martha Graham, who performed in Phoenix in February 1940; Richards designed the program. A period photograph records her standing second from the left in front of the mural. The artist is at the right.

Painted in bright primary colors, the effect of the strong reds, blues, and yellows must have been singular. Two walls were finished in copper paint, and two others in light yellow and sage green. A blend of Art Deco style and Native American designs, his elegant patterns provided an appropriate backdrop for the classes held there. Richards's mural marks a curricular change, for courses in modern dance were now offered for the first time.

John Porter Leeper, who taught at the Phoenix Art Center, executed *Women in Sports and the Arts* (fig. 4.20) for the lounge of the Moeur Building. His mural pictures the broad scope of physical education offerings at the college, including drama, music, visual arts, dance, and sports. It was intended to produce a "restful attitude," whereas Richards aimed his to be "stimulating and vigorous."[37] Yet Leeper's young women are active and engaged, as they prepare themselves for future careers and families. Born in Tennessee, Leeper had been raised in Phoenix, studying at Phoenix College and then the Otis Art Institute in Los Angeles. He also executed murals for a tuberculosis sanitarium in Phoenix, but his inclusion of nude figures led officials to hire David Swing to paint landscapes over some of them so as not to offend patients.

Springerville and Flagstaff

While most mural commissions went to painters, some sculptors were given work. Robert Kittredge produced reliefs for the Springerville (1939) and Flagstaff (1940) post offices. He had moved to Sedona in 1930, settling in Oak Creek Canyon. His two Springerville reliefs, *Apache Chiefs Geronimo and Vittorio* (fig. 4.21), were

FIGURE 4.19. Sim Bruce Richards, Modern dance murals, 1939, 20' high × 70' long, Women's Activity Building (now the Moeur Building), Arizona State University.

FIGURE 4.20. John Porter Leeper, *Women in Sports and the Arts*, 1939, oil on canvas, 9' × 24', Women's Activity Building (now the Moeur Building), Arizona State University.

FIGURE 4.21. Robert Kittredge, *Apache Chiefs Geronimo and Vittorio*, 1939, plaster relief, 4' diameter, Post Office, Springerville.

inspired by events during the territorial period. The sculptor has represented the two warriors on a raiding party, suggesting the many skirmishes made on the town by the fierce Apaches. The highly stylized composition is compact, yet energized by the galloping horses, the sense of forward movement reinforced by the long spear held by one of the riders. They were the last two chiefs to be subdued during the Indian wars, and the history was fresh enough that the father of the then-current postmaster had been wounded in an engagement with them. In contrast to Fogel's experience in Safford, Springerville's residents had no qualms about

FIGURE 4.22. Robert Kittredge, *Arizona Logging,* 1940, plaster relief, 6' long × 4½' high, Post Office, Flagstaff (unlocated).

celebrating an American Indian theme, especially as "it fitted in so well with the favorite legends of the town—spun around these two local red devils."[38] Context could significantly shape local opinion.

Kittredge was also awarded the commission for Flagstaff in 1938, taking as his theme *Arizona Logging* (fig. 4.22). Lumbering was one of the major industries of Coconino County, and he pictured a team of powerful Percheron horses pulling the ten-foot-tall dolly wheels that were used to bring the timber from the forests to the railroad for shipping. Three men struggle with their task, with the forests from which the great logs have been cut suggested by the growth of trees above the wheel.

FIGURE 4.23. Jay Datus, *Arizona Pageant of Progress,* 1937–38, oil on canvas.

The Arizona Department of Library and Archives

Murals installed in state buildings share content and aesthetic agendas with those in federal structures, giving regional reinforcement to national perspectives. Funded by supplemental federal funds from the Public Works Administration, between 1937 and 1938, Jay Datus executed eight historical murals in the newly constructed west wing of the Capitol, which housed the Department of Library and Archives. His theme was the *Arizona Pageant of Progress* (fig. 4.23), and in the four main panels, the artist portrayed ancient civilizations before the Anglo discovery of North America, and the Spanish missionary, the pioneer, and the modern eras. Four side panels pictured Apaches sending smoke signals. In his "epic in paint," Datus "put the emphasis on periods rather than events, types rather than individuals, the character of people rather than of persons, the collective achievements of men and women who never gained fame but who did their parts faithfully and well, rather than the roles of any one or a few of them."[39]

In the section depicting modern Arizona, a young man and woman stand hand in hand at the edge of the cornice, pausing in purposeful stride toward the future. Behind them are arrayed figures who are contemporary allegories of key aspects of the state's economy—a miner, a cowboy, a logger, and agricultural laborers. Behind them, the Phoenix bird, wings spread, provides a triumphant backdrop for a community looking toward the prosperity that will come from their collective efforts. Datus's broad sweep of Arizona history was both appropriate to the context and typical of the treatment of state history in other murals.

The Navajo Nation Council Chamber, Window Rock

The Depression was devastating for reservation populations, already at the bottom of the economic ladder. To aid them, the federal government established a series of separate programs for Native Americans, broadly known as the Indian New Deal.[40] These were administered by John Collier, who served as commissioner of Indian Affairs between 1933 and 1945. The centerpiece of his agenda was the Indian Reorganization Act of 1934, which aimed to shift federal mandates from assimilation to tribal economic and political autonomy.

The arts (especially as arts and crafts) were an important component of the Indian New Deal and were featured at Interior's headquarters. The establishment of the Indian Arts and Crafts Board, in 1935, sought to foster cultural pride in tribal heritage while stimulating commercial development within Native American communities. The tourist market would be an important adjunct to these efforts. Representations of Native Americans were common in thirties murals, and artists broadly portrayed popular archetypes of Indian life, as well as notable historical events. However popular Indians were as imagery, only a small number of Indian artists received New Deal commissions (this reflected both their smaller numbers nationally and the narrower opportunities available to them under the Indian New Deal), the most prominent being the six who produced murals for the new headquarters of the Department of the Interior in Washington, D.C.[41] It is within this cultural context that the only Indian New Deal mural in Arizona was created.[42]

In 1933, Collier selected Window Rock as the site for the new capital of the Navajo Nation. Funded by the Public Works Administration, the large sandstone Council Chamber (1934–35) was constructed of indigenous materials, its octagonal design inspired by the traditional hogan form.[43] Designed by the firm of Mayers, Murray, and Phillip of New York City, the structure can best be characterized as Navajo Revival. Indeed, many tribal members disapproved of Anglo use of their historic structure type.[44]

Collier intended that art by Navajos be a prominent feature in this handsome new building. The main door into the chamber was flanked by a pair of carved wood panels by Charles K. Shirley: *The Livelihood and Religious Rites of the Navajo Indians*. On one side, a silversmith and a weaver are set against a mountain backdrop, with a dramatic cloud-filled sky enlivened by a rainbow and lightning bolts, while on the other a hunting scene is portrayed. Hoping to employ a team of seven or eight Navajo artists, Collier wanted murals to be installed not only in the council chamber but also in day schools on the reservation. A lack of funding prevented the realization of his plan. In 1937, the mural scheme was revived, this time to be executed by Shirley and Andy van Tsinnajinnie. Once again no monies were authorized.

Five years later funds finally became available from the Civil Works Administration, and Navajo painter Gerald Nailor was awarded the commission. An accomplished artist, he had studied at the famed Santa Fe Indian School with Dorothy Dunn between 1935 and 1937. In undertaking this project, the artist was challenged with creating a mural in a space consisting of about eleven thousand square feet, that was seventy feet wide and thirty feet high.

Nailor's *The History and Progress of the Navajo Nation* (1942–43) dynamically portrayed the broad sweep of the Diné chronicle in a series of eight panels covering the walls of the chamber. Beginning with the arrival of the Spanish missionaries in the seventeenth century, he depicted key events from earliest colonial contact through the present day. Nailor portrayed the traditional lifestyle of his ancestors, including the hunting and gathering of wild food and the cultivation of corn, squash, and melons. With the arrival of the Spanish, the Navajo began to raise sheep and engaged more intensively in agriculture and raising livestock. Weaving and silversmithing became important activities during this period.

His portrayals also included painful events from Navajo history as well, including the many misunderstandings and broken peace treaties with the United States government the tribe had experienced, culminating in Kit Carson's final campaign. In Canyon de Chelly, their crops and livestock destroyed, the starving Navajo surrendered. Marched nearly five hundred miles to Fort Sumner in New Mexico, they began a four-year detention at Bosque Redondo under miserable conditions that resulted in the death of nearly three thousand Navajos.

In 1868 a new treaty granted them reservation lands of nearly three and a half million acres, enabling them to finally return home. Once settled, they built up their flocks of sheep and herds of horses. The establishment of trading posts and schools, along with the arrival of the railroad, meant they were firmly linked to the Anglo community. The twentieth century continued to bring many changes to the reservation, and Nailor's cycle concludes with the modern Navajo world, in which education played an important role. Adaptable, with values grounded in family, agriculture, and livestock, they continued to negotiate a balance between Navajo tradition and the dominant white culture.

Photographer Milton Snow posed Nailor in front of a section of his completed mural (fig. 4.24). Visible is a rug on a loom and a silversmith at work, with a cluster of horses and sheep suggesting a settled life. Such scenes were common subjects for Anglo painters and photographers, and reference the arts and crafts that were a significant point of intersection between the Indians and the tourists who sought an authentic experience of the American West. In depicting traditional ways, the image suggests neither political turmoil nor the economic devastation of the Depression.

FIGURE 4.24. Gerald Nailor at work on *The History and Progress of the Navajo Nation*, Navajo Nation Council Chamber, Window Rock, 1943. Photograph by Milton Snow.

Nailor's paintings are typical of the studio style in their decorative abstraction, muted palette, and elegant outlines. His Interior and Window Rock murals marked a promising beginning to the career of a talented young painter who would die tragically young a decade later at the age of thirty-five.

The reception of Native American imagery in Arizona's New Deal murals depended significantly on the context. Absent in Window Rock are the fierce warriors who were celebrated in the post office in Springerville. Nor was there the controversial clash regarding whose history would be represented, such as the one that greeted the original proposal for Safford. Nailor had experienced first-hand the mission boarding schools that suppressed Indian cultural identity in an attempt to "Americanize" them (for instance, students were forbidden to speak their own language). Implicit in the paintings at Window Rock are both a critique of federal Indian policy and a strong affirmation of Navajo culture. The celebration of community values and heritage typical of these murals reinforces the distinctive civic character of the towns where they were installed and may be understood within the matrix of government support for the arts.

CHAPTER 5

THE GOVERNMENT LENS
Documentary Photography in Arizona

The best-known government documentary work was done for the Farm Security Administration (FSA), and the photographs sponsored by the FSA came to define "documentary" for many years thereafter. The iconic image of the Depression remains Dorothea Lange's *Migrant Mother* (1936), which she made while employed by the FSA. In this chapter I focus on the work of Lange and Russell Lee. Both are well known, though their Arizona work is not. Russell Lee traveled widely throughout Arizona on three extensive trips, producing the largest number of Arizona images of any of the government photographers who visited the state.[1] A little more than half of the nearly fourteen hundred Arizona FSA/OWI images are by Lee. Because they traversed the country on numerous road trips, Lange and Lee gained a sense of regional difference and identity.

The head of the FSA's Historical Section was Roy Stryker. He had grown up in Colorado, and after graduating from Columbia University with a major in economics in 1924, he remained in New York to work with Rexford Tugwell, collaborating with him on his text *American Economic Life* (1925). In compiling illustrations, which included images by earlier reformist photographers Jacob Riis and Lewis Hine, Stryker realized how powerfully photographs could convey a fundamental concept: "Economics is not money. Economics is people."[2] Tugwell became a member of FDR's "brain trust," and went to Washington to organize the FSA's predecessor, the Resettlement Administration (RA). It was he who hired Stryker to head the Historical Section. Stryker, an administrator not an artist, in turn assembled a team of more than a dozen photographers who for nearly eight years traveled extensively throughout America taking pictures.

The role of the FSA photographers was to record the condition of American agriculture ravaged by the Depression, but Stryker expanded his agency's mission to document what he regarded as "The American way of life."[3] Landscape artists like Ansel Adams dismissed the imagery that was the hallmark of the FSA, observing to Stryker: "What you've got are not photographers. They're a bunch of sociologists with cameras."[4] Stryker's photographers created an extraordinary archive of more than 150,000 images, "done in a search for the heart of the American people."[5]

The Depression challenged the nation at every level, but the economic devastation that confronted ordinary Americans also served to unite them as they faced uncertain times. The overarching theme of shared experiences that was the foundation of the FSA file conveyed a sense of community through a visual record that aimed to portray fundamental American values. Because the identities of their subjects were often not recorded, they necessarily read as types, reinforcing the fact that theirs was a national story grounded in local conditions. The photoessays they produced presented an ideology of shared visual symbols. Close-up shots of individual faces, views of the homes in which individuals lived, scenes of their work, and images of their participation in public events reveal the cooperative civic life fundamental to a democratic society.

Photographs taken by Dorothea Lange and Russell Lee clearly document just how hard Arizona's rural areas were hit by the Depression. The state was a crossroads for transients, both displaced people passing through and migratory laborers in search of seasonal work. That the state's economic base was not diversified—agriculture, mining, and tourism remained the main industries—left it vulnerable to economic fluctuation.[6]

Russell Lee: Community Portraits

Russell Lee, possessed of a keen eye for the specifics of social geography, eloquently captured this spirit of the local in his Arizona photographs. Attuned to the shifting economics of thirties America, his images present a fluid definition of what constituted a community. It could be temporary, as in the many views he took of migratory labor camps, whose unsettled populations constantly changed, coming together seasonally, and dispersing when whatever had brought them there was harvested. Long-established communities like Concho were also pictured, conveying the strong familial values of an old town whose original Mormon settlers had been supplanted by Hispanic sheepherders. In the case of Taliesin, the community was an artistic one led by architect Frank Lloyd Wright. Wherever it was found, copper mining created scrappy communities, like the Phelps Dodge company town of Bisbee. The agricultural cooperatives set up by the FSA at Casa Grande, Chandler, and Camelback Farms were another form of constructed community.

Born in Ottawa, Illinois, Lee graduated from Lehigh University in 1925, with a major in chemical engineering. His first wife, whom he married in 1927, was painter Doris Emrick, also an Illinois native. He pursued a business career, and not until they moved to Kansas City in 1929, so she could study at the Kansas City Art Institute, did he begin to paint. A year later they relocated to San Francisco, where they met Mexican muralist Diego Rivera, whose highly public paintings had a strong social purpose. In 1931, they moved east, dividing their time between Woodstock, New York, an art colony favored by progressive and modernist artists, and New York City.

Russell Lee realized he wanted to engage subjects drawn from everyday life, but he had not yet discovered the right medium to express what he wanted to say. That changed when he acquired his first camera in 1935. Frustrated with his slow progress as a painter, he took to the medium of photography right away. Although their media now diverged, Russell and Doris Lee overlapped thematically. Throughout her career, she favored scenes of rural life and ordinary people engaged in everyday activities, subjects portrayed by regionalist painters and FSA photographers.

Ben Shahn, an artist with a strong social consciousness who worked for the RA, introduced Lee to Stryker in 1936. The agency soon hired him. Russell Lee and Roy Stryker established a good working relationship from the start. As "a great cataloger of facts,"[7] Lee "was the ideal FSA photographer."[8] Not only did he take more photographs than any other FSA artist, Lee remained with the Historical Section until 1942, the longest tenure of any of Stryker's photographers. Lee's idealism was typical of the Historical Section staff, and he believed in the work of the agency that employed him, describing himself straightforwardly in 1941: "I am a photographer hired by a democratic government to take pictures of its land and its people."[9] In wanting to make "photographs of America and Americans,"[10] he spoke to a broad national interconnectedness, which the government sought to reinforce during a period of economic challenge.

In 1938, Lee met Jean Smith, a Texas reporter, and, after he divorced Doris, they married the next year. Jean proved to be an excellent partner in her husband's career, taking field notes, editing images, and writing narrative captions to accompany them. A skilled journalist, she conversed easily with people, freeing Russell to take pictures undistracted. The Lees arrived in Phoenix in April 1940, "after a trip through about all the extremes you could imagine—windstorms, rain, dust storms, sleet, driving snow, and finally tropical heat."[11] Lee was impressed with the desert city: "It seems to be a most modern community—beautiful schools, lawns, stores, swimming pools, etc., with all the irrigated crops."[12] Still, when it was time to leave Phoenix, he was glad to do so, as he reported to Stryker when he arrived: "what a *hot* sun."[13]

The dry state's urban areas were sustained by water, and he wrote Stryker that he planned to shoot images that would add a great deal to "our story of water— the final result of water when used to irrigate the desert,"[14] making possible the agriculture and citrus orchards that were central to the region's economy. As he also wanted "to show the end result of water use—buildings, parks, etc,"[15] his photograph of the municipal golf course (fig. 5.1), whose grass was also sustained by irrigation, was a fitting image. Golf remains a sport indelibly associated with

FIGURE 5.1. Russell Lee, Municipal golf course, Phoenix, May 1940.

the region's tourist industry. In addition to a band shell (which Lee also photographed), the Public Works Administration had built a clubhouse, a boathouse, and an office for the golf club in this park.

Lee's major photo essay in Phoenix portrayed the United Producers' and Consumers' Cooperative. With more than twelve thousand members, most of whom were small farmers, it was very successful. Items were bought in bulk so that its members could get the lowest prices. Just about anything a farming family could possibly need was available. One image records a salesman demonstrating the virtues of a new refrigerator to a pair of older women (fig. 5.2), reminding viewers that new products, as well as traditional ones, were available for purchase. The cooperative was a gathering place for those who made their living from agriculture, and other members were photographed with their happy children, reinforcing the idea that it was the strength of families that kept operations like this in business. The emphasis was on both community values and self-sufficiency, qualities Lee sought to convey in much of his Arizona work.

The New Deal was a period of social experiment, and in Maricopa County the government established several different residential models, including temporary camps for migratory workers, and full- and part-time farms for permanent residents. Agua Fria was the first FSA camp to be built in Arizona. Efficiently arranged in a pentagon plan, it permitted the orderly administration of large numbers of people (fig. 5.3). Throughout the Depression and the World War II years, the issue

FIGURE 5.2. Russell Lee, Salesman demonstrating an electric refrigerator to members of the United Producers' and Consumers' Cooperative of Phoenix, May 1940.

of affordable child care became an issue when both parents worked. Day care was a progressive benefit available at Agua Fria during this period. Community buildings were centrally located, and a photograph of the camp buildings presents a tidy (if impermanent) community with everything laid out for modern democratic life for those on the move (fig. 5.4). To bring residents together, a range of social outlets was made available for the leisure entertainment of residents, including Saturday

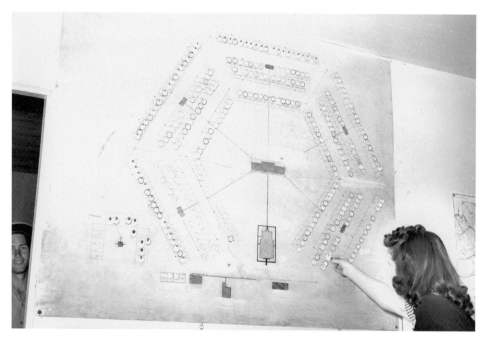

FIGURE 5.3. Russell Lee, Agua Fria Farm Security Administration Camp for migratory workers. Chart showing occupants of shelters, May 1940.

FIGURE 5.4. Russell Lee, Agua Fria Farm Security Administration Camp for migratory workers. View from the water tower, May 1940.

night dances, horseshoes, and baseball. A standard plan meant housing that could be built quickly and inexpensively wherever needed. An oddly prescient image, it forecasts the coordinated construction of internment camps, and even the master-planned communities that were constructed in the region after the end of World War II. Although Sun City, the first of these latter communities, did not open until 1960, Del Webb, its developer, got his start during the New Deal era, constructing military facilities and factories under defense contracts, so he may very well have been influenced by the FSA camp plan and its successors.

Photographs recorded families staying together, with determination, hard work, and some relaxation carrying them through a difficult time. The ideal of stalwart character the government hoped to convey of camp residents is exemplified in a photograph Lee took of a migratory laborer and his wife (fig. 5.5). Their jaws resolute, with his hand on her shoulder, suggesting both protection and partnership, the pair gazes as if to the future. Together they form one of the most basic social units of American society: two were better than one, allied against adversity. That the picture evokes movie stills from John Ford's 1940 film of *The Grapes of Wrath* reveals how thoroughly embedded were FSA photographs in the broader visual culture of the period.[16]

The government camps for migrants offered many more basic services and were far cleaner than those constructed by growers (which were recorded by Lange), but public health remained a major concern for a mobile population. Visiting nurses treated residents in their temporary homes, while doctors were available at the clinic for more serious illnesses and injury. Those with contagious diseases were placed in isolation units. Individual shelters had no plumbing, but there were shared sanitary and laundry units. Many tasks remained gender-specific, and it was the women who did the washing and ironing. Residents were encouraged to keep clean, as Lee recorded in the caption he wrote to accompany his image: "The appearance of migratory workers when hot water and laundry facilities are available is striking and indicates that hard work in the fields and life on the road has not dulled their personal pride."

Tidy metal shelters provided short-term lodging for individual families, with houses constructed for permanent laborers. Workers, who could stay up to a year, often made small improvements, like planting flowers (fig. 5.6). One photograph shows a cat and dog—America's most popular pets—resting companionably on the porch. The lace curtains visible in the front-door window convey a sense of settled domesticity to those with no fixed address. Another recorded the wife of a migratory worker holding a crocheted bedspread she had made, and the caption concludes: "This is one of the indications that these migratory workers are still interested in homes."

Eleven Mile Corner was the second FSA camp in the state, and it shared many features with similar establishments. The presence of a modern medical facility, the Burton Cairns General Hospital, was part of the government's efforts to

FIGURE 5.5. Russell Lee, Migratory laborer and his wife at the Agua Fria FSA Camp, May 1940.

FIGURE 5.6. Russell Lee, Migrant agricultural worker planting flowers in front of his metal shelter, Agua Fria FSA Camp, May 1940.

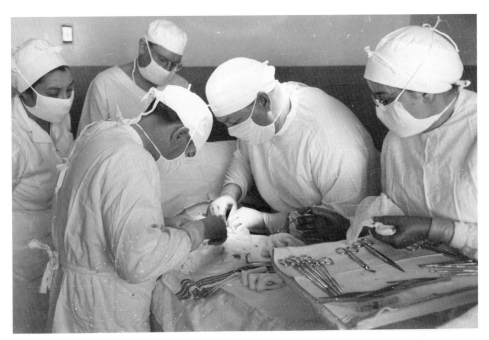

FIGURE 5.7. Russell Lee, Operation at Cairns General Hospital, Eleven Mile Corner, February 1942.

pursue long-term pragmatic solutions to the persistent health-care problems of a mobile population (fig. 5.7).[17] Improved medical care ensured healthier workers, and the government became increasingly involved in public health. Doctors in well-established practices resisted such federal initiatives as "socialized" medicine, but the fact that medical care became increasingly available to those at the bottom of the economic ladder improved their lives, at least when they were at the camps. A full range of health services was available to both camp residents and low-income agricultural workers in the region. The Cairns' facilities, which included a modern surgery, were in stark contrast to the conditions faced by many migrants. At a weekly well-baby clinic, infants were weighed and measured and mothers given instruction in the best practices regarding their care and feeding, giving a hopeful start to the next generation. Federal programs were organized around traditional gender norms, and in the community's home economics building National Youth Administration girls were trained to be nurse's helpers, while vocational classes were offered for boys, who learned gardening, woodworking, and automotive skills.

To accommodate the state's many seasonal laborers, the FSA established a farm workers' community in Yuma, a town that boasted that it was the "Sunshine Capital of America." Its good weather made Yuma a major agricultural center, and Lee recorded the region's bountiful harvests that employed large numbers of migratory workers. As Lee had done plenty of coverage of other FSA settlements, he did not feel he needed any more pictures of daily life in the camps. Instead, he attended an annual field day. Young men from the local Army base participated in the activities that had been organized, as did farm workers from camps nearby. The events concluded with a dinner in the community auditorium, followed by a dance that included an energetic jitterbug contest (fig. 5.8).

Lee did extensive coverage of three experimental ventures that had been organized by the FSA—Casa Grande Valley Farms, Chandler Farms, and Camelback Farms. Government officials hoped that by creating "more stable conditions" for potential residents, the result would be "happy and useful citizens instead of discontented drifters floating hither and yon in search of seasonal employment."[18] Despite the optimistic tone taken by the government, the cooperative model remained controversial. Most ambitious of these experiments was Casa Grande Valley Farms, a cooperative, large-scale mechanized farm, the only full-time settlement organized by the FSA in Arizona.[19] Completed in fall 1937, sixty families were responsible for about four thousand acres. The government sought to assist the new community to become self-sufficient. Members grew and harvested their own crops and maintained their equipment. Collectively, residents could farm more efficiently and cheaply, and in creating a more permanent version of the labor camps, government officials asserted that it represented a "chance for the little man."[20]

Community buildings were the center of the fledgling settlement. Residents participated in many social events and business meetings, all of which were designed to show "democracy in action." Lee's images convey a sense of cooperation between members and FSA officials, with board meetings resembling old-fashioned town meetings. The Sunday school held in the community building enabled residents to further bond through Bible study and singing hymns.

Ideals and reality diverged in practice, with government representatives remaining firmly in control, reluctant to delegate meaningful authority, a situation that was a source of resentment among residents. Lee observed further problems: "There is some feeling at this project among some of the members that they are simply working for a salary and that's all they're getting out of it. However there are plenty of stronger men who are making it go, but one of the big drawbacks is that the members have a rather difficult time getting Oklahoma and Texas out of their minds and getting accustomed to Arizona and all its aridity. The matter of water alone is curbing the project."[21] Many had already left to take jobs elsewhere.

Livestock was a source of pride, especially the dairy operations, and detailed records were kept on all cows, their healthy production of milk signaling an end to the desperate hunger seen in Lange's photographs. A woman holding her prize-winning canned goods from the state fair conveys, if not prosperity, at least the idea that her family did not want for food (fig. 5.9). In another photograph, a woman and her pet look into the refrigerator, with Lee's caption reminding viewers: "Even the cat knows that the refrigerator contains plenty of food." A stable society provided well for all living creatures. These scenes may not have been "true" everywhere, but they spoke to governmental aspirations to improve conditions.

FIGURE 5.8. Russell Lee, Jitterbug contest, Second Annual Field Day, FSA Camp, Yuma, March 1942.

FIGURE 5.9. Russell Lee, Casa Grande Valley Farms, wife of a member displaying canned goods with which she won prizes at the state fair, May 1940.

In contrast to Casa Grande, Chandler Farms was established as a part-time farming and cooperative project. Here participants worked at regular jobs, devoting only part of their energies to the cooperative. One unusual feature was a trench silo for underground storage (fig. 5.10). Cheaper to construct than upright silos, trench silos created the difficulty of maintaining the earthen walls, which meant that they were a temporary storage solution until something more permanent could be built. Families occupied what was described in the FSA literature as "highly attractive and unusual two-story adobe apartments"[22] (fig. 5.11). Housing was simple in design, tidily functional, and sparsely furnished. They were models for other developments: "Low-cost but comfortable and reasonably modern

FIGURE 5.10. Russell Lee, Chandler Farms, trench silo, May 1940.

housing is a feature of all units."[23] Their design had received national attention, as Stryker wrote Lee: "At Chandler, you will observe a pretty interesting style of architecture. The Museum of Modern Art and that whole group of modern architects have practically run us ragged around here trying to get good atmospheric shots of the Chandler buildings."[24] The apartments featured modern kitchens and specially designed furniture.

The most spread out of the three cooperatives was Camelback Farms. Located several miles north and northeast of downtown Phoenix, it was established on three tracts—Glendale, Baxter, and Phoenix Homesteads. The three sites were set up to serve the specific needs of three different income levels, and many of the families in Phoenix Homesteads were white-collar workers employed in Phoenix. Regarded as "socially more sophisticated than at the other projects,"[25] Camelback Farms in the official version was not always what the photographers found on-site, as Lee wrote Stryker in 1940: "Camelback Farms are not all they're cracked up to be. The social life at the community is a flop—the only activity now is a bridge club—once every two weeks. The nursery school was disbanded two or three weeks ago. There are no dramatics or such activities. The main trouble seems to be rent and location."[26] Rent was approximately $25 a month, but with the other expenses, overall monthly costs for individual families came to about $150. If a family could afford that, they preferred to buy houses closer to town, nearer friends, schools, and employment. The lack of public transportation made a car

FIGURE 5.11. Russell Lee, Chandler Farms, apartment house, May 1940.

a necessity. On his first visit, Lee found a third of the homes were vacant, though things had improved by the time he returned. He recorded the small but tidy houses there, showing families enjoying leisure time together. Outside, neighbors were shown visiting, reinforcing the community values that were fundamental to the success of such projects.

Baxter's residents were intended to be largely citrus workers, whereas Glendale's were occupied by lettuce and cantaloupe packers and vegetable harvest hands: "The aim is to provide decent homes and assured employment for people of the low-income laborer or lettuce shed worker group."[27] Units set on one-third-acre lots were of adobe construction, with electricity, modern plumbing, and city water. Ending migratory patterns was a goal, with permanent homes meaning that the workers would no longer have to be "fruit tramps."[28]

Most of Lee's Arizona work was done outside the Phoenix area. Copper mining was as important to the Arizona economy as agriculture, and Lee documented the state's many mining communities. In encouraging tourists to visit points of interest through the state, the WPA guide linked mining and tourism, and five of the eleven cities it highlights were grounded in this industry. When mines reopened after economic slumps, "tourist traffic increased."[29] He understood the economic volatility of the industry: "Here are Globe, Bisbee, Douglas, and other towns, thriving when copper is high, depressed when copper is low, dead when copper is gone—such is the fate of a mining town."[30] Mining faced many challenges during the thirties, including "restricted demand, falling prices, foreign

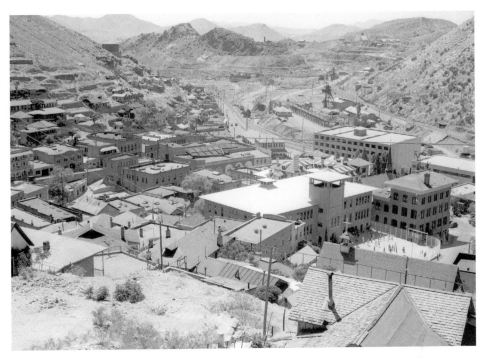

FIGURE 5.12. Russell Lee, Bisbee, May 1940.

competition,"[31] and the depletion of ore reserves. The Depression left many such towns "only half alive."[32]

Copper had long been Arizona's dominant business, expanding rapidly throughout the first two decades of the twentieth century, with the huge open pits challenging the scale of the surrounding landscape. Extensive mining operations existed throughout the state, but it was Bisbee that was Arizona's leading copper mining town (fig. 5.12). By the beginning of the Depression, Arizona led the nation in copper production. Lee recorded the main features of a community whose buildings were cobbled up the sides of the surrounding mountain, overlaying a classic western grid plan on the pattern of random growth typical of mining camps, which were "built for a shifting population."[33] As noted in the WPA guide, "Bisbee's history is essentially the story of its mines,"[34] and they are clearly visible adjacent to the center of town and in the distance. Bisbee owed its survival to a single company, as Lee observed in his caption: "Phelps Dodge practically owns this town, the mines, the principal mercantile company, the hospital, and the hotel." His photograph of the 435-foot-deep Sacramento Pit (fig. 5.13), abandoned in 1929 due to a lack of ore, conveys the immensity of above-ground extraction operations.[35]

A visit to Concho gave him a chance to make a series of photographs documenting a well-established Hispanic community, recording the businesses and adobe houses along the main street (fig. 5.14), and the growing and harvesting of chili peppers hung in *ristras* to dry on the sides of houses. The town, whose residents were directly descended from early Spanish settlers, was located forty miles

FIGURE 5.13. Russell Lee, Sacramento Pit, Bisbee, May 1940.

FIGURE 5.14. Russell Lee, Home of a merchant, Concho, September 1940.

FIGURE 5.15. Russell Lee, Members of the last remaining Mormon family, Concho, October 1940.

from the New Mexico border and had been settled by Spanish-speaking sheep-herders from New Mexico territory in 1861. The sheep industry had once been Concho's major source of income, though the creatures that had made possible its former prosperity appear in only one of Lee's photographs. The Candelarias, a prominent local family, had once owned half of the hundred thousand sheep that had grazed in the area, but the condition of some of the adobe houses, which although tidy, are in need of replastering, indicates the changed economics of the region. Lee noted in his caption that Juan Candelaria, who still owned several thousand acres of land, was "considering selling to the government for FSA use." The Candelarias, among the earliest non-Indian sheep raisers, preceded the Mormon settlement of the late 1870s. By the time Lee came through, only a single Mormon family remained (fig. 5.15). He photographed this last remnant of a social transition that had occurred gradually over many decades.

Lee made about a dozen shots of Frank Lloyd Wright's winter headquarters, Taliesin, which had been established at the foot of the McDowell Mountains in north Scottsdale in 1937 (fig. 5.16). Just three years old, Taliesin was a pioneer artistic community in the region, but it was also transient, as its members returned to the fellowship's Wisconsin headquarters during the summer months. The complex of redwood and native stone structures with an open plan evolved gradually, coexisting comfortably with the landscape. No one is visible, and the apprentices and their famous leader may not have been in residence at the time Lee visited.[36]

FIGURE 5.16. Russell Lee, Taliesin, May 1940.

Stryker encouraged his photographers to take pictures of distinctive regional features. Some subjects were quirky individuals, like Homer Tate, an Arizona "outsider artist," who operated a tourist shop:

> At Safford I ran into one of those rare characters who specializes in primitive sculpture—this man had been in Safford for about 45 years—had never traveled much but was setting down in sculpture and diorama some of his interpretations of what "Dixie" was like, what the Arkansas (Ozark) mountains were like, etc., along with heads of animals, people done in papier maché, cactus, bone and other mediums. I took about 15 or 16 shots. When you see them you'll think you're having a nightmare, but they're all full of humor and very, very good. The man really deserves an exhibition of his work in New York.[37]

He photographed Tate's creations, which were displayed in a shop loaded with strange stuff for sale, ranging from what the proprietor claimed were shrunken heads to mummified rattlesnakes and Gila monsters. One directly referred to the WPA, showing a group of men laboring on a public works project. A sign advertising that they were supported by a government program is prominent in the background (fig. 5.17).

While FSA imagery is necessarily grounded in the contemporaneous, one of Lee's subjects derives from early state history: the Madonna of the Trail (1924–29),

FIGURE 5.17. Russell Lee, WPA work, as visualized by Homer Tate, Safford, May 1940.

a sculpture by August Leimbach located in Springerville (fig. 5.18).[38] The statue had been commissioned by the Daughters of the American Revolution as part of an effort to place markers along the routes taken by early pioneers. Twelve casts were made and installed at regular sites between Bethesda, Maryland, and Upland, California.[39] Standing ten feet tall, she is a strong figure of maternal virtue, clutching her baby in her left arm, while firmly holding a rifle in her right hand. Her son clings to her skirts as she strides purposefully forward, ready to face whatever unknown danger has befallen her unseen husband, her sturdy boots crushing a prickly pear cactus.

A widely recognized figure by this period, her iconography is grounded in a long history of gendered representations of Manifest Destiny justifying the divine right of western settlement. Her sunbonnet was a dual symbol of femininity and civilization and was also an article of clothing worn by the thirties migrants, making her emblematic of a new generation, one that feared economic ruin rather than Indian attack. Modern women displayed a similar determination in facing the adversities of the Depression as they made their migrations west. What Lee recorded was a public monument to a strong white woman who was part of the westward expansion, contrasting with a long tradition of masculinist imaging.

If the Springerville Madonna represented the strength of early families, another variation on the theme of familial connection could be seen in the town of Salome. Located in central western Arizona, it had been founded in 1904 by

FIGURE 5.18. Russell Lee, Madonna of the Trail, Springerville, April 1940.

FIGURE 5.19. Russell Lee, Marriage mill, Salome, February 1942.

humorist and "auto poet" Dick Wick Hall, who published his "laughing gas" in his paper, the *Salome Sun*. As a regional character, he was remembered long after his death, which occurred three years before the beginning of the Depression, and several of his tall tales are mentioned in the WPA guide.

But it wasn't Hall's populist literary legacy that attracted Lee in Salome but its marriage mills (fig. 5.19). California, about sixty miles away, had a three-day wait-ing period, making the town a mecca for those more impatient to wed (there were also wedding chapels in Yuma). The town Lee visited was similar to what one writer described in 1949: "complete with air-field, modern accommodations, auto-mobile facilities, and the legal machinery for quick marriages, squats invitingly on the floor of the desert. And it's only 150 miles to Old Mexico if you feel the need of a quick divorce so, among other advantages, everything is handy for legalized emotional happiness."[40] Rapid personal ups and downs thus paralleled economic ones during the Depresssion.

One justice of the peace offered twenty-four-hour service and claimed to have married more than three thousand couples in ten years. Another boasted on his small building: "Add a thrill to your trip of romance, no publicity, marriage license issued day or night, No waiting, no delay! Get married here today, Day time just walk in, Nite time just ring bell." The Holsum Bread truck parked nearby adds a mundane touch to the more colorful advertising of the signs.

Dorothea Lange: Documenting Migratory Labor

In stark contrast to the work of Russell Lee, whose view of life was fundamentally optimistic, was that of Dorothea Lange, who took a sharper view. Yet her deep compassion for people in difficult circumstances is evident in her photographs. Lee's subjects often appear more settled than those of Lange, who regarded the dislocation of those she photographed with a toughness in which one senses the essence of how many coped with the Depression.

Lange's understanding of Depression issues came from her experience as a westerner, and her Arizona work was deeply rooted in her personal chronicle. She had settled in San Francisco in 1918 and opened a commercial studio there the next year. Favoring a pictorialist style, even in the formalism of her studio portraits, she connected directly with people, especially women. By the time she took her first images of the Depression, she had been a professional photographer for a decade and a half. Lange, born in the East, was an active part of artistic circles in San Francisco, and in 1919, she met painter Maynard Dixon. Despite the considerable differences in their ages and personal experiences—she was twenty-four and he was twenty years her senior—the pair married in 1920. The fifteen years of their marriage proved an artistically productive relationship, if fraught with the personal challenges of a partnership between two independent individuals, both of whom were artists.

Dixon had first visited Arizona at the turn of the twentieth century and returned regularly to the state for the rest of his career. Lange sometimes accompanied him on his extended summer travels throughout the Southwest in search of subjects, and together they made several trips to Arizona, visiting the Navajo and Hopi reservations in 1922 and 1923. In Dixon's company, she entered aesthetic and geographic territory that was emphatically his, for the landscape and Native peoples of the West were the subjects of his signature work. She had always lived in cities, and her experience of the remote beauty of the state was memorable: "We went into a country that was endless and timeless."[41]

For Lange, it was the first time she had worked outside the studio without the constraints of a commission, and she now attempted to record the faces of people she did not know in an unfamiliar setting over which she had no control. Her first photographs of southwestern subjects took their cue from Dixon's paintings, revealing her tentativeness with subjects completely new to her. Like so many visitors, she was fascinated by the Native Americans she encountered, and the romantic pictorialism of Lange's first Arizona photographs reflect popular imaging stereotypes in the tradition of Edward S. Curtis and others, who, fascinated by an exotic "other," created pictures symbolic of a vanishing people.

However, Lange's response to those she encountered laid the foundation for her later government work, and when she visited the Indian School in Tuba City, she "was filled with surprise and disgust at the harsh and unjust treatment of the

Indian children by those in authority."[42] She may not have yet found her independent artistic voice, but her sympathy for those in unfortunate circumstances had clearly already been formed. Within a decade her style would change dramatically.

Lange did her first street photographs around 1933, exhibiting them the next year. Her social conscience quickly emerged in a photographic vision grounded in the concerns of ordinary people. Her strong technical and compositional skills and deep personal empathy had found a subject that enabled her to find her voice as an artist. Using a large-format camera, her deliberate method of working, combined with strong compositional skills, gave strength to her formal vision.

She felt driven to photograph the effects of the Depression, and, wanting to improve the lot of those she recorded, found employment first with state agencies, and then with the federal government. Dixon and Lange diverged artistically and personally. Although he worked for the PWAP and executed a strong series on "The Forgotten Man," Dixon continued to portray the sustaining grandeur of the vast western landscape, and the mythic strength of the region's indigenous residents. Lange's focus was firmly on contemporary life. Ultimately his vision remained with the timelessness of the Old West and hers with the complicated changeable economics of the new.

Lange was committed to an art of social responsibility, her marriage to Dixon finally unraveled, and they were divorced in 1935. Lange met Paul Schuster Taylor, a labor economist at the University of California at Berkeley, whose specialty was migratory workers. More interested in people than statistics, he recognized that Lange's photographs could graphically convey the human problems central to his research.

Taylor and Lange began to collaborate early in 1935, and together they produced a series of reports for state and federal agencies. She found more or less steady employment with RA and FSA, though for the next few years she was hired, laid off, and rehired several times by Stryker, who found her distance from Washington and her independence troublesome. Taylor and Lange's marriage in 1935 provided her both financial and emotional security and the prospect of a shared professional life; it was a true intellectual collaboration—he with words, she with pictures. She thus possessed a more extensive understanding of the conditions affecting her subjects than any other government photographer.

Both Lange and Taylor were highly practical and empirical in their approach, preferring fieldwork to theory. Lange had learned from Taylor the value of being a good listener and a careful note-taker, and her captions and reports reveal an attention to specific local detail and a broad acquaintance with regional problems.

Documenting the desperate economic plight of poor migratory agricultural laborers nationwide, Lange had both a strong personal vision and a deep human sympathy that gave to her work a powerful blend of art and historical record that remains resonant. The New Deal era was the most productive of her career, and her documentary work helped define "public photography."[43] The FSA, for which she took some of her most compelling images, sent her on assignment to more than two dozen different states, though her work was concentrated in the South and the West, especially in California, where she lived. Her Arizona work remains little known, though the photographs she took in this state are as compelling as any she took elsewhere.

The migratory laborers who were Lange's photographic specialty had long been central to Arizona's agricultural economy. She recorded workers in caravans on the highway, as ragged roadside squatters, and in the appalling squalor of the growers' camps. Although an essential component of the state's crop harvest, these seasonal workers were not made welcome. Lange soon established herself as the chronicler of the desperate and displaced individuals and families.

Arizona's harsh and unforgiving desert climate did not encourage lingering, and the rickety vehicles of the Okies, Arkies, and Texies fleeing the Dust Bowl to what they hoped would be better economic conditions in California regularly broke down in Arizona. Some had already planned to harvest cotton there, while others could afford to go no further. Most aimed to continue on to California when they had earned enough money to do so. Often they were simply people with "no place to stay and no place to go."[44] Typical was the comment made by a mother with seven children whose husband had died in Arizona: "We'd have gone back to Oklahoma from Arizona, but there wasn't anywhere to go to."[45]

This massive westward migration was impelled by economic crisis. The goal of fellow travelers, as least regarding Arizona, was succinctly articulated by Tom Joad in John Steinbeck's 1939 novel, *The Grapes of Wrath,* when he responded to a New Mexico border guard's query: "How long do you plan to be in Arizona?" with "No longer'n we can get acrost her." The guard put a sticker on their car certifying that they were carrying no plants, and warned them: "Go ahead, but you better keep movin.'"[46] The states that welcomed tourists were not eager for the unemployed to linger. Steinbeck's protagonists motored across Route 66 as quickly as they could, though they would soon discover that plenty of misery awaited them in California.

The slow-moving, overloaded cars of refugees crossing the state were distinctive, as Lange's husband Taylor wrote in an article published in 1935, "Again the Covered Wagon": "The refugees travel in old automobiles and light trucks, some of them home-made, and frequently with trailers behind. All their worldly possessions are piled on the car and covered with old canvas or ragged bedding, with perhaps bedsprings atop, a small iron cook-stove on the running board, a battered trunk, lantern, and galvanized iron washtub tied on behind. Children, aunts, grandmothers and a dog are jammed into the car, stretching its capacity incredibly."[47]

Lange captured his words in her 1940 photograph of a single migratory cotton picker standing beside his car, which had broken down (fig. 5.20). The landscape looks as bleak as his prospects for employment, and what little his family

FIGURE 5.20. Dorothea Lange, Highway 87 near Coolidge, migratory cotton picker stopped by engine trouble alongside the road, November 1940.

possesses is tenuously attached to his vehicle. In this image, the auto dominates the composition. Formally, the man plays a comparatively minor role, echoing his diminished status as a marginal worker in an increasingly mechanized agricultural industry. The car, one of the symbols of modernity and the American dream, here provides its owner neither pleasure nor status, but is simply the unreliable means of travel from one meager job to another. Like many of Lange's images, this one is part of a small series, endowing her photographs with a narrative character (this storytelling character is true of FSA images generally). She first shot from a distance, gradually coming in closer to her subjects. The one that precedes this image reveals that there were three carloads of families stopped by the roadside. As Lange observed in her caption: "Related family groups frequently travel like this, in pairs or in caravans of three or four." In the final photograph, only the very back of the car is visible.

These travelers, impelled by economic necessity, were the victims of a "social erosion"[48] as serious as that which afflicted the land they fled. This new western migration was sustained by the sheer need to survive rather than the dreams of a new beginning. These were folks who were "starved, stalled, and stranded."[49] Such bands of cars represented the conditions pictured in *An American Exodus*, the landmark book about the drought-impelled migration westward and its human cost published by Lange and Taylor in 1939.

Lange traveled in Arizona for the RA/FSA in 1936, 1937, and 1938, but took only a small number of photographs for that agency in the state. Lange's most significant body of work in Arizona was done in 1940 under the sponsorship of the Bureau of Agricultural Economics (BAE), which sent her to document cotton workers in Arizona and California. This assignment gave her the chance to do what she did best, an extended photo essay on a topic with which she was thoroughly familiar.

Arizona was an important part of the western cotton belt. Although Native Americans had grown cotton in the Southwest long before the arrival of the pioneers, the role of "white gold"[50] as a significant agricultural industry in the region dates from the second decade of the twentieth century, when World War I cut off African imports. Irrigated by the extensive canal system made possible by a series of dams constructed by the Bureau of Reclamation, cotton became the state's principal crop.

While not as volatile as copper mining, the cotton industry was still subject to significant fluctuations, and the onset of the Depression dealt a serious blow to Arizona growers. Recovery came late in the decade, by which time it had been transformed into a large industrialized agribusiness, pushing aside the small-scale farmer. This situation had even been noted in the WPA guide: "Machine farming has been adopted widely in Arizona, and this has an inevitable effect of increasing the size of the farm unit and decreasing the number of owner-operators."[51] Huge tracts of land owned by absentee corporations concentrated economic control in the hands of a few, effectively ending the agrarian ideal that had long been part of the American ethos. Cotton became increasingly mechanized, huge in scale, and irrigated, comprising "factories in the field."[52] Large holdings of land supplanted the small, family-owned farm. Within such a corporate structure, a large migratory labor force was easily exploited.

Much of Lange's BAE work was done near Eloy, the regional center for Arizona's agricultural trade. It was there that the cotton was collected and processed, and where temporary and permanent residents came to shop. On Saturday afternoons during cotton harvest, pickers crowded the main street of Eloy, where they would buy what supplies they could afford for the coming week.

Agriculture on this scale was dependent on low-paid seasonal migratory labor, caught in a nearly inescapable cycle of poverty. Lange's image of one of the region's many cotton fields (fig. 5.21) is virtually interchangeable with that of any other state. The broad expanse of the field in which the workers labor, burdened by their heavy sacks, conveys the arduous length of time it took to fill them. Individual bolls had to be methodically plucked from the sharp-edged pods. The workers led lives completely absorbed by their temporary employment, camping adjacent to the fields to maximize their picking time.

In the West, the forerunner of the large industrialized farm was, as Lange observed in her caption, "the plantation system of slave days." But Arizona's sparse population meant there was an insufficient supply of local labor to harvest the crop when it was ready to be picked. To attract workers to the state, the Arizona

FIGURE 5.21. Dorothea Lange, Cortaro Farms, Pinal County, November 1940.

Farm Labor Service, representing the growers, mounted an extensive recruitment campaign in Texas, Oklahoma, Missouri, and Arkansas. Arizona was presented as "a promised land which could solve for them the problems which they could not solve at home."[53] The cotton growers optimistically reported that a good worker "could pick from 300 to 400 pounds of cotton a day, which would mean an income from $14 to $19 a week per picker."[54] In practice, it was nearly impossible to earn these wages. Within the precarious economic hierarchy of seasonal agricultural labor, cotton picking was the lowest paid, making it "the least desirable of all migratory agricultural work."[55]

The campaign resulted in an oversupply of labor that benefited growers, not migrants, who did not discover the low wages and poor living conditions until after they arrived, at which point they could not afford to leave. Lange's picture of a truckload of pickers who have recently pulled in from Arkansas (fig. 5.22) must have been a familiar sight. That they had driven across Texas and New Mexico in their journey to Arizona underscores their desperation, belying the neighborly tone of Lange's caption: "We come over to help these folks pick their cotton." The discomfort they experienced throughout their trip must have been considerable, and the off-angle view of the truck and the range of ages of the occupants simultaneously convey their uncertain economic situation and their powerlessness to change it.

By 1939, the problems generated by the labor surplus had reached crisis proportions. Pickers endured hardship and miserable odds that their situation would improve, for although these temporary workers were essential to the state's farm industries, permanent Arizona residents disdained cotton pickers as "poor white trash."[56]

FIGURE 5.22. Dorothea Lange, Truckload of cotton pickers from Arkansas, Pinal County, November 1940.

FIGURE 5.23. Dorothea Lange, Cotton picker coming down the row, Maricopa County, November 1940.

Picking cotton involved long days of exhausting labor in the hot Arizona sun. A close-up image of a single worker's hands makes no reference to age or race, and the emblematic quality of a widely shared experience suggested by an image of a single anonymous individual (fig. 5.23) implies a depth of visual reference evoking a long art-historical tradition of picturing European peasants engaged in endless back-breaking labor, as defined by nineteenth-century French painters Jean-François Millet, Gustave Courbet, and others. Heavy bags were hoisted up for weighing, so field supervisors could calculate wages, and then dumped into trucks to be taken to cotton gins for processing. Those who could afford to do so moved on at the end of the season, hoping never to return.

Lange recorded one cotton picker as he paused to rest against a ladder, his empty cotton sack slung over his shoulder (fig. 5.24). He stares directly at the photographer, the leathery palm of his hand turned outward as he wipes his mouth with the back. Simultaneously he indicates the heat of the day, his weariness from working long hours, and his mistrust of the intrusive camera held by a stranger employed by a government from which he received little benefit.

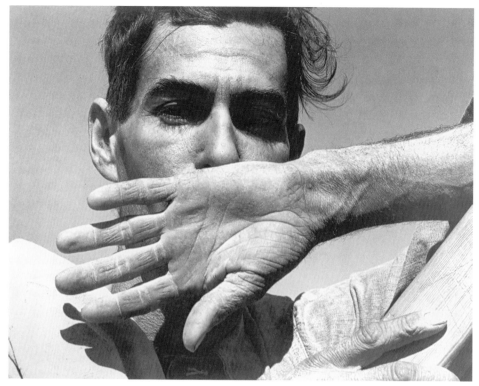

FIGURE 5.24. Dorothea Lange, *Migratory Cotton Picker, Eloy, Arizona*, 1940, gelatin silver print, 10 ⅜" × 13⅜".

Many pickers had little choice but to live in camps located near the fields, the majority run by growers. Close attention to profit margins and scant concern for the easily replaceable workers they had hired gave them little incentive to improve the deplorable and crowded living conditions. The shacks in these camps provided meager material comfort for their temporary occupants. Set in landscapes devoid of vegetation, they graphically show the degraded circumstances of those who occupied them, which, with minimal water and sanitation, posed a major public health problem. The contrast to the orderly government camps photographed by Lee is heartbreaking.

One family set up camp by the side of the road, next to an open field (fig. 5.25). The children's grandmother, aged beyond her years, and the four children live in appalling conditions that were little worse than the growers' camps. The family had picked cotton in Amarillo, Texas, and Roswell, New Mexico, and planned to return to Texas at the end of the season. The nurturing maternal archetype of the Madonna and child here conveys neither familial nor social stability. She holds the sick baby awkwardly with one arm, its struggle emblematic of their anguished circumstances, and as he kicks and pushes against her, he receives little comfort. The mother and father may be at work with their older children, and Lange's image starkly illustrates their abandonment by society. The future looked grim for these ragged children on the margins of the Depression.

Figure 5.25. Dorothea Lange, On Highway 87, south of Chandler, November 1940.

FIGURE 5.26. Dorothea Lange, Near Coolidge, young girl works in cotton field on Saturday morning, November 1940.

Many of the workers Lange recorded were children, who spent their days picking cotton with their parents (fig. 5.26). Her young subjects are shown nearly engulfed by the prickly vegetation that surrounds them, dragging long heavy bags on their small shoulders. Exhausted, they often seem unaware of their surroundings. They concentrate with quiet dignity, and their averted gazes suggest good workers dutifully engrossed in their assigned tasks. Such young laborers were among the most helpless of those she photographed, and her images powerfully express the painful ironies facing their parents, who might have hoped for a better life for the next generation but who were forced by economic reality to put their children to work alongside them. Enforcement of school attendance rules was lax, and except for the sporadic education of their children, pickers remained "almost completely isolated from the social life of the community in which they work."[57]

FIGURE 5.27. Dorothea Lange, Children in a democracy. Bus carries migratory cotton pickers' children from FSA mobile camp for migratory laborers to the Eloy district school, Pinal County, November 1940.

Their separateness is starkly conveyed by her picture of a group about to leave for school (fig. 5.27). Their expressions are wary, and that the side of the bus separates subject from viewer connotes the social barriers they would soon face in town.

The children's meager earnings painfully reinforce the marginality of their existence, the subject of *Children in a Democracy,* a scathing 1942 government report whose title Lange referred to in her captions. She realized that simply documenting these conditions would not be enough to effect the substantive change for which she and her fellow New Dealers hoped. Government officials, too, recognized that while they could provide some temporary assistance, "a permanent solution of the difficulties presented by the migratory worker in the Southwest cannot be expected until far-reaching social and economic readjustments occur in the areas from which the great bulk of these migrants come."[58] The problems of the Southwest, economically linked to the Dust Bowl and to the South, affected ordinary and powerless people, requiring federal initiatives on a national scale if anything was to change on the local level.

Race, labor, and economics have long been flash points in Arizona, and Lange's photographs strongly convey the ethnic diversity of the labor force. For

FIGURE 5.28. Dorothea Lange, Children of drought refugee family, Chandler, May 1937.

people of color, the Depression was especially devastating. Hispanics comprised the largest minority in Phoenix, and, already at the bottom of the economic ladder, first felt the effects of what this community referred to as *La Crisis.* Many Mexicans crossed the border into Arizona during the thirties. When jobs were plentiful, American employers were eager for Mexican workers, but with so many white American citizens unemployed, those once welcomed as cheap labor now became the focus of anger and resentment from jobless Anglos. Once a major component of the Arizona labor force, they now found their subsistence-level positions taken by unemployed white Dust Bowl refugees from the southern plains. As Lange noted in the label she wrote accompanying a picture taken in Chandler in 1937: "Drought families are now mingling with and supplanting Mexican laborers in the Southwest." Two children stand uneasily outside the adobe building where they live, the gestures of the young girl to the left reflecting the uncertainty of their future[59] (fig. 5.28).

No agriculture was possible without water. In a series of handsome photographs, Lange recorded the work of a *zanjero,* the Mexican overseer of irrigation ditches who siphoned water into a field on a large farm (fig. 5.29). In addition to opening the gates to let allotments of water flow, he also collected fees for the canal company.[60] He was more fortunate than most in that he was employed year round and did not have to make seasonal relocations. The monumentality

FIGURE 5.29. Dorothea Lange, *Zanjero,* Eloy District, Pinal County, November 1940.

FIGURE 5.30. Dorothea Lange, Weighing cotton at the truck, Cortaro Farms, Pinal County, November 1940.

with which Lange imbues her figure conveys both the stability of his job and the responsibility of his position.

African Americans fared no better than their Hispanic counterparts. Government agencies operated under policies shaped by widely held racial views; the camps were segregated, with worse facilities for people of color, and white laborers were paid more for the same work. Black pickers appear in Lange's Arizona photographs, but their imaging by government photographers generally was shaped by national perceptions. Stryker suggested that Lange emphasize white workers, "since we know that these will receive much wider use."[61] Her photograph of an African American woman hoisting the heavy sack that nearly overwhelms her at the weighing truck reinforces the sense that the problems facing those who were not white were neglected within the federal system of assistance[62] (fig. 5.30).

Only a few images of Native Americans were documented by FSA and BAE photographers in Arizona, and Lange recorded Yaqui Indians who were employed off the reservations as pickers (fig. 5.31). These were neither the picturesque Native Americans featured in the tourist trade nor the favored research subjects of archaeologists and anthropologists. In her caption, she reveals that many chose not to live in housing provided by the growers, but rather in the traditional desert

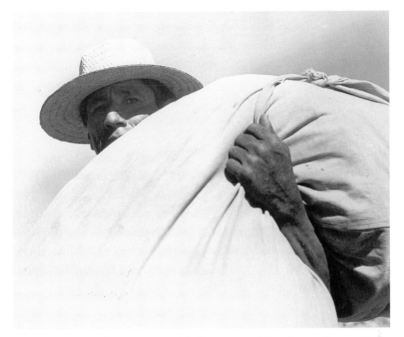

FIGURE 5.31. Dorothea Lange, Yaqui Indian cotton picker, Cortaro Farms, Pinal County, November 1940.

FIGURE 5.32. Dorothea Lange, Yaqui Indian *Jacal*, Cortaro Farms, Pinal County, November 1940.

structures of their ancestors called *jacals* (an Aztec word for "straw house"), made of mud, cactus ribs, and mesquite timbers, and roofed in thatch (fig. 5.32).

The documentary work by Dorothea Lange and Russell Lee done during the New Deal era is informed by consistent thematic interests, and their Arizona images grounded a universal story within a matrix of local experience. Lee's extensive coverage of Arizona captures the essence of FSA programs and collectively remains an invaluable visual record of the state during the Depression. The many photographs he took of subjects unrelated to government projects give fascinating texture to what could have been simply a straightforward report of good deeds done and lives improved through federal intervention. Lange's Arizona BAE photographs emerge as a significant body of her work, in which she produced an extended visual essay on a subject about which she was both well informed and held strong views. Lange's and Lee's powerful images of these forgotten men, women, and children who endured the Depression with fortitude enabled their Arizona experience to resonate nationally.

CHAPTER 6

THE LANDSCAPE OF ARIZONA
The Natural and Unnatural Sublime

The sublimities of the western landscape in Arizona might seem above the desperate economic conditions that engendered the programs established to mitigate them.[1] The state offered an artist stunning formalist possibilities grounded in a long tradition, but within this matrix of awesome grandeur was a swirl of human activity and enterprise. A key early intrusion was the construction of the transcontinental railroad that exemplified "the inevitable encounter between the natural and technological sublime in the American West."[2] But later endeavors were equally significant, conducted on an impressive scale. The western landscape was majestic in both its natural and altered states.

The Landscape of Extraction

Mining was the transformative industry of the American West and was indelibly associated with the Arizona known as the "copper state." Its many mining towns were intertwined with the ore-rich mountains into which they were nestled and comprised "man-made canyons"[3] that colorfully echoed natural landscape formations, competing with it in scale and scenic qualities. Mining caused an immense alteration of the landscape, prefiguring what would be put *on* the land in the form of dams and other public works during the New Deal era.

Arizona's mining and smelting towns were extensively documented by FSA and OWI photographers. Writers for the WPA guide published vivid descriptions for the tourist who might pass through. Globe was given a romantic account: "But on a green and rose-colored hillside at the northern limits the remains of a great copper mine stand on the landmark of a famous old mining camp. Below the dark skeletons of the abandoned buildings lie the black slag dumps and the weathered tailings dumps (gigantic accumulations of copper ore residue). The tailings, leached to colors as fine as those of the surrounding mountains, occupy the creek valley like mellow sand dunes." While guide writers noted that this

FIGURE 6.1. Russell Lee, Copper smelter, Douglas, May 1940.

made "a pleasing picture," old miners regarded the scene as "a grave stone," a sad reminder of the town's once flourishing days.[4] Nearby Miami also was colorfully described: "[T]he smelter's coal-black slag dumps and the cement-colored tailings from the concentrators stretch for miles over the heights and down in to the flat alongside the town. At night, when the smelter is working, the mounds of slag glow red with streams of molten rock dumped from the furnaces."[5]

The typical structures of such communities comprised "houses perched in groups on the hills dominated by the tremendous smelter and waste piles."[6] Russell Lee took photographs in Douglas, a place characterized as a "smelter city"[7] located near the Mexican border, about twenty-four miles from Bisbee (fig. 6.1). He recorded its tall, active smokestacks, the dominant features of such western communities. Smaller towns might feature one tall stack; that there were three here indicates intense activity. His view is panoramic, and the deep foreground, demarcated by the fence that kept the photographer at a distance, combined with an expansive sky, imbues the scene with an impressive industrially scaled grandeur. That it was shot for the FSA denotes that Lee was aware of the contemporary social and economic realities of places like Bisbee and Douglas, subject to a volatile economy where copper prices steadily declined throughout the Depression. But it was not a connection that Ansel Adams, who also worked for the government, would make.[8]

The Sublime Federal Landscape

Mining was not the only large-scale incursion on the western landscape. Wilderness was made increasingly accessible and encroached upon, with the Department of the Interior serving as a key agency in this endeavor. The federal government controlled vast tracts of land in the West, including national parks, forests, and reservations. Art was one means the government used to advance agency policies to the general public. Photographer Ansel Adams would be a key player in visualizing these endeavors to a broad public.

Throughout the New Deal years, painted murals were regular sources of commissions for artists. Installed prominently in highly trafficked government buildings, they were powerful conveyors of national values and government policies. Although less common, in part because of the technical challenges of working in a large scale, photographers, too, received public commissions, and a 1932 exhibition at the Museum of Modern Art of contemporary murals presented work in both media. Although this show took place before the beginning of the WPA, its prominent venue suggested new possibilities for photographers. Of the nearly fifty artists shown, a dozen were photographers, of whom Julien Levy observed in the accompanying catalogue were "particularly well equipped to meet the problems of mural decoration as posed by the modern architect and builder."[9] Quickly executed and installed, the photographic murals cost considerably less than those on canvas. They could be easily moved to a new location or replaced with something of more topical interest. Adams was intrigued by the aesthetic and technical problems of producing large-scale photo-murals.

Between 1941 and 1942, Adams worked on a commission from the Department of the Interior to execute a series of photo-murals for its Washington offices. His broad subject was America's national parks in the West, and in Arizona he made images of several well-known sites—the Grand Canyon, Canyon de Chelly, Walpi, and the Saguaro National Monument. He also worked on both the Navajo and Hopi reservations and at the Hoover Dam, whose lands were under Interior jurisdiction. The commencement of World War II halted work on the project, and although Adams returned to many of these same subjects throughout his career, the murals were never realized as planned.

Harold Ickes had been appointed Secretary of the Interior in 1933 and the next year had received authorization for a new building to house the offices of his greatly expanded department.[10] Ready for occupancy in the spring of 1937, it was one of the most modern structures in Washington and featured a museum and an Indian arts and crafts shop, as well as the many offices and meeting rooms essential to the running of a large federal bureaucracy. Ample space for art works that would underscore the department's mission was provided, and between 1938 and 1943 the Department of the Interior commissioned a series of painted murals, each of which portrayed subjects inspired by key areas of agency responsibility, much of it in the West. The twenty-three artists who executed works in various parts of the building drew on both historical and contemporary themes for their paintings that portrayed the full range of agency mandates.

Adams was first contacted in June 1941 regarding "the possibility of making one or more photographic murals to be placed in the Interior Department. He [Ickes] has the very beautiful screen which you made some time ago in his office, and while we have quite a number of murals painted on the walls of our corridors, we would like to have some made by the photographic process."[11] Adams enthusiastically proposed a body of work that would convey "the grandeur and influence of the Natural Scene," while also displaying "the benefits of conservation, good administration, and careful long-term planning,"[12] all values fundamental to Interior New Deal initiatives.

The project was an ideal assignment for him, as he recollected, with some self-serving hyperbole: "It sounded perfect to me—one of the best ideas ever to come out of Washington."[13] Adams, who functioned well in the public realm, relished government work. The commission would enable him to make money and undertake his favorite activities: traveling and photographing the spectacular western landscape. If biography is destiny, the Mural Project was surely fated. The National Park Service had been established in 1916, the year Adams first visited Yosemite and the year he got his first camera; thereafter, photography and the national parks were intertwined for him. Not only was he a native of the West, he had a long personal and photographic connection to Yosemite National Park, the site of some of his most memorable images. He had been married there, and his wife's family had long operated a concession on park property, a business that Adams eventually took over.

It is hard to imagine Adams's work without the national parks. Not only were they "phenomena of an advanced society," they were, in the artist's opinion, "America's unique contribution to the democratic idea."[14] His heroic view was well suited to a federal agency with a national vantage and big plans. More than handsome propaganda and bureaucratic decoration, the murals would be seen by those visiting the building, who, Adams hoped, would subliminally absorb his message. For Adams, national identity was embodied in nature, and, rather than emphasize challenging societal issues in need of a solution as did the FSA photographers, he would patriotically celebrate American values as denoted by the grandeur of the wilderness.

Adams began work in October, but with the declaration of war in December, he was informed that all nonessential government projects would be terminated in June 1942. Adams tried to convince officials that his photographs were a worthy contribution to the war effort: "I believe my work relates most efficiently to an emotional presentation of 'what we are fighting for.'"[15] His request was turned down, but he was able to take most of the photographs he wanted by the end of the fiscal year, and Interior reimbursed him for the printing expenses he incurred in the following year.

FIGURE 6.2. Ansel Adams, Grand Canyon National Park, 1941.

Nearly half of the images he shot in Arizona for the Mural Project were made at the Grand Canyon, the state's signature symbol (fig. 6.2). For Ansel Adams, a true citizen of the American West, the region's breathtaking landscape embodied a quasi-religious mythic sublime. Natural monuments were both visual spectacle and sacred space, with the divergent agendas of conservation and massive public works construction projects challenging the natural on its own scale and terms.

Adams's imagery contrasts with that of an image shot by Russell Lee for the Farm Security Administration (fig. 6.3). For that agency, Lee was a national traveler for whom the Grand Canyon was part of a mosaic portrait of America created by a team of government-sponsored photographers who criss-crossed the United States for the better part of a decade. His darkroom practice was different from that of Adams as well. Lee would mail his film back to Washington for developing and printing and was little concerned about the technical quality in which Adams took such pride. He also had no control over the uses to which his imagery was put. Transcending agency mandates, Lee's image conveys something fundamental about our national character, positioning the landscape as a counterpoint to the more mundane aspects of everyday life that had been buffeted by the economics of the Depression. For Adams, however, transcendent landscape trumped everything.

FIGURE 6.3. Russell Lee, Grand Canyon of the Colorado River, October 1940.

In Canyon de Chelly, Adams photographed the famous White House Ruins, first recorded by Timothy O'Sullivan (1873), who, as a member of the Wheeler Expedition, was also sponsored by the government (fig. 6.4). Adams's trip was a memorable one, as he wrote photo historians Beaumont and Nancy Newhall from Mesa Verde National Park, fully aware of the historical resonance of his work:

> We have had a spectacular and dangerous trip. All went well through Death Valley, Boulder Dam, Zion, North Rim, South Rim, Cameron. Then we spent the night on Walpi Mesa, proceeded to Chinle, and had two spectacular stormy days at Canyon de Chelly. I photographed the White House Ruins from almost the identical spot and time of the O'Sullivan picture!! Can't wait until I see what I got. Then our troubles began. They had had the worst rainy season in twenty-five years and the roads through the Indian country are unbelievable. The road from Chinle to Kayenta was so terrible that it took us fifteen hours to go sixty miles; then we ended up at midnight flat on our chassis in the worst mud hole you ever saw—with lightning and thunder and rain roaring on us. We slept in the car that night and worked from 5 A.M. till noon getting the old bus rolling again.[16]

They continued on to Monument Valley and into Utah. He declared: "Never such a trip. We have only 4000 miles to go!"[17]

FIGURE 6.4. Ansel Adams, White House Ruins, Canyon de Chelly, 1941.

FIGURE 6.5. Ansel Adams, Navajo woman and infant, Canyon de Chelly, 1941.

His image of a young Navajo woman with her child (fig. 6.5), taken in Canyon de Chelly, is a classic Native American portrait and is embedded in a rich tradition of nineteenth-century ethnographic work by Adam Clark Vroman and Edward S. Curtis, scenic images from *Arizona Highways,* and prints made by native-son politician Barry Goldwater in his many trips around the state. As in similar images shot by Laura Gilpin during this period, the woman is dressed up and formally posed. Shot close up as one might in a studio, the image made no reference to the landscape in which she and her family lived, which, as reservation, was federal land. The image Adams portrays is of a traditional culture apparently little touched by the Depression. In truth, the reservations had been severely affected by the nation's economic crisis, and the future of the child was an unsettled one, though in contrast to the ragged children pictured by FSA photographers, this one appears well fed and cared for. The mother may have been wary of the motives of a government photographer, but whatever her private feelings may have been, she could not refuse to pose for him.

Only a few photographs of Native Americans were made by the agencies that sponsored the artists who are the focus of this book. They appear, however, heavily stereotyped in painted murals. When Native Americans worked off the reservations, they were recorded by FSA/OWI photographers. There is little evidence of John Collier's Indian New Deal in these images, and those taken of Navajo

FIGURE 6.6. Ansel Adams, Walpi, 1941.

mothers and children by Ansel Adams emphasize traditional ways. The timeless calm of Adams's formal portrait is comparable to the great natural formations he favored. More attuned to landscape than people, he nonetheless understood their strength in facing the challenges of a steadily encroaching modern world, though the young woman whose portrait he made would appear to resist change.

For the Mural Project, Adams also visited the Hopi mesas, and his photograph of Walpi presents the ancient community on its rugged nub of land (fig. 6.6). A wide range of artists had already visited the Hopi, fascinated by their distinctive clothing and ceremonies. By the time Adams arrived, the Hopi, resentful of intrusive artists and anthropologists, no longer permitted the recording of their sacred practices. This may be why no figures are visible in his photograph, which was taken at a distance. Adams portrays the architecture of Walpi more as an element of the landscape than as a community of dwellings.

The Conquest of the Landscape: Dams and the New Deal

The tension between the spectacular landscape of the West and the construction of dams, among the most triumphal and striking building efforts of the New Deal era, spoke to the ideal of accomplishing a large social good at the heart of federal

FIGURE 6.7. Russell Lee, Roosevelt Dam, Gila County, May 1940.

programs. The dams competed in scale with their surroundings, and the tremendous New Deal public works projects undertaken during the thirties were powerful governmental symbols in the midst of the Great Depression. Providing jobs and stimulating local economies, they represented the promise of modern technologies that were the key to the nation's future prosperity. The immense structures imposed on the landscape as a result of extensive federal public works projects were extensively recorded by government photographers, as well as by some painters.

Arizona was the site of several famous dams, and there was a notable shift in scale in the quarter century between the construction of the Roosevelt and Hoover dams. For the FSA, Russell Lee visited the Roosevelt Dam (fig. 6.7), located about sixty miles from Phoenix, photographing the full sweep of the handsome masonry dam, then the highest in the world. Built between 1903 and 1911, and named for the man who was president when the Reclamation Act became law in 1902, it was the Bureau's first big structure. In a dry state, growth followed water, and, primarily a large-scale irrigation project (some hydroelectric power was also generated), Roosevelt Dam spurred development and the expansion of agriculture in central Arizona. Able to grow a wide range of seasonal crops, agribusiness then depended on migratory labor, a staple of FSA photographers. By the Depression, the Roosevelt Dam would be overshadowed by even bigger developments.

Dams were emblematic of such large-scale efforts in the West, and none were bigger than the Hoover Dam. The project was authorized in 1928; construction

FIGURE 6.8. Ansel Adams, Hoover Dam, 1941.

began in 1931 of what was the largest dam in the world when it was dedicated in 1935.[18] It "was the first major federal project based on multi-purpose objectives,"[19] including flood control, irrigation, hydroelectric power, recreation, and the generation of thousands of jobs. At 726 feet in height, the sublime scale of one of Interior's most massive projects aligned with the breathtaking landscape of which it was a part.

While project management was headquartered in Nevada, half of the dam is in Arizona, with the Colorado River flowing between. Further, water rights issues connected with it involved a large percentage of the Bureau of Reclamation's mandated constituency of seventeen western states. To regard it only as a Nevada project, as is done in some historical accounts, belies the contentious complexities of modern water politics. It was sufficiently Arizonan to be included in the WPA guide to the state.

Painters and photographers working for federal agencies were commissioned to record these ambitious enterprises, both under construction and after completion. The Hoover Dam was a magnet for overlapping artistic agendas, and artists were hired to record the site at various stages, including before any work was begun.[20] At the Hoover Dam, Ansel Adams made dramatic shots of the spillway as part of his Mural Project (fig. 6.8). His prints present the great structure in all its precisionist beauty. Adams's vision is strongly formal in aesthetic and idealistic in content, pairing the grandeur of nature that he so admired with grand construction within nature. As the projects were for the public good, the connection with the betterment of human society is always implicit.

The most extensive documentation of the Hoover Dam was undertaken by the Bureau of Reclamation, which hired photographer Ben Glaha to record the entire construction process. Stylistically, he had interesting connections with the f.64 group, and the artistic merit of his work so impressed Maynard Dixon that in 1935 the painter convinced officials at the M. H. De Young Museum of Art in San Francisco to mount an exhibition, in connection with which Ansel Adams gave a lecture. The face of the strong, youthful figure is concealed by the container from which he drinks (fig. 6.9), his anonymity suggesting the universality of hard physical labor involved in massive public works projects. The image also speaks to the intense heat under which such labors took place.

In April 1934, Maynard Dixon was hired by the Public Works of Art Project to document construction activities at the dam.[21] He was given free choice of subjects, and he made many paintings and sketches during the six weeks he was there. He was overwhelmed by the site: "I found there a dramatic theme: Man versus Rock; the colossal dam an immense work compared to man, but a peanut compared to its setting. A bewildering display of engineering for the understanding of which I had not the least preparation in past experience. It gave me an impression of concealed force—and of ultimate futility."[22] That Dorothea's brother, Martin Lange, worked there as a laborer gave Dixon additional insight into the conditions of those constructing this huge edifice. The armed guards at Boulder City, Nevada, the town built to house workers, made it seem like a prison camp to him. The housing and concessions were typical of a company town. Dixon boarded with a family and saw firsthand the many young men forced by economic necessity into hard, dangerous manual labor for which they were unsuited. They would return from work exhausted, and one of his paintings, *Tired Men* (1934) (fig. 6.10), shows a group in the back of a truck at the end of their shift. The men are weary, their legs dangling over the end gate, revealing that they are at the end of their physical resources, rather like the migratory laborers recorded by Lange. Dixon emphasized not the heroism of labor, but the human price. In describing the courage of these bronzed, hardy men battling nature, Dixon observed: "It's like war."[23]

Despite the great efforts the workers exerted, Dixon felt "All these things merged in a sense of the tragedy of men's labors; the great treadmill drama of lost endeavor—but in the long run, the desert will have the last laugh."[24] The efforts to harness the turbulent waters of the Colorado River were impressive:

> The painting of the mechanical and engineering end of it had been taken care of by other people. So I decided to make my main theme "Pigmy man against everlasting rock." The men seemed like robots to me. I didn't get near enough

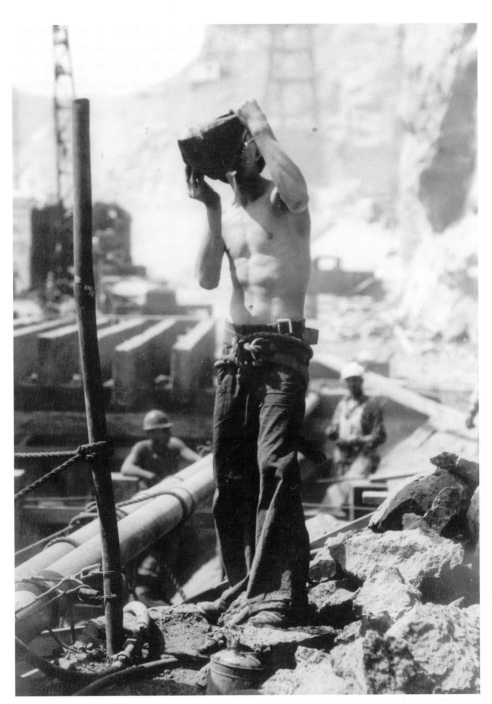

FIGURE 6.9. Ben Glaha, Workman with water bag, 1934.

FIGURE 6.10. Maynard Dixon, *Tired Men,* 1934, oil on canvas, 25" × 30".

to know them. But there they worked in the blazing sun at 140 degrees. The water boys—important persons there; high-scalers working on the faces of stupendous cliffs; men riding huge cement buckets in the middle of space, over canyons a thousand feet deep; flesh-and-blood men opposed to immutable rock. These are the things I tried to paint. America doesn't realize what a dangerous undertaking it is. Four were killed while I was there and the hospital was full all the time.[25]

Dixon's *High Scalers* (fig. 6.11) dramatically shows the dangerous conditions under which they worked. Similar views of men standing on platforms dangling from a web of ropes were also recorded by Glaha. Such carefully coordinated acrobatics of laborers were often recorded close-up, but if they were to fall, their bodies would plummet hundreds of feet to certain death.

Commissioned by the Department of the Interior for its headquarters, *Construction of the Dam* (1938–39) (fig. 6.12), by William Gropper, portrays a strong labor theme.[26] The mural was based on sketches Gropper made when he visited both the Hoover and Grand Coulee dams in 1937, as part of a trip he took on his Guggenheim Fellowship. His painting embodies a passage from the Arizona WPA guide, whose writers proudly declared that the pair of dams were

FIGURE 6.11. Maynard Dixon, *High Scalers,* 1934, oil on board, 19½" × 15½".

"the greatest water and power projects ever undertaken."[27] The entire composition
of his huge mural, which measures ten by thirty feet, is linked by the slate-blue
sky. Groups of men in flanking panels contrast the human labor with the massive
canyon in which the dam is being built. Man and landscape maintain their own
spheres. Gropper's composition is full of the drama of masculine labor.

Each of the three panels portrays a specific construction task. At the left,
a group of high scalers, connected by ropes, prepares the rock for blasting.
Although suspended in safety belts, that they hang perilously over the edge

FIGURE 6.12. William Gropper, *Construction of the Dam*, 193839, oil on canvas, 27¼" × 87¼".

reminds viewers that this was a hazardous task. The strong workers glorified in the mural contrast with the human cost of their efforts. At the right, another group of men work to erect the framework of the dam, their construction balancing that of nature in the rocks at the left. The curving metal structure they form will reinforce the concrete. Their muscles straining against the rigid steel, they struggle to brace and hammer the cables together. The central panel of Gropper's dramatic mural is the largest. Visible is a huge half-section of a conduit hung by a hook; the crane that swings it into position is unseen. A man standing near the hook signals to another on the ground. The precariousness of the workers contrasts with the sturdiness of the landscape and the unfinished dam. Two men study the blueprints that indicate each stage of construction.

Projects like the Hoover Dam heralded the end of the Depression, and the beginning of World War II began to renew America's economic strength. Industrialization was an integral part of American life, with the modern what Leo Marx defined as the "machine in the garden"[28] played out in dams on a colossal scale. These sublimely scaled machine-age artifacts would be the ultimate realization of Manifest Destiny. Landscape, whether in an apparently natural state or as the site for immense federal works projects, remains a defining element of the American West. Gropper and Glaha portrayed the workers who realized the vision, while the images of Ansel Adams remain a classic statement of the intersection of the awesome landscape with constructions on a scale commensurate

with the place of which they were a part, and which they were intended to control, tame, and civilize. The natural and the constructed coexisted in the sublime federal landscape of the American West. No other Arizona subject except the Grand Canyon engaged artists as did the Hoover Dam. Adams's heroic view of the dam conveys the implicit ideology of a democratic government responsibly harnessing the nation's natural resources for the greater public good.

The balancing of public and private needs was at the core of New Deal policies. Adams had been commissioned to make prints that would be installed in a prominent government building in Washington, D.C., and he positioned the dam within the context of the natural beauty that surrounded it. He was attuned to the enduring values of landscape that would ultimately prevail over any construction, though his federal patrons undoubtedly placed greater value on the dam itself.

Seeing Straight: The Social Work of Landscape

If the "social work" of the FSA remains emblematic of New Deal documentary photography, these images of mines, dams, and natural wonders suggested a different human connection. But some found it hard to make a convincing imperative between conditions in Depression America and the images of those who made landscape their primary subject. Because his landscapes are largely absent of people and their daily problems, Adams was criticized for his evident lack of an overt social conscience, a charge also leveled at abstract painters during a period when regionalism was the dominant style. Novelist Wallace Stegner observed of Adams: "He did not much like the documentarians, with the exception of Dorothea Lange and Walker Evans, and he liked *them* not because they were documenting social significance but because they were artists."[29]

If Adams's art did not directly deal with the important social issues of the day, it could still be put to political ends. In 1941, the Museum of Modern Art mounted a photography show entitled Image of Freedom, and curator Beaumont Newhall recalled its purpose: "Ansel had suggested positive statements by photographers about America and its people would reaffirm faith in our country during the critical and difficult war years."[30] The exhibition prospectus stated:

> What gives our lives meaning? Why do we feel that, with all its faults, this is the place we want to live? Why do we feel that the foundations of our national life are not only unshaken but capable of supporting a greater, more human structure than any nation, or combination of nations, has yet built? In this immense panorama, what, to you, most deeply signifies America? Can you compress it into a few photographic images? Not with the hysteria and jingle of superficial patriotism, with the bitterness of protest, but profoundly, simply, with insight and emotion? In the belief that you, photographers of America, can through photography express and confirm our faith . . . . You are invited to a competition.[31]

While Adams admired Lange's Depression work as a "grand photo-document," declaring: "She has done beautiful stuff,"[32] he was also critical of it, as he complained to his friend, fellow California photographer Edward Weston, whose sere formalism had engendered similar assessments:

> I am getting very tired of just the same thing—of being called 'dead' because I do not include 'social' material and subjects of 'class-significance.' . . . It is not that we would refuse to apply our work to the general good—but I feel that the work of the creative artist—the free and intimate expression—is much more important than any phase of direct propaganda or an artistic medium. . . . I feel that all *propaganda-expression* [emphasis in original]is transitory anyway. But a rock seems to last some little time![33]

Adams may have admired Lange as "a humanitarian and an artist,"[34] but he questioned the use of photographs for propaganda purposes to support a particular ideology. Yet he supported the ideologies of the Department of the Interior every bit as much as did the FSA photographers. He resisted showing "the land and the sky as settings for human activity,"[35] writing photographer Alfred Stieglitz in 1944: "As the war moves to a climax, the only enduring things seem to be the aspect of Nature—and its reciprocal, the creative spirit."[36] It was the timelessness of the landscape that engaged his social consciousness, rather than people.

Many years later Adams wrote to Dorothea Lange, whose work from the thirties was emphatically grounded in the present: "What bothers me is a deep-seated resentment over the one-sided direction of most documentary work. As I said, I get no *human* emotion from pictures of this type; I get only a sense of *group, mass, class condition* [emphases in original]. As it is only a small part of the whole framework of humanity—and a damned negative one at that—I find myself entertaining an increasing tension about it."[37] Publicly optimistic by nature, Adams in his patriotism reveals just how different his personal and professional experiences had been from Lange's: "America is a land of joy—more than any other land. With all the misery, all the economic troubles, and the crack-pot politicians, we are still the most liberal, the best off, and the most beautiful country in the world."[38]

Adams was a member of the California group f.64, which first exhibited together in San Francisco in 1932. Although these more formalist photographers made no obvious references to economic problems and were more aligned with exploring modernist strategies than with portraying the daily social conditions of contemporary life, they still had many connections with the FSA in terms of "seeing straight."[39] The word "documentary" suggested too many aesthetic and personal limitations to Adams, who simply was not drawn to an art of activist social purpose as was Lange.

The purist principles of group f/64 were familiar to Roy Stryker, who once suggested to Russell Lee, who was at the time (1940) traveling through Arizona and New Mexico, that he "try a few 'Westons by Russell Lee.' You have no idea how important these highly pictorial syrupy pictures are going to be, especially when someone comes in here who isn't particularly sold on our other photography, and is in a position to do a lot of talking."[40] Lee's view of the Grand Canyon is the closest he would get to a "Westonized"[41] image.

THE DEPRESSION ENDS
The World War II Years

The image of the Battleship USS *Arizona* sinking amidst clouds of dense black smoke after the Japanese bombing of Pearl Harbor on December 7, 1941, is one of the most dramatic in the history of photojournalism. The events that propelled America into war in the European and Pacific theatres signaled yet another societal upheaval. America's entry into World War II effectively ended the Depression and the relief programs the government had put in place to mitigate its effects.

Federal agencies continued to provide art patronage, but the relationship between artists and the government was transformed as the wartime context made the need for propaganda more urgent. Agencies were mandated to support the war effort, and Roy Stryker urged his staff to seek out particular kinds of subjects for their photographs: "Pictures of men, women and children who appear as if they really believed in the United States."[1] The Farm Security Administration became the Office of War Information (OWI) in June 1942, and many of the artists continued to work for the renamed agency. If the FSA had focused on the desperate needs of rural agricultural workers, the OWI visually positioned a recovered and unified nation ready to wage and win a war. Emphasis was now placed on well-fed, gainfully employed workers who were able to contribute productively to winning the conflict in which America was now thoroughly engaged, and activities signifying military preparedness and strength were highlighted.

Propaganda and the Office of War Information

The Office of War Information sent Jack Delano and Fritz Henle to Arizona to record the railroad operations and the mining industries critical to the nation's home-front military strategy.[2] The image projected was patriotically affirmative and prosperous. In Arizona, their photographs exemplify a shift in priorities from agricultural agencies and the needs of the rural poor to those related to mining and transportation—enterprises essential to the war effort. The OWI was more frankly propagandistic than the FSA, though the artists who were more idealistic than their employers did not think of their images in those terms, and despite his government employment as an FSA/OWI photographer, Delano regarded his work as apolitical: "Speaking for myself, I felt that I was part of an organization which was basically interested in the cultural values of America, which had nothing to do with politics but had to do with the American tradition, with the bad things, the good things, the difficulties, the problems, the joys and inspirations and everything that went with it."[3]

Issues of national defense were as important to the home front as they were abroad, and the propaganda devices employed by these photographers were overt and artful. Propaganda had remained a fairly neutral term until the First World War, when the sense that it was incompatible with democratic values resulted in its rhetoric becoming increasingly euphemistic. By World War II, *information* replaced *propaganda,* and in supporting a new agenda on a global scale, aesthetics and ideology were linked when the government was the patron.

Jack Delano and the Railroad

Jack Delano had immigrated to the United States from Ukraine with his family, settling in Philadelphia in 1923. In 1932, he enrolled at the Pennsylvania Academy of the Fine Arts, and, supported by financial aid provided by the National Youth Administration, a New Deal job-training program aimed at unemployed youth, he pursued courses in illustration in addition to his academic art classes. He did well in his studies, and when a scholarship enabled him to travel in Europe in 1935, he bought his first camera: "[N]ow I began to think that perhaps in photographs I could show the same concern and understanding of ordinary people that I found so compelling in the work of the artists I admired so much."[4]

Job opportunities were few for someone with no professional experience, but as an "unemployed artist" he found support under the New Deal from the Federal Art Project, which assigned him to photograph furniture and folk art for the Index of American Design. Although more interested in social conditions and current events than in recording artifacts of the past, he was grateful to have a job. The FAP was little interested in photography as a creative medium, but Delano was able to persuade FAP administrators to let him work on a project documenting unemployed coal miners in the anthracite region of Pennsylvania. When Delano exhibited this work, photographer Paul Strand's praise convinced him to move to New York City to freelance.

He was soon introduced to the work of several of the leading FSA photographers, and he was struck by "the simplicity, sureness, power, and grace"[5] of their images. Still, some of it disappointed him: "they seemed to be too cool, precise, and emotionally aloof, like technically perfect, interesting specimens of humanity rather than human beings of flesh and blood and joys and sorrows."[6]

Already committed to produce art that was "seriously concerned with the plight of the dispossessed, the needy, and the landless,"[7] Delano decided he wanted to work for the agency that had sponsored such photographs, and sent Roy Stryker some of his anthracite images. When Arthur Rothstein resigned in 1940 to take a position with *Look* magazine, Delano was offered a job at the FSA. Stryker's vision was very much in line with that of Delano, who felt "anything I saw that reflected social conditions in America was fair game for my camera."[8]

He found an ideal subject in the American railroad. Trains are an iconic feature of American cultural identity, and in them Delano discovered a powerful visual narrative to which he responded deeply. For Stryker, the railroad represented a "big transportation story which is just begging to be told,"[9] and Delano portrayed "The Iron Horse at War" in a series of documentary images he shot as he traveled across the country. Stryker observed: "The railroad has been a part of the everyday affairs of a large proportion of the villages and towns in the United States."[10] Central to American life, trains had long been "the tie to the outside world"[11] for small communities. But he recognized that they were gradually being supplanted by "the bus, pleasure car, and the truck,"[12] although with gas rationing and the need to transport servicemen, rail travel increased during this period.

In 1942, Jack Delano began a two-year study of the nation's railroads for the OWI, a project that brought him to Arizona in March 1943. His subject was the Atchison, Topeka, and Santa Fe Railway, which had been largely taken over for military purposes for the duration of the war. Chicago, where it was headquartered, was a major transportation hub, with forty-one different lines, freight transfer handled by eight switching lines, and several passenger terminals. Delano decided to begin his journey there. Leaving Union Station early in March, he traveled for nearly a month across the country, making many stops and detours along his two-thousand-mile route. As the train made its way west, Delano, who rode in the locomotive with the engineer, recorded the full range of the company's operations, structures, and employees by the time he arrived in Los Angeles on the first of April.

As Delano traveled through northern Arizona, he passed through towns with busy train yards, as well as through others that were desolate and remote, before crossing the Colorado River into California. Delano's captions for his Arizona photographs reveal how hard it was for him to know exactly where he was in the great expanses of the high desert during the three days it took to traverse the state.

The railroad transported military personnel and materiel, and his image of tanks that were being shipped west (fig. 7.1) serves as a reminder of how close the war was even to people not on the coast. His narrow vantage through the window was typical of the "train's-eye-view" he had throughout the long journey. Delano

FIGURE 7.1. Jack Delano, Train load of military tanks on the Atchison, Topeka, and Santa Fe Railway, March 1943.

recalled: "We were hauling a long train of more than a hundred cars and going up a slight hill, with one engine up front pulling and another behind pushing. We were carrying, among other things, tractors, bombs, trucks, electrical equipment, steel, mines, military tanks, engines, and other military goods. From the window of the engine cab, I could see the whole train in a great arc behind us."[13] The sheer mechanical power of the big trains inspired him.

In addition to recording the ordinary activities of the railroad, Delano's photographs reveal the dramatic social changes that occurred in wartime. Workers became more diverse in gender and race, as a shortage of white males enabled women and Native Americans to enter the railroad work force in increased numbers. Conditions on the reservations were difficult during the Depression, and Navajo laborers found employment opportunities in the Flagstaff area with the Santa Fe Railway. The young man he photographed was part of a large crew at work in the railroad yard (fig. 7.2).

FIGURE 7.2. Jack Delano, Young Indian laborer working in the Atchison, Topeka, and Santa Fe Railway yard, Winslow, March 1943.

Fritz Henle and Mining

The OWI photographs taken in Arizona by German-American artist Fritz Henle were concentrated on the copper and tungsten mining industries.[14] He grew up in Germany's heavily industrialized Ruhr Valley, and he had begun taking pictures by the mid-twenties. His photographs appeared in *Fortune* in 1936, the year he immigrated to the United States. Hired by the OWI in 1942, the year he became an American citizen, Henle remained with the agency until 1945. The government, so paranoid about Japanese Americans, had no problem with hiring a recently nationalized German American. It was harder to be prejudiced against other Caucasians, whose features were not readily identified as the "other."

The copper industry had enjoyed boom years during the twenties, but after the crash, the price of copper fell rapidly. Diminished demand and foreign

FIGURE 7.3. Fritz Henle, Open-pit copper mine of the Phelps Dodge Mining Corporation, Morenci, December 1942.

competition further eroded prosperity, and many operations were either reduced or closed. Underground mining had ceased at Morenci in 1932, but when World War II revitalized the industry, the OWI sent Henle to Arizona to shoot a photo essay there in December 1942. Henle recorded the massive Phelps Dodge extractive and processing operations (fig. 7.3). Henle's industrial work at Morenci was not his first foray into such subject matter, as his first published photograph was of a German blast furnace, and for the OWI he recorded a number of industrial sites.

Like Bisbee, Morenci was a company town, comprising a landscape of intense production. Morenci was "one of the largest copper mines in the United States." A town of extremes, it was also described as "one of the most precipitous towns" in the nation: "Tier upon tier of houses cling to the steep hillside and look as if they were built on top of each other. Children are tethered to keep them from rolling down the slope." Until 1912, there were no regular streets, and homes were

FIGURE 7.4. Fritz Henle, Electric shovel, open-pit copper mine, Morenci, December 1942.

accessible only by burro and ladder. When the paths were widened to accommodate cars, it was recommended *"but only by experts without nerves."*[15] The italics were put in for emphasis in the WPA guide. Their open-pit mine challenged the scale of the surrounding landscape, busy with the immense electric shovels that could load seven tons in a scoop into huge carts that dumped eighty tons a minute into crushers (fig. 7.4).

The war put people back to work, and Henle's image of two workers who transport and dispense the explosives used for blasting in the open-pit mine (fig. 7.5) graphically documents how things had changed from the Depression. The hunger so evident in Lange's gaunt and dirty migratory laborers and their families has been replaced by an image of two obviously well fed men with good jobs. Their broad smiles contrast with the grim hopelessness of those forced to be constantly on the move.

FIGURE 7.5. Fritz Henle, Phelps Dodge Mining Corporation workers, Morenci, December 1942.

Phelps Dodge had begun to extensively develop the site even before America entered the war, and with the beginning of World War II expansion continued. Russell Lee had already photographed the impressive operations there for the FSA: "Morenci is quite an amazing mining town (active) and should be a good place to concentrate on a story of copper mining later on. The town is really precipitous—houses one on top of the other and there was a lot activity apparent which was quite a contrast to Bisbee."[16] Lee took only four photographs, including images of the immense open pit, the mill (fig. 7.6), the tailings, and the new copper smelter then under construction. His emphasis was on the structures rather than on the spacious landscape.

Vital to munitions manufacture, the Morenci operations were on a scale greater than any other in Arizona. At full production and running twenty-four hours a day, Morenci was the site of "the most efficient mining/smelting plant

Figure 7.6. Russell Lee, Morenci copper mine mill, May 1940.

in the world," making the town "the centerpiece of the Phelps Dodge copper empire."[17] Ore was hauled to crushers and mixed with water, then pulverized in "the huge revolving cylinders of the ball mills of the concentrator plant,"[18] before being transferred to flotation cells for further processing. Waste was put in massive tailings ponds covering two thousand acres, and the "copper-laden froth"[19] from the concentrator was prepared for the smelter, which could process 650 tons daily. After more processing, the molten metal was cast into seven-hundred-pound anodes and shipped to the refinery at El Paso, which Henle also photographed that month.

The War Relocation Authority: Art and Internment

The Depression and the New Deal ended with World War II in Arizona much as it began, with uprooted citizens bewildered by circumstances beyond their control, residing in rickety shacks in a bleak desert, their economic hopes shattered. The patriotic portrayal of American home-front strengths by the OWI contrasted sharply with the work of the War Relocation Authority (WRA). With the bombing of Pearl Harbor, long-simmering anti-Japanese sentiment burst into racist rhetoric and wartime hysteria, spurring the Civilian Exclusion Order (Executive Order 9066), which President Roosevelt signed into law in February 1942. The WRA oversaw the removal of some 110,000 Japanese Americans from the Western Defense Command, an area comprising the coastal states of California, Oregon, and Washington, and parts of southern Arizona. Two thirds of those transported to domestic concentration camps were American-born citizens.[20]

In June 1942, Manzanar in California was the first of ten hastily constructed camps to be opened on remote federal land in seven states, with populations ranging from eight to twenty thousand individuals. Of the ten, two camps each were set up in California and in Arkansas, and four more in Colorado, Wyoming, Idaho, and Utah. Arizona was the site of two of the largest internment camps.

Built to a standard plan, the barracks were crude one-story, wood-frame structures a hundred feet long, covered with tar paper held down with wood strips that frankly revealed their temporary nature. They provided bleak comfort during the hot summer heat. Up to 10,000 residents could be housed in thirty-six blocks of 250 to 300 people. Five to eight people might be assigned to a twenty-five-foot-square room. Conditions were similar in all camps.

The two Arizona camps were established on Indian reservations at Gila River (near Casa Grande) and at Poston (near Parker, on the California border), collectively holding nearly thirty-five thousand prisoners.[21] Both opened during the summer of 1942 and remained open until late 1945. With a population of twenty thousand internees, Poston, the largest in the nation, was organized into three units, scornfully named "Duston, Roaston, and Toaston"[22] by residents. Arid desert conditions featuring brutal summer temperatures, dust storms, and rattlesnakes must have been shocking to those forced to move to Arizona. One of the few ways out of the camp for internees was either to obtain defense employment or to volunteer for the armed forces. With tragic irony, although not free, they could die in service to the country of which they were until recently legal citizens.

The WPA Writers' Project gave editorial assistance to the Arizona Civilian Defense Coordinating Council in publishing its newsletter, *Arizona Defense News*. The government-regulated tone was upbeat, putting a positive spin on federal actions:

> The great majority of persons in Arizona who are of Japanese extraction, were born here and are full-fledged Americans. There is no reason to doubt their loyalty. Their allegiance to their and our Country is genuine; this we may believe. Of the 632 residents of Japanese blood among us, the 1940 census lists only 220 as of foreign born aliens. Four hundred and twelve are native born. These people are confronted with a difficult situation, which can be mitigated only by the understanding of their white brothers. Every consideration should be shown to those who are loyal to our country. None should be condemned, nor accused without provocation. The few among foreign born Japanese, who are suspected of alien sympathies or activities are well known to the FBI. Those who have not been taken into custody are under close surveillance. The real test of the loyalty of the citizen Japanese will come in their own attitude toward subversive elements that may exist among them. Their duty is to report such persons promptly to the FBI.[23]

Toyo Miyatake in Arizona

The camps were extensively recorded by the government, though in contrast to the FSA, few of the WRA photographers established reputations as artists. Lange, Lee, and Adams all worked for the WRA, but not in Arizona. A surprising exception is Japanese American photographer, Toyo Miyatake, a Los Angeles pictorialist. Born in Japan, in 1909 Miyatake came with his family to Los Angeles, where he became a professional photographer, opening his studio in Little Tokyo in 1923.[24] His business was successful, and, in addition to his commercial work, he also achieved recognition as an artist for his pictorialist photographs. In 1942 he was interned with his family at Manzanar, where he remained until his release in November 1945.

It was Manzanar that was celebrated in Ansel Adams's polemical volume *Born Free and Equal* (1944). An officially approved "documentary," it was as blatant a piece of propaganda as any produced by the FSA, despite his criticism of its work on those very grounds. In contrast to Lange, Adams was inclined to trust what he perceived as the government's good intentions, portraying a tidy community functioning collectively under difficult circumstances, contrasting the beauty of the surrounding landscape, which he characterized as "spiritually uplifting and emotionally sustaining,"[25] with the inner strength of camp residents, of whom he made close-up portraits, including one of Miyatake.

Adams, who maintained his belief in government actions, tried to make a distinction between "loyal citizens of Japanese ancestry," and those who were "disloyal" or "Japanese-loyal."[26] And although even he realized that "the big-business boys have the unfortunate gift of vaporizing the Constitution when their selfish interests are concerned,"[27] he remained patriotic and declared with unintended irony: "The War Relocation Authority is doing a magnificent job, and is firm and ruthless in their definitions of true loyalty. In effect these pictures imply a test of true Americanism, and suggest an approach to treatments of other minority groups."[28] Lange, however, who also photographed at Manzanar, was irked that Adams "could find beauty in such an immoral place."[29] In sharing the government view, Adams failed to recognize that he was free to come and go; his livelihood had not been destroyed as a result of wartime racial hysteria.

Miyatake smuggled in a lens and a film holder with the small cache of personal belongings each internee was allowed and constructed a crude wooden box camera. He declared: "As a photographer, I have a responsibility to record camp life so this kind of thing will never happen again."[30] Japanese Americans were forbidden to take photographs, but, ordering film from Los Angeles, he managed to work clandestinely for about nine months recording the daily life of the internees before he was caught by camp police.

Once his activities were discovered, Miyatake explained his desire to make a historical record of camp life to director Ralph P. Merritt. It was he who had given Adams permission to work there, and, sympathetic to Miyatake's goals, permitted him to continue taking pictures. Although no specific regulations were imposed regarding what he could shoot, he understood the parameters implicit in his "freedom" to work. Because of his work at Manzanar, he remains one of the most famous Japanese American photographers of his generation. Despite the notoriety of his California work, his Arizona photographs have been ignored.

During Miyatake's internment at Manzanar, Allen Eaton was beginning his research for his book *Beauty behind Barbed Wire: The Arts of the Japanese in Our War Relocation Camps.* Eaton was an early historian of American folk art and craft and had become interested in the arts programs set up at the camps. In need of illustrations, he approached Merritt, who in turn asked Miyatake if he would be willing to take photographs of the Arizona camps for Eaton's book. He accepted the assignment and was issued a special travel pass. While Miyatake did not work directly for the WRA, he had the official sanction of the camp's director. At Gila River, Miyatake shot *Garden of Native Cactus* (fig. 7.7), and his caption reads: "The dispossessed residents made use of local materials to make their new habitations

FIGURE 7.7. Toyo Miyatake, *Garden of Native Cactus,* Gila River, c. 1944–45.

more attractive."[31] Internees ingeniously adapted what materials they could scavenge to their cultural traditions, and at the center, surrounding by prickly cacti, a small Japanese shrine is visible.

Isamu Noguchi at Poston

Isamu Noguchi's experiences in Arizona suggest the complexities of the intersection of art and government with race and international and national events. Born in Los Angeles but raised in Japan from the age of two, he had returned to America in 1918. His mother was American and his father Japanese, making him too Western to be comfortable in Asia, and in America, too Asian to be accepted as American. His sense of personal identity would remain ambiguous. When Pearl Harbor was bombed, Noguchi experienced an epiphany: "With a flash I realized I was no longer the sculptor alone. I was not just American but Nisei [a second-generation Japanese American]. . . . I felt I must do something." He hoped to be able to "counteract the bigoted hysteria that soon appeared in the press."[32]

In Washington, D.C., he met with John Collier, commissioner of the Office of Indian Affairs, whose agency was part of the Department of the Interior, which had jurisdiction over the reservations on which the relocation camps would be established (though in terms of control, WRA agendas trumped those of the OIA). Both were idealists, and Noguchi, taking as his goal that his art might serve a public good, hoped to design a cooperative utopian community that would improve life for the internees by providing them "with useful work, educational opportunities, and other services to ease their postwar rehabilitation."[33] He volunteered to go to one of the camps and was given permission to proceed to Arizona.

As a Japanese American attuned to the uneasy position of individuals of color in America, he thought he could blunt the searing racism inherent in the internment: "Thus I willfully became a part of humanity uprooted."[34] To those who questioned his actions, he explained: "When people ask me why I, a Eurasian sculptor from New York, have come so far in the Arizona desert to be locked up with the evacuated Japanese from the West coast, I sometimes wonder myself. I reply that because of my peculiar background I felt this war very keenly and wished to serve the cause of democracy in the best way that seemed open to me."[35] Though Noguchi soon realized that the WRA, brutally impelled by wartime racism, had little interest in fostering the kind of community he and Collier envisioned, he was initially optimistic: "I sought some place where I might fit into the fight for freedom."[36]

Noguchi arrived at the Colorado River Relocation Center in Poston in mid-May 1942, when the barren and makeshift camp was still under construction. A barbed wire fence surrounded the periphery, with guard towers and machine guns pointing inward placed at regular intervals. At night searchlights swept the camp interior. Although he was self-incarcerated, except for his private room, his daily routine was similar to that of the rest of the internees.

He had never lived under such harsh conditions, and at first he was inspired by the extremes of hot and cold in Arizona: "The desert was magnificent—the fantastic heat, the cool nights, and the miraculous time before dawn."[37] A distinctive camp personage, one resident recalled of Noguchi: "He tramped the desert collecting ironwood in his pith helmet, high-top shoes, and dusty denims."[38] He never fit in with his fellow internees, who distrusted him because of his special connection to camp administrators.

Encouraged by Collier, Noguchi drew up designs for park and recreation areas for the camps and began to organize activities to improve the quality of life of the residents. His plans, which included art instruction and craft guilds for internees (all the camps had art programs), was broad in its goals, aiming to "contribute toward a rebirth of handicraft and the arts that the Nisei have so largely lost in the process of Americanization."[39] This was just the sort of thing Eaton wanted Miyatake to photograph. Excited by the possibilities, Noguchi scavenged leftover lumber and mesquite from the desert to use in the woodcarving and carpentry shop he set up for adult education programs, though the only available tools were those he had brought with him. His proposals included an elegantly

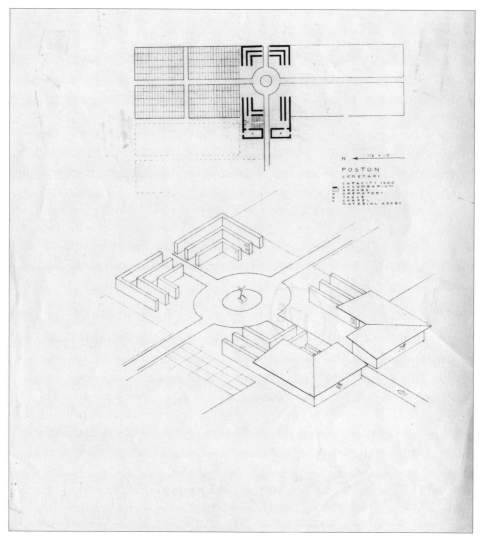

FIGURE 7.8. Isamu Noguchi, Plans for Poston Cemetery, 1942, blueprint.

spare cemetery (fig. 7.8), with columbarium, chapel, and gravesites, but none of these were ever realized: "They wanted nothing permanent nor pleasant."[40]

As with Miyatake's, Noguchi's work falls into an ambiguous area of government patronage. Although Noguchi's Arizona designs had not been officially commissioned by the WRA, that agency had given his work its tacit approval by permitting him to become a resident of the camp. Further, his plans had been supported by the head of the Office of Indian Affairs. But WRA mandates took precedence over those of Interior during wartime, and federal artistic patronage by one agency was decidedly not welcomed by another at a time of suspicion and paranoia.

Within weeks of his arrival, Noguchi realized he had made a huge mistake in coming to Arizona, writing artist Man Ray: "This is the weirdest, most unreal situation—like a dream—I wish I were out."[41] His vision was doomed, as he bitterly observed: "[T]his must be one of the earth's cruelest spots."[42] By the end of July he requested permission to leave. But although he had voluntarily interned himself and had the support of an important agency head, the government balked at releasing him. The WRA, uninterested in his humane vision, further resented Collier's interagency meddling. That Noguchi had spent part of his childhood in Japan meant his loyalty was questioned by federal officials who dismissively characterized him as a "half-breed."[43]

Despite endorsements from an impressive array of prominent individuals, including Collier, Francis Biddle (United States Attorney General), and Henry Allen Moe (secretary of the Guggenheim Foundation), his request to leave was initially denied. Seven months after his arrival, he was finally released, in November 1942. Frank Lloyd Wright invited him to Taliesin to organize a program with other talented Nisei, but Noguchi had no interest in remaining in Arizona. Disenchanted with social causes, he fled east from what had turned out to be a misguided social experiment, and immersed himself in his New York studio.

The Army as Federal Art Patron

The military employed many artists and established extensive art programs during World War II, and this area of government patronage is an important part of the Arizona story. Noguchi's chronicle of racial prejudice stands in sharp contrast to the work of Arizona artist Lew Davis, who portrayed Native American and African American themes within the context of a segregated Army base. Between 1943 and 1944, Davis executed a series of remarkable paintings in Sierra Vista, Arizona, at Fort Huachuca, where he had been sent on special assignment. The post maintained separate clubs for white and black officers.[44]

At the white officers' club (called Lakeside), Davis's central panel portrayed *The Founding of Fort Huachuca* (1943) (fig. 7.9) in 1877. It was flanked by two smaller panels portraying the *Apache Scouts* who assisted the Army in subduing their fellow hostile Apaches. *The Surrender of Geronimo* (1943, unlocated) showed the capitulation in 1886 of Native American warriors, including Geronimo and Cochise, an event that ended the Southwestern Indian wars. The Indian conflicts that were so troubling for Saffordians were a source of historical pride for the Army, whose victory was celebrated in Davis's painting. For one race, it was an image of subjugation with a long tradition in art, literature, and movies, and for the other a source of affirmation. Had these been Davis's only murals at the fort, their standard iconography of authority and surrender could be regarded as yet another example of a colonialist government asserting control over the state's indigenous peoples. But they were paired with a series of paintings whose themes were exceptional for a white artist in Arizona during the 1940s.

FIGURE 7.9. Lew Davis, *The Founding of Fort Huachuca,* 1943, oil on board, 8' high × 12' wide.

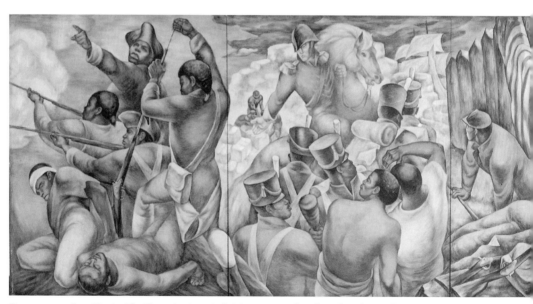

FIGURE 7.10. Lew Davis, *The Negro in America's Wars,* 1944, oil on board, 60" × 144".

Davis executed a series of remarkable paintings for the black officers' club (named Mountain View). His five-part mural, *The Negro in America's Wars* (1944) (fig. 7.10) portrays incidents of African American participation in the American Revolution, the War of 1812, the Civil War, the Spanish-American War, and World War I. The contemporary resonance for those stationed there during the forties was considerable, and the murals were inspiring to them, as reported in the post newspaper: "Today, Black soldiers are again marching through an enemy land at the summons of duty, face to face with great labors, great dangers in the swamps and jungles of New Guinea, through the marshes and among the hedgerows of Normandy, and the mountainous terrain of northern Italy, to fight again, along with the freedom-loving men of all races and creeds, the forces of evil."[45]

Few white artists were interested in African American history during this period, and Davis's work is even more unusual when one considers that the sixty-panel series *The Migration of the Negro* (1940–41), portraying events from recent black history, had been executed only a few years before by noted African American painter Jacob Lawrence. That the Fort Huachuca murals were done by a white artist in an era of rigid racial segregation makes them extraordinary celebrations of black history. To teach soldiers skills they might use when they returned to civilian life, Davis organized a mural-painting workshop at Fort Huachuca, and several soldiers assisted him in his work (fig. 7.11). He also set up a silkscreen poster shop. To improve post morale, with the assistance of the soldiers

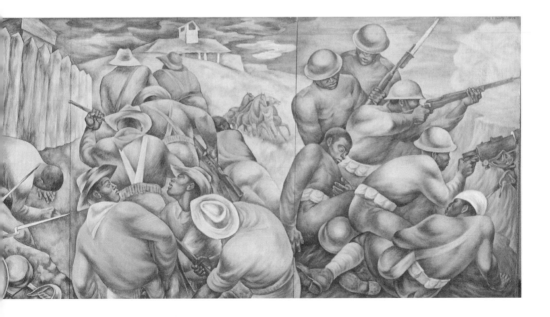

FIGURE 7.11. Art Workshop, Fort Huachuca, Sergeants Dillard and Shearer assist Sergeant Lew Davis in finishing *The Surrender of Geronimo*.

stationed at Fort Huachuca, Davis produced a series of work-incentive posters featuring black, rather than white, faces. These were in contrast with imagery featuring, in Davis's words: "smiling, blond, blue-eyed guys . . . waving a war bond or something."[46] Government propagandists featured mostly white imagery, and nationwide, only a few black faces were ever printed on these posters.

Davis's posters reminded viewers to be discreet in their public conversations, lest sensitive information be inadvertently passed on to the enemy. Lips needed to be zipped and rumors stopped. Other posters addressed sexually transmitted venereal diseases (gonorrhea and syphilis). Posters advised that if soldiers wasted food at mealtime, there would be less for their families at home. Buying war bonds today would insure money in their pockets in the future. Equipment needed to be taken care of, and training remembered, so that injury, even death, could be avoided. *History Will Judge Us by Our Deeds* (c. 1943) (fig. 7.12) is one of the most forceful in the series. Like many of the New Deal murals and FSA photographs, the figure looks seriously ahead, as if to the future, when both the war and the New Deal will come to an end.

The last art effort at Fort Huachuca came also in 1943, when the Army sponsored an art exhibition comprised of eighty-six works by thirty-seven African American artists in response to a request for "works of art by Negro artists of Negro subjects."[47] Included were several canvases by Illinois painter Archibald J. Motley, Jr., whose striking works of contemporary social life were inspired by

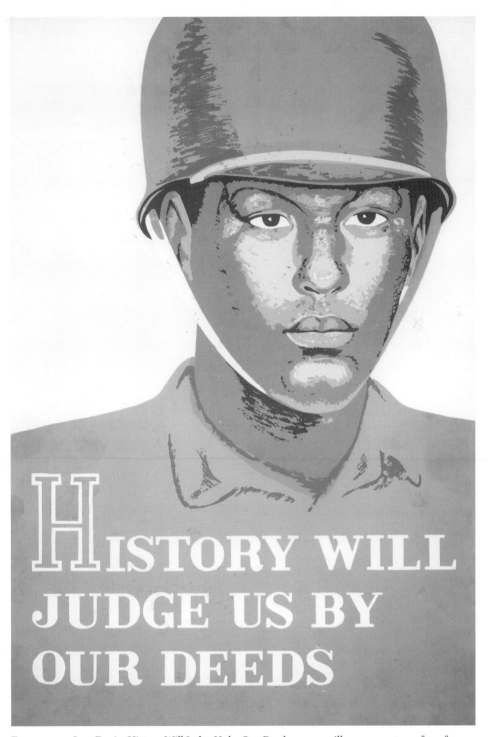

Figure 7.12. Lew Davis, *History Will Judge Us by Our Deeds*, c. 1943, silkscreen poster, 21″ × 15″.

neighborhoods in Chicago and Washington, D.C.[48] *Progress of the American Negro* (1939–40, Howard University Art Gallery) by Charles White was also shown. The allocation of art sent to Fort Huachuca included prints and paintings by many other notable African American artists, including painter Hale Woodruff and printmaker Dox Thrash. Images of scenes from black culture by white artists were also shown and included *Harlem Dancers* by printmaker Elizabeth Olds. The display would have been remarkable anywhere, but given the small minority representation of African Americans and national and local racial politics, that it took place in Arizona makes it an extraordinary historical event.

The end of World War II concludes a dozen years of remarkable federal support for the arts in Arizona. Not until the sixties, with the establishment of the NEA and NEH, would the government once again become a major art patron.

CHAPTER 8

CONCLUSION
The Legacy of the New Deal in Arizona

Two final photographs—one by Dorothea Lange for the Bureau of Agricultural Economics, and the other by Fritz Henle for the Office of War Information—bracket this chronicle of New Deal Arizona and reveal how much things had changed during the period that has been explored in this book. Lange's image is of a car parked on a Saturday in the cotton town of Eloy in November 1940 (fig. 8.1). Nearby is a market for second-hand clothing and furniture. The dealer is little better off than those who come to peruse what is for sale and will follow potential customers from crop to crop. The car that dominates the right foreground is dusty and battered, as its occupants must have been on arrival. The vehicle had been registered that year in Oklahoma, before its owners embarked on the long drive to Arizona in hopes of finding employment picking cotton. "FOR SALE" is written in block letters on the rear window. Whoever buys the car won't get much, but they will still have a little more than those who sold it. It is a life of increments for those on the move. And what will the Okies who once owned the car now do for transportation to that next meager job? They can't afford to keep it, but how can they follow the crops that are the source of their marginal livelihood without it? Eloy could not have offered many options to those who found themselves there with no way out. Similar impossible choices faced other Arizona migratory laborers in comparable circumstances at the bottom of the economic ladder. These people must have thought the Depression would never come to an end.

Henle's photograph (fig. 8.2), though made only two years later at Morenci, conveys the shift from the Depression to wartime, from unemployment to a steady job (at least as long as copper prices were high), from on the move to more or less settled. The image is replete with telling symbols. A vigilant white man with a gun is a classic western image. Cigarette dangling from his mouth, he stands alert and ready "for any approaching trouble," as the caption informs us. It evokes movie stills of stalwart sheriffs protecting their rough and ready towns from the bad guys. It is December, and a small Christmas wreath hung from his

FIGURE 8.1. Dorothea Lange, Saturday afternoon, Eloy, November 1940.

guardhouse marks the holiday season, though with the mines in full production, one day will be much like any other. In an emergency, first aid is available, affirming that people there will be cared for if needed. The sign above him instructs No Loafing, and the pair of American flags waving above remind the viewer that hard work and a war brought an end to the Depression. So it happened in Arizona, as it did in the rest of the nation.

Underlying the goals of many New Deal programs was a fundamental optimism that assumed that hope would trump hopelessness. People proved resilient in facing immense economic challenges and dislocation. For Baby Boomers like me, only a generation separates us from the Depression era that shaped my parents, and the stories they shared of this period were their collective histories. Habits of thriftiness and caution not to waste were the result of those years. Russell Lee's photograph of a young family at Chandler Farms (fig. 8.3) could be any young couple beginning their family during this period. Both parents smile with pride and affection at their young son, who returns the gaze of the photographer. His calm expression represents their hope for the future.

Framed by the Depression and World War II, the New Deal era demarcates the transformation from the period of early statehood to modern Arizona. The state, which was less than two decades old at the beginning of the Depression, had

FIGURE 8.2. Fritz Henle, Guard, Phelps Dodge copper mine, Morenci, December 1942.

changed dramatically by the mid-forties. A collision of national and international events marked the transition. President Roosevelt died on April 12, 1945, and the war ended on the European and Pacific fronts on May 8 and August 12, respectively. As it had the nation, the New Deal era indelibly changed the state, whose economy had become more diversified with the growth of manufacturing spurred by war industries. The expansion of military bases in the region stimulated private industry as well, and, aided by advances in air conditioning, by the war's end the state was poised for the dramatic development that began in the early 1950s. Construction surged, and manufacturing overtook the state's traditional economic base, though tourism remained a staple.

The chronicle of New Deal art support in this state emerges as an important Arizona story, and the collective view gained from a consideration of the visual arts is a remarkable lens through which to consider its cultural history. For a state that prides itself on its independent conservatism grounded in a fiercely held view

FIGURE 8.3. Russell Lee, A member of the Chandler Farms FSA part-time farming and cooperative project, with his wife and child May 1940.

of "states' rights," where would Arizona be without the federal government? The scope of federalization within Arizona remains extensive, with vast acreage under governmental control in the form of reservations, national parks, and military bases.

Federal art patronage under the New Deal was emblematic of this process. The issues suggested by the subjects portrayed by artists working in Arizona under the New Deal retain ongoing significance for Arizona, and in many ways represent broad archetypes of the American West as well. Art is a powerful instrument of historical record and cultural construction, and what is missing in its portrayals is as important as what is there. The five Cs that were the historical foundation of Arizona's economy—cotton, citrus, copper, climate, and cattle—are all represented, but with varying degrees of emphasis. It is during this era that culture emerges as a sixth significant C.

The population boom signaled increased cultural life, and for the many people who moved to Arizona during the thirties and the war years, that boom meant the arts grew as well. The government bureaucracy that gave cultural support under the New Deal created a sense of community among the state's artists where there had been none before. Spurred by the WPA and the Federal Art Project, one result of the initiatives implemented by federal agencies was that an arts community gradually coalesced as a result of these pioneering cultural efforts, as Mark Voris later recollected: "I think that one of the very nice things that came out of

the whole thing, for all of us in the state was getting to know one another."[1]
A fledgling art community had taken root in this desert state.

The challenges faced by Arizona artists during the thirties and early forties remain familiar ones today, and the themes portrayed by these image-makers are significant still. The proper role of the government in the arts on the federal and state level remains the subject of heated debate. Whether state funds appropriated for the arts should be reserved for resident artists is another area of ongoing discussion that is familiar to those working in the arts today, as is the question of whether the government should be (or is perceived to be) in competition with private enterprise in a free-market economy. The imagery portrayed in paintings and photographs by New Deal artists remains by surprising familiar, and their considerable resonance for twenty-first-century Arizonans derives from subjects that suggest water rights and usage in a dry state, migrant and immigrant labor, and the economic and environmental impact of the volatile mining industry. The flash points of economics and race continue to be played out politically.

How the arts developed in Arizona under federal patronage during the New Deal is an important and multifaceted story, and one with many implications for contemporary discussions regarding public funding for the arts. Current initiatives relating to heritage and cultural tourism raise the question of the role of the arts in economic development. How Arizonans defined their cultural identity and how it should be preserved and interpreted were issues during the thirties and forties, as they are now.

Most chronicles of Arizona, including those on art, have emphasized the pre-statehood period, and the New Deal era has received little scholarly attention, in part because it falls between the more "romantic" pre-statehood period of the pioneers (the era that is marketed to tourists), and the explosive expansion that followed World War II through the efforts of developers like Del Webb and others, some of whom got their start under the New Deal. This is very recent history.

As aggressive development and burgeoning population growth erase the tangible artifacts of the physical memory of Arizona's historical identity, these images sharpen our appreciation of the ongoing dialogue between past and present. As the last territory in the continental United States to achieve statehood, Arizona's (Anglo) history is brief. Because many current residents (like me) were not born here, the state has been slow to come to grips with much of its true heritage, preferring hoary Old West stereotypes of the noble cowboys, bad Indians, and lazy Mexicans of a mythologized Arizona, at odds with the diversely textured view portrayed by those who made images for government agencies. The artists who came to Arizona during the thirties, whether they were permanent residents or just passing through, portrayed the rich range of the state's residents (migrant and permanent, white, Mormon, Hispanic, black, and Native American), their professions (mining, agriculture, railroads), and the landscape in which they lived during a period of considerable economic, political, and social transition.

The subjects that were portrayed by artists during the New Deal era contribute to the iconography of Arizona. State identity, set against a broad discussion of cultural nationalism, a subject reinvented with each generation of American artists, proves to be a slippery concept, complicated by the mobility of modern society, and was slippery for the artists who have been the focus of this book. Where, then, may Arizona be found? The multiple perspectives of painting, sculpture, photography, and literature represent a cultural collage that even today we recognize as characteristic of Arizona. Although constructed, the themes have infused state identity. In the WPA guide, the ethnic and occupational contrasts of Flagstaff were suggested in footwear worn by people casually seen on the street: "the cowboy's spurred boots, the lumberjack's hobnailed shoes, and the Indian's moccasins."[2] And the guide addresses the issue directly:

When one speaks of an Arizonan, does he mean one of the 46,000 Indians whose ancestors were here first? Does he mean one of the 145,000 Mexicans who may be descended from seventeenth century invaders or have crossed the international line only yesterday as an immigrant? Does he mean the grizzled pioneer who may have come half a century ago to fight Apaches and brave other dangers of a perilous frontier? Does he mean one of the 200,000 or so who have come in the last decade from every other state in the Union and from almost every country on the face of the earth?[3]

State identity, grounded in a range of icons of visual culture, evolved and changed over time.

Arizona's New Deal photography, painting, and sculpture remain significant exemplars of federal art patronage and offer telling lessons positioned at the intersection of community history and culture. In presenting a broad range of themes and images of the state's historical development, they reinforced a sense of identity for this young western state. As Arizona moves forward in the twenty-first century, there is much to be learned from the historical events chronicled in this book regarding state identity and shared cultural values. Arizona's art history is emblematic of the story of the modern West. The past informs our view of the present, and reclaiming this significant period in the state's artistic history reveals that the broad issues addressed by New Deal artists and their federal patrons remain critical ones today. History may not have an opinion, but those who write it do. In reflecting on past events, we may better understand not only where we have been, but also where we are going. Photographer Russell Lee's hope that his work would be part of a visual archive that might "help the people of tomorrow understand the people of today, so they can carry on more intelligently,"[4] reminds us of the potent lessons that cultural history has to offer a state not yet one hundred years old.

NOTES

Abbreviations Used in the Notes

AA	Ansel Adams	NARA	National Archives and Records Administration
AAA	Archives of American Art		
AWP	Arizona Writers' Project	OWI	Office of War Information
CH	Carl Hayden	PCC	Philip Campbell Curtis
CWA	Civil Works Administration	PWAP	Public Works of Art Project
DL	Dorothea Lange	RA	Resettlement Administration (1935–1937)
DSD	Daniel S. Defenbacher		
EBR	Edward B. Rowan	RG	Record Group
EW	Edward Weston	RK	Robert Kittredge
FAP	Federal Art Project	RL	Russell Lee
FERA	Federal Emergency Relief Administration	RS	Roy Stryker
		RSP	Roy Stryker Papers
FSA	Farm Security Administration	SF	Seymour Fogel
FWP	Federal Writers' Project	TCP	Thomas C. Parker
HABS	Historic American Buildings Survey	TRAP	Treasury Relief Art Project
HC	Holger Cahill	WPA	Works Progress Administration (August 1935–September 1939), and the Work Projects Administration (September 1939–March 1942).
JD	Jack Delano		
JDP	Jack Delano Papers		
LC	Library of Congress		
LM	Lon Megargee	WRA	War Relocation Authority
MHV	Mark H. Voris		

Chapter 1. The Government as Patron

1. See Otero, "Refusing to be 'Undocumented,'" 42–59. No works by Hispanic artists have been located.

2. Many figures in the history of photography did not begin as artists, but after being included in museum collections, published in volumes on art history, and having influenced other artists, their images became works of art. Some were consummate professional photojournalists with as sharp an "eye" as any professionally trained artists. And the gold standard for those like FSA photographer John Vachon, who was first hired to write captions for RA before beginning to shoot pictures in his spare time, was the work he saw by artists like Dorothea Lange, Walker Evans, and others. In my chronicle, I reframe the presentation typical of many FSA albums that privilege the image over the maker. See "Farm Security Administration Photography and the Dilemmas of Art" and "Farm Security Administration Photography in the Aura of Art," in Raeburn, *Staggering Revolution*.

3. Excellent studies included Contreras, *Tradition and Innovation in New Deal Art;* Harris, *Federal Art and National Culture;* Larson, *The Reluctant Patron;* McDonald, *Federal Relief Administration and the Arts;* and McKinzie, *New Deal for Artists.* On the West, see Lowitt, *New Deal and the West;* and Nash's *American West Transformed* and *Federal Landscape.*

4. Excellent general studies of FSA photography include William Stott's *Documentary Expression and Thirties America;* Pete Daniel et al., *Official Images: New Deal Photography;* James Curtis's *Mind's Eye, Mind's Truth;* Fleischhauer and Brannan's *Documenting America, 1935–1943;* and Finnegan, *Picturing Poverty.* Of the many state studies, Mary Murphy's Montana study, *Hope in Hard Times,* is one of the most compelling in its narrative approach and nonalbum format. See

also Colorado: Leonard, *Trials and Triumphs;* Florida: Carlebach and Provenzo, *Farm Security Administration Photographs of Florida;* Illinois: Reid and Viskochil, *Chicago and Downstate;* Russell, *Southern Illinois Album;* Indiana: Reid, *Back Home Again;* Iowa: Zielinski, *Unknown Iowa;* Kansas: Schulz, *Bust to Boom;* Kentucky: Brannan and Horvath, *Kentucky Album;* Maine: Doty, *Acadian Hard Times;* Michigan: Schulz, *Michigan Remembered;* Minnesota: Reid, *Picturing Minnesota;* New Mexico: *Far from Main Street, Threads of Culture,* and Wood, *Heartland New Mexico;* Ohio: Carr, *Ohio: A Photographic Portrait;* Pennsylvania: Cohen and Filippelli, *Times of Sorrow and Hope;* South Carolina: Schulz, *South Carolina Album;* Texas: Reid, *Picturing Texas;* Utah: Briggs and Cannon, *Life and Land,* Swensen, "Dorothea Lange's Portrait"; Vermont: Graff, *Looking Back at Vermont,* Hastings and Hastings, *Up in the Morning Early;* and Virginia: Johnson, *Mountaineers to Main Streets.*

5. For New Deal post office murals, see Marling's *Wall to Wall America* and Park and Markowitz's *Democratic Vistas.* Beckham's imaginative *Gentle Reconstruction* juxtaposes both painting and photography. In *Engendering Culture,* Melosh considers gender issues in New Deal art. State mural studies include Arkansas: Gill, *Post Masters;* Indiana: Carlisle, *Simple and Vital Design;* New York: Park and Markowitz, *New Deal for Art;* and Texas: Parisi, *Texas Post Office Murals.* For Illinois, Becker (*Art for the People*) studied WPA-era murals in Chicago public schools, and Gray's excellent general Chicago guide (*Guide to Chicago's Murals*) includes New Deal murals.

6. Both paintings are in the collection of the U.S. Department of the Interior and are on loan to the Smithsonian American Art Museum.

Chapter 2. Arizona Welcomes You

1. Sonnichsen, *Tucson,* 237.
2. Sherwood, *Petrified Forest,* 11.
3. Sonnichsen, *Tucson,* 230.
4. Ibid., 240.
5. Luckingham, "Promotion of Phoenix," 87.
6. Sonnichsen, *Tucson,* 258.
7. Ibid., 238.
8. *WPA Guide to 1930s Arizona,* 12.
9. For the history of the magazine, see Thomas Cooper, "*Arizona Highways,*" and Topping, "Arizona Highways," as well as two articles by Raymond Carlson: "Yesterdays Remembered" and "Report to the Publishers."
10. Holt, "Arizona through the Eyes of One Who Knows It," 21.
11. For information on the Santa Fe Railway, the Fred Harvey Company, and tourism in the Southwest generally, see Berke, *Mary Colter;* D'Emilio and Campbell, *Visions and Visionaries;* Howard and Pardue, *Inventing the Southwest;* Rothman, *Culture of Tourism;* and Weigle and Babcock, *Great Southwest.*
12. Powell, *Arizona: A Bicentennial History,* 124.
13. For more on Megargee, see Fahlman, *Cowboy's Dream.*
14. The WPA Guide noted that it was the paintings of Moran, Remington, and others that "gave the world its first conception of Arizona." (137) See also James K. Ballinger, *Frederic Remington's Southwest.*
15. Murray, *Cinema Southwest,* 53.
16. *WPA Guide to 1930s Arizona,* 3.
17. George W. P. Hunt to Commission of State Institutions, 13 August 1918. George W. P. Hunt Papers, Arizona State Archives, Department of Library, Archives, and Public Records.
18. Maynard Dixon, "Arizona in 1900," 17–18.
19. Davis quoted in Chanin and Chanin, *This Land, These Voices,* 226.

20. For more on New Mexico, see Flynn, *Treasures on New Mexico Trails;* Hoefer, *More Abundant Life;* Nunn, *Sin Nombre: Hispana and Hispano Artists of the New Deal Era* (despite its title, this book is about New Mexico only); and Wilson, *Myth of Santa Fe.*

21. For Arizona's artistic development in the early twentieth century, see especially Ballinger and Rubinstein, *Visitors to Arizona;* and Sarah Moore's "No Woman's Land." One of the most concise accounts of this era is "The Depression and the New Deal," in Sheridan's excellent *Arizona: A History.* See also Wagoner, *Arizona's Heritage;* and Trimble's *Arizona: A Cavalcade of History* and *Arizona 2000.* William S. Collins's *New Deal in Arizona* is thorough, but in 436 pages, he devotes barely a page to cultural agencies. For New Deal art in Arizona, see Bermingham, *New Deal in the Southwest;* Hall, "Federal Art Patronage of Art in Arizona"; and Morrissey and Jensen, *Picturing Arizona.* For the New Deal in Arizona generally, see the Autumn 1991 issue of *Arizona History,* with articles by Booth, "Cactizonians"; Keane, "Cotton and Figs"; and Weisiger, "Mythic Fields of Plenty." There is a growing literature focused on this era in Arizona. See LeSeur, *Not All Okies Are White;* Meeks, *Border Citizens;* Melton and Smith, *Arizona Goes to War;* Moore, *Civilian Conservation Corps in Arizona's Rim Country;* Vilander, *Hoover Dam;* Weisiger, *Land of Plenty;* and Westerlund, *Arizona's War Town.* For modern Arizona, see Luckingham's several publications, especially *Phoenix;* and Luey and Stowe, *Arizona at Seventy-Five.*

22. Raymond Phillips Sanderson, interview with Sylvia Loomis, 1965, AAA.

23. Davis quoted in Chanin and Chanin, *This Land, These Voices,* 237.

24. Ibid., 229.

Chapter 3. The Cultural Desert

1. "Federal Sponsored Community Art Centers," WPA Technical Series, Art Circular no. 1 (8 October 1937): 1.

2. Ross Santee to Henry G. Alsberg, NARA/RG 69/WPA.

3. Cosulich, "Old Pueblo Authors and Artists," 32.

4. MHV to DSD, 29 September 1936, AAA/WPA/FAP/DC-60/NARA.

5. Ibid.

6. MHV to DSD, 12 November 1936, AAA/WPA/FAP/DC-60/NARA.

7. Ibid.

8. MHV to DSD, 27 February 1937, NARA/RG 69/WPA.

9. MHV to Mr. Stallcup, 12 October 1936, NARA/RG 69/WPA.

10. MHV to Mary-Russell Ferrell Colton, 26 October 1936, AAA/WPA/FAP/DC-60/NARA.

11. See Chadwick et al., *American Dreamer* and Philip Curtis's recollections, "Phoenix Art Center." Master's theses by Hight and Walczak have useful biographical material.

12. PCC to TCP, 27 May 1937, AAA/WPA/DC-63.

13. "Art Center Opens Today," *Arizona Republic,* 15 July 1937.

14. PCC to DSD, 27 May 1937, NARA/RG 69/WPA.

15. Ibid.

16. Joseph A. Danysh to TCP, 22 November 1938, NARA/RG 69/WPA/.

17. Jane H. Rider to HC, 16 July 1937, AAA/WPA/DC-63.

18. Ibid. Rider is quoting from a conversation she had with Maie Heard at the opening of the Federal Art Center.

19. Ibid.

20. MHV to Trevor Browne, 6 November 1936, DC 60: AAA, WPA/FAP/NARA.

21. Agnes Hunt Parke to Florence Kerr, 19 August 1940, AAA/WPA/DC-63.

22. PCC to TCP, 15 October 1938, NARA/RG 69/WPA.

23. Ibid.

24. PCC to DSD, 19 April 1939, NARA/RG 69/WPA.

25. PCC to TCP, 21 July 1937, AAA/WPA/DC-63.

26. Louise R. Norton to HC, 11 February 1936. AAA/WPA/DC-63.

27. PCC to DSD, 16 September 1937, NARA/RG 69/WPA.

28. PCC to HC, 11 September 1937, AAA/WPA/DC-63.

29. Ibid.

30. Ibid.

31. Ibid.

32. PCC to HC, 24 September 1937, AAA/WPA/DC-63.

33. HC to PCC, 31 January 1938, AAA/WPA/DC-63.

34. Ibid.

35. The names appearing on relief rolls vary, and the largest number were from Phoenix (Creston F. Baumgartner, Mary Edith Brooke, Will W. Colby, Joseph Morgan Henninger, Harriet Morton Holmes, Barnett Kapland, Emery T. Kopta, Lucy Drake Marlow, Lon Megargee, J. Glen W. Scott, David Carrick Swing, Burdell Tenney, and J. D. York). Three from Tucson received funding from the project (Louise R. Norton, Stella McLennan Roca, and Mark H. Voris). Also on the lists were artists from Flagstaff (Jade Fon Woo, who had studied at Northern Arizona University, and Edna P. McGrew), Prescott (Kate T. Cory and Doris B. Hanson), Tempe (Howe A. Williams, Juanita Watkins), Scottsdale (Marjorie Thomas), Springerville (Curt Maxwell), Adamana (Alva Hermetet), Warren (Phillip Sanderson), Globe (Maybelle Mercer), Wickenberg (Eugene Upton), Mesa (Bernhart Mickelson), Winslow (Joe Rodriguez), and Holbrook (George Keyes). Additional names mentioned in correspondence include Elmer Curley of Leupp; and Lew Place, James Powell Scott, Salvador Camacho, and Andres Anderson of Tucson. Most of these remain little known.

36. See Robbins's MA thesis "The Hardrock Miner" and her exhibition catalogue, *Lew Davis*.

37. Lew Davis to Cecil H. Jones, 22 February 1937, NARA/TRAP/DC-16.

38. Ibid.

39. Cecil H. Jones to Lew Davis, 1 March 1937, NARA/TRAP/DC-16.

40. PCC to HC, 24 November 1937, AAA/WPA/DC-63.

41. Ibid.

42. MHV to TCP, 28 November 1937, AAA/WPA/DC-63.

43. Ibid.

44. Carl T. Hayden (1877–1972) represented Arizona in Washington for fifty-seven years, serving first in Congress (1912–27), and then in the Senate (1927–69). *The Sheepherder* (1934, Archives and Special Collections, Arizona State University), by Marjorie Thomas, who received support under the PWAP, hung in his office in Washington, D.C., and came to ASU as part of his archives.

45. MHV to TCP, 28 November 1937, AAA/WPA/DC-63.

46. Jane H. Rider to Ellen S. Woodward, 28 December 1937, AAA/WPA/DC-63.

47. Donald Bear to HC, 21 January 1936, AAA/WPA/DC-63.

48. Bermingham, *New Deal in the Southwest*, 14.

49. Agnes Hunt Parker to Florence Kerr, 19 August 1940, AAA/WPA/DC-63.

50. Weadock, "Dedication to the Memory of Ross Santee," 184.

51. For information on Santee, see Bell, "Ross Santee Cowboy Artist"; Carlson, "Arizona Sketchbook"; Ford, "Ross Santee"; Kirkpatrick, "Ross Santee"; Powell, "How He Pictured the West"; Weadock, "Dedication to the Memory of Ross Santee"; and articles written by Santee for *Arizona Highways*.

52. Penkower, *Federal Writers' Project,* 41. For more on the FWP and the state guides, see also Bold, *WPA Guides;* Mangione, *Dream and the Deal;* and Schindler-Carter, *Vintage Snapshots.*

53. Ross Santee to Henry Alsberg, 21 April 1936, quoted in Penkower, *Federal Writers' Project,* 41.

54. Joseph I. Miller to J. D. Newsom, 13 February 1942, NARA/RG 69/WPA.

55. Carlson, "Yesterdays Remembered," 1.

56. Powell, *Southwest Classics,* 178.

57. Ibid., 181.

58. Weadock, "Dedication to the Memory of Ross Santee," 185.

59. *WPA Guide to 1930s Arizona,* 137.

60. Carlson, "Arizona Sketchbook," 14.

61. Ibid.

62. Ibid., 28.

63. *WPA Guide to 1930s Arizona,* 137.

64. Ibid.

65. Franklin Delano Roosevelt to Florence Kerr, assistant commissioner, WPA, 30 September 1941, AWP/NARA.

66. Report of J. M. Scammell, quoted in letter Reed to Mary Barret et al., 26 January 1938, FWP Files, quoted in McDonald, *Federal Relief Administration and the Arts,* 745.

67. Thomas J. Tormey, "Foreword," in *Arizona: A State Guide,* v. Arizona State Teachers College had published the guide.

68. Florence Kerr and J. D. Newson to W. J. Jamieson, FWP/LC.

69. Santee's first show was at the Phoenix Art Center in January 1938.

70. Christensen, *The Index of American Design,* xii. See also Clayton et al., *Drawing on America's Past.*

71. Christensen, *The Index of American Design,* v.

72. Louise Norton to Ruth Reeves, 7 May 1936, NARA/RG 69/WPA, 651.315.

73. Holger Cahill, "Introduction," in Christensen, *The Index of American Design,* xii.

74. Louise Norton to Ruth Reeves, 7 May 1936, NARA/RG 69/WPA, 651.315. Although not part of the Index of American Design, there was a copper craft project in the Tucson and Phoenix weaving unit (sponsored by the University of Arizona). What was made was strongly utilitarian in nature, and a press release stated that it "provided employment for disabled war veterans, women and others not able to do manual labor." (NARA, RG 69) Artists were not involved, and the aim was clearly to train participants in a technical skill with which they could earn a living.

75. She grew up on her family's ranch. See *Lazy B,* the memoir she wrote with her brother.

76. "Index of American Design," Phoenix Federal Art Center, 10–30 October 1937, exhibition brochure. NARA/RG 69.

77. Charles E. Peterson, "The Historic American Buildings Survey: Its Beginnings," in *Historic America,* 9. See also Davidson and Perschler, "Historic American Buildings Survey;" and *Recording a Vanishing Legacy.*

78. *WPA Guide to 1930s Arizona,* 243.

79. John P. O'Neill, "Memorandum to the Chief Architect," 30 June 1937, NARA/HABS/RG 515.

80. WPA publicity photograph caption, NARA.

81. Bindas, *All of This Music Belongs to the Nation,* xiii.

Chapter 4. Art in Public Places

1. LM to Olin Dows, 6 October 1935, TRAP AZ, DC 16, NARA/AAA.

2. LM to Olin Dows, 26 November 1935, NARA.

3. Joseph Morgan Henninger to his parents, 24 January 1934, Joseph Morgan Henninger Papers, Department of Archives and Special Collections, Arizona State University Libraries. See Cripe, "New Deal Revisited."

4. Joseph Morgan Henninger to his parents, 24 January 1934, Joseph Morgan Henninger Papers, Department of Archives and Special Collections, Arizona State University Libraries.

5. *WPA Guide to 1930s Arizona*, 3.

6. O'Kane, "Emry Kopta: Sculptor of Indians," 34. See also Hurst, "Emry Kopta."

7. *Bisbee Daily Review*, 12 May 1935, quoted in Snively, "The Sculpture of Raymond Phillips Sanderson," 17–18.

8. Ibid., 36.

9. William G. Hantranft to EBR, 8 April 1937, NARA/RG 121. Richards is best known as a San Diego architect. See *Nature in Architecture*.

10. LM to CH, 6 April 1937, NARA.

11. Ibid.

12. CH to C. J. Peoples, 10 April 1937, NARA/RG 121.

13. EBR to CH, after 10 April 1937, NARA.

14. EBR to Florence H. Sture, 17 May 1937, NARA.

15. Lew Davis ro Cecil Jones, 22 February 1937, NARA/TRAP/DC-16.

16. Ibid.

17. A memorial exhibition of Black's work was held at the Federal Art Center in June. Artists were not then aware of the potential dangers their materials and working conditions posed. Gerald Cassidy (1879–1934) worked in an empty store building, and the fire he kept for warmth enhanced the fumes: "He succumbed to carbon monoxide and turpentine poisoning incurred while working in a temporary studio on a mural of the Canyon de Chelly for the federal building in Santa Fe. When stricken Mr. Cassidy was painting on a platform high above the floor, where several of his assistants had been previously affected by the fumes." "Cassidy, Painter of Southwest, Dies at 54," *Art Digest* 8 (1 March 1934): 23.

18. For more on Fogel, see Berman, "Self-Knowledge into Form"; and two articles by Jared Fogel on his father.

19. Farmer, "Art Controversy Falls Upon Safford Valley."

20. Ibid.

21. H. P. Watkins to W. E. Reynolds, 8 December 1939, NARA/RG 121.

22. Ibid.

23. H. P. Watkins to EBR, 17 December 1939, NARA/RG 121.

24. CH to W. E. Reynolds, 3 January 1940, NARA/RG 121.

25. SF to H. P. Watkins, 18 January 1940, NARA/RG 121.

26. SF to EBR, 18 January 1940, NARA/RG 121.

27. Ibid.

28. SF to EBR, 12 February 1940, NARA/RG 121.

29. SF to EBR, 18 April 1940, NARA/RG 121.

30. SF to EBR, 10 November 1941, NARA/RG 121.

31. Ibid.

32. SF to EBR, n.d. [February 1942], NARA/RG 121.

33. Martin Layton to EBR, 10 February 1942, NARA/RG 121.

34. SF to EBR, 22 December 1941, NARA/RG 121.

35. RK to Inslee A. Hopper, 1 March 1940, NARA/RG121.

36. Murphy, *History of Women's Physical Education*, 31. Those depicted were Anna Pavlova, Vaslav Nijinsky, Doris Humphrey, Yvonne Georgi, Helen Tamiris, Charles Weidman, Martha Graham, Ruth St. Denis, Ted Shawn, Kurt Jooss, Ruth Sorel, Senia Gluck-Sandor, Mary Wigman, Isadora Duncan, and Harald Kreutzberg.

37. "The B. B. Moeur Activity Building, Arizona State Teachers College," dedication pamphlet, 29 September 1939.

38. RK to EBR, 3 October 1938. NARA/RG 121.

39. Lamar, "Arizona's Department of Library and Archives," 13.

40. See Parman's *Indians and the American West,* and *Navajos and the New Deal;* Prucha, *Great Father;* and Faris, *Navajo and Photography.* For Arizona specifically, see "The Indian New Deal" in Collins, *New Deal in Arizona,* 237–72.

41. None were from Arizona. See Doss, "Between Modernity and 'the Real Thing,'" and Nelson, "Indian Art in Washington."

42. No other New Deal murals by Indian artists have been discovered in the state. Several Native American artists established teaching careers in Arizona, though none received federal commissions for murals in the state. Fred Kabotie (Hopi) returned to Arizona in 1937 to teach art in the new high school at Oraibi, and Lloyd Kiva New (Cherokee) assumed leadership of the art department at the Phoenix Indian School in 1939.

43. The best source on this commission is Rachel Leibowitz's brilliant dissertation, "Constructing the Navajo Capital." See especially chapter 5, "Murals, Models, and Modernity: Representing Window Rock." A generous scholar, she shared her research with me and also provided the previously unpublished photograph of Nailor that is published for the first time in this book. I am very grateful for her assistance. See also Dunn, *American Indian Painting;* Brody's two volumes, *Indian Painters and White Patrons* and *Pueblo Indian Painting;* Karaim, "Of Trading Posts, Hogans, and Navajo Tacos"; and Burt's detailed National Register nomination. There has been considerable recent scholarly interest in the Indian New Deal and the visual arts, and several recent dissertations have explored this topic. In addition to Leibowitz, see Jennifer McLerran, "Inventing 'Indian Art'"; and Stephanie Jones, "American Indian Painting and Visual Rhetorics."

44. See Leibowitz, "Constructing the Navajo Capital," 271.

Chapter 5. The Government Lens

1. His trips were April–May 1940, September–October 1940, and February–March 1942.

2. Roy Stryker quoted in Calvin Kytle, "Roy Stryker: A Tribute," in Anderson, *Roy Stryker: The Humane Propagandist,* n.p. For more on Stryker, see Hurley, *Portrait of a Decade;* Keller, *Highway as Habitat;* Plattner, *Roy Stryker, U.S.A.;* and Stryker and Wood, *In This Proud Land.*

3. RSP, AAA/NDA-8.

4. Stryker and Wood, *In This Proud Land,* 8.

5. Jack and Irene Delano, interview with Richard K. Doud, 1965, AAA.

6. Since the publication of Meltzer's biography in 1978, the literature on Lange has expanded considerably. Of the most recent, see Heyman et al., *Dorothea Lange: American Photographs;* Tsujimoto, *Dorothea Lange: Archive of an Artist;* and Partridge's *Dorothea Lange: A Visual Life.* For her work in Arizona, see Fahlman, "Cotton Culture." The first major study of Lee was published by Hurley in 1978. His New Mexico photographs have received the most attention. See Wroth's volume on Chamisal and Peñasco and Myers's *Pie Town Woman.* Most recent is Szarkowski et al., *Russell Lee Photographs.* For Lee's Arizona Work, see Jensen, "'It Was Just a Job.'" See also Jensen, "Dorothea Lange and Russell Lee: Documenting and Imaging Women," in Morrissey and Jensen, *Picturing Arizona,* 80–101.

7. Lange quoted in O'Neal, *A Vision Shared,* 183.

8. Ibid., 135.

9. Lee, "Life on the American Frontier," 40.

10. Ibid., 42.

11. RL to RS, 20 April 1940, RSP/AAA/NDA-31.

12. Ibid.

13. RS to RL, 22 April 1940, RSP/AAA/NDA-31.

14. Ibid.

15. RS to RL, 22 April 1940, RSP/AAA/NDA-31.

16. John Steinbeck studied RA/FSA photographs when writing his novel, as did John Ford as he directed the movie version. In 1938, photographer Horace Bristol traveled with Steinbeck, intending to collaborate with him on a picture book. Steinbeck, however, decided to proceed on his own. *Life* published some of Bristol's images in 1939, and in 1940 included some of his pictures in an article comparing them with movie stills. See *Stories from Life: The Photography of Horace Bristol.* Thomas Hart Benton illustrated the novel in 1940 for the Limited Editions Club, and producer Darryl Zanuck commissioned six prints to advertise the movie.

17. See Michael Gray, *New Deal Medicine,* and Stoeckle and White, *Plain Pictures of Plain Doctoring.*

18. "New Resettlement Plans: Resettlement Administration Selects Arizona for Historic Trials in Rural Housing and Cooperation," *Arizona Producer,* 1 March 1937.

19. See Banfield, *Government Project,* and Keane, "Cotton and Figs." See also Brian Q. Cannon, "Casa Grande Valley Farms," as well as his *Remaking the Agrarian Dream.*

20. "New Resettlement Plans: Resettlement Administration Selects Arizona for Historic Trials in Rural Housing and Cooperation," *Arizona Producer,* 1 March 1937.

21. RL to RS, 11 May 1940, RSP/AAA/NDA-31.

22. "Data for Photographers," undated typescript, RSP, AAA, NDA-31.

23. "New Resettlement Plans," 1.

24. RS to RL, 22 April 1940, RSP/AAA/NDA-31.

25. "Data for Photographers," undated typescript, RSP/AAA/NDA-31.

26. RL to RS, 22 April 1940, RSP/AAA/NDA-31.

27. "New Resettlement Plans," 31.

28. Ibid.

29. *WPA Guide to 1930s Arizona,* 199

30. J. Russell Smith and Phillips, *North America,* 578.

31. Cleland, *History of Phelps Dodge,* 227.

32. *WPA Guide to 1930s Arizona,* 305.

33. *WPA Guide to 1930s Arizona,* 203.

34. *WPA Guide to 1930s Arizona,* 174.

35. See Cleland, *A History of Phelps Dodge;* Hyde, *Copper for America;* and Schwantes, *Vision and Enterprise.*

36. In 1941, Weston spent three days in the Phoenix area, shooting six negatives at Taliesin, as part of his trip in connection with a commission to provide illustrations for Whitman's *Leaves of Grass.*

37. RL to RS, 19 May 1940, RSP/AAA/NDA-31.

38. See Simpson, "Pioneer Mother Monuments," and A. Stott, "Prairie Madonnas and Pioneer Women."

39. The other nine were erected in Pennsylvania, West Virginia, Ohio, Indiana, Illinois, Missouri, Kansas, Colorado, and New Mexico.

40. Cardwell, "Salome," 14.

41. *Thunderbird Remembered,* 45.

42. Wallace, "Maynard Dixon: Painter and Poet of the Far West," 44, University of California Library, Berkeley.

43. Keller, *In Focus: Dorothea Lange,* 9.

44. Pare Lorentz incorporated these words in his famous 1935 film, *The Plough That Broke the Plains.*

45. Taylor, "Again the Covered Wagon," 348–51.

46. Steinbeck, *Grapes of Wrath,* 274.

47. Taylor, "Again the Covered Wagon," 348–51.

48. DL, interview with Richard Doud, 22 May 1964, AAA.
49. Lorentz and Taylor, "Dorothea Lange: Camera with a Purpose," 105.
50. Sheridan, *Arizona: A History,* 213.
51. *WPA Guide to 1930s Arizona,* 85.
52. This was the title of Carey McWilliams's 1939 history of California farm labor.
53. Brown and Cassmore, *Migratory Cotton Pickers in Arizona,* xix.
54. Ibid., xvii.
55. Ibid.
56. Ibid., 8.
57. Ibid., 8.
58. Ibid., 7.
59. See Hoffman, *Unwanted Mexican Americans;* Luckingham, *Minorities in Phoenix;* Meeks, *Border Citizens;* and Sheridan, *Los Tucsonenses,* as well as Morrissey, "Migrant Labor Children in Depression-Era Arizona," in Morrissey and Jensen, *Picturing Arizona,* 22–41.
60. The term *zanjero* remains in use, and *zanjeros* are still employed by the Salt River Project in Phoenix.
61. RS to DL, 18 June 1937, RSP/AAA.
62. See LeSeur, *Not All Okies Are White,* and Natanson, *Black Image in the New Deal.*

Chapter 6. The Landscape of Arizona

1. Resident and visiting artists continued to be inspired by Arizona subject matter during the thirties, favoring either landscape or Native American themes. The iconography of Charles Sheeler and Edward Weston both complements and contrasts with that of Adams. Sheeler's patronage came from *Fortune,* the nation's leading business magazine, while Weston was supported by a fellowship from the Guggenheim Foundation. In working on federal land, either recording the landscape wonders of the national parks or the period's great public works projects, their subject matter parallels that of Ansel Adams and other New Deal agency artists. Although not government sponsored, their work serves as a counterpoint to the documentary photographers and muralists, reinforcing the national significance of their imagery.
2. Nancy K. Anderson, "'The Kiss of Enterprise': The Western Landscape as Symbol and Resource," in Truettner, *West as America,* 244.
3. *WPA Guide to 1930s Arizona,* 202.
4. Ibid., 193.
5. Ibid., 202.
6. Ibid.
7. James, *Arizona: The Wonderland,* 403.
8. Adams is not generally thought of as a mining photographer, but commercial work netted him assignments that stretched his vision. His photograph of Kennecott Copper's immense mine at Bingham Canyon near Salt Lake City was published in *Fortune* in 1951. The bibliography on Adams is considerable. In addition to the sources already cited in the notes, see Alinder, *Ansel Adams: A Biography;* Haas and Senf, *Ansel Adams in the Lane Collection;* Nyerges, *In Praise of Nature;* and Szarkowski, *Ansel Adams at 100.*
9. Julien Levy, "Photo-Murals," in *Murals by American Painters and Photographers,* 11.
10. For more on Ickes and Interior art programs, see Look and Perrault, *Interior Building,* and Watkins, *Righteous Pilgrim.*
11. E. K. Burlew to AA, 18 June 1941, quoted in Spaulding, *Ansel Adams and the American Landscape,* 181.
12. Hammond, quoting AA in *Ansel Adams: Divine Performance,* 110.
13. Adams, *An Autobiography,* 271.

14. Ansel Adams, "The Meaning of the National Parks," in Stillman and Turnage, *Ansel Adams: Our National Parks,* 15.

15. Letter quoted in Wright and Armor, *Mural Project,* vi.

16. AA to Beaumont and Nancy Newhall, 26 October 1941, in Alinder and Stillman, *Ansel Adams: Letters and Images* (hereafter *AA: L and I*), 131–32.

17. Ibid., 132.

18. First named the Boulder Dam after the site originally selected, the dam, in 1930, was being called the Hoover Dam. With the election of Franklin Delano Roosevelt, Harold Ickes changed the name back to Boulder Dam in 1933. Not until 1947 was it renamed Hoover Dam.

19. Lowitt, *New Deal and the West,* 82. See also Billington and Jackson, *Big Dams of the New Deal Era;* Reisner, *Cadillac Desert;* Stevens, *Hoover Dam: An American Adventure;* Vilander, *Hoover Dam: The Photographs of Ben Glaha;* and Richard Guy Wilson, "American Modernism in the West."

20. In 1929, before construction commenced, Arizona artist Kate Cory was commissioned by the Bureau of Reclamation to record the site of the future dam, and the result was her painting, *Boulder Canyon Dam Site* (1929, Sharlot Hall Museum).

21. Major sources on Dixon include Burnside, *Maynard Dixon: Artist of the West;* Gibbs, *Escape to Reality;* Hagerty, *Desert Dreams;* and *Thunderbird Remembered.*

22. Wallace, "Maynard Dixon: Painter and Poet of the Far West," 77, University of California Library, Berkeley.

23. Ibid., 79, quoting a reviewer from the *Oakland Tribune,* 1 May 1934.

24. Ibid., 78.

25. Ibid.

26. See Lozowick, *William Gropper;* and Vigneault, "The Hidden Life."

27. *WPA Guide to 1930s Arizona,* 337.

28. Marx, *Machine in the Garden.*

29. Wallace Stegner, "Introduction," in Alinder and Stillman, *AA: L and I,* viii.

30. Newhall, *Focus,* 66.

31. Ibid., 67. Ellipses in original quotation.

32. AA to Alfred Stieglitz, 16 May 1935, Alinder and Stillman, *AA: L and I,* 78.

33. AA to EW, 6 August 1935, Alinder and Stillman, *AA: L and I,* 79.

34. Ansel Adams, "Unpublished Statement of Group f/64," in Nancy Newhall, *Ansel Adams: The Eloquent Light,* 82.

35. AA to David McAlpin, 4 November 1938, Alinder and Stillman, *AA: L and I,* 110.

36. AA to Alfred Stieglitz, 25 December 1944, Alinder and Stillman, *AA: L and I,* 154.

37. AA to Dorothea Lange, 15 May 1962, Alinder and Stillman, *AA: L and I,* 281.

38. AA to David McAlpin, 4 November 1938, Alinder and Stillman, *AA: L and I,* 108.

39. See Heyman, *Seeing Straight: The f.64 Revolution in Photography.*

40. RS to RL, 28 March 1940, RSP/AAA/NDA-31.

41. Charis Wilson and Weston, *California and the West,* 150.

Chapter 7. The Depression Ends

1. Field Work Outlines, 19 February 1942, RSP/AAA/NDA-8.

2. See Bendavid-Val, *Propaganda and Dreams;* Clark, *Art and Propaganda in the Twentieth Century;* and Winkler, *Politics of Propaganda.*

3. Jack and Irene Delano, interview with Richard K. Doud, 1965, AAA.

4. Delano, *Photographic Memories,* 20. For Delano's railroad photographs, see Valle, *Iron Horse at War.*

5. Delano, *Photographic Memories,* 28.

6. Ibid.

7. Ibid., 29.

8. Ibid., 34.

9. RS to JD, 27 July 1942, JDP/AAA.

10. Shooting script, probably 1940, in Fleischhauer and Brannan, *Documenting America,* 278. Shooting scripts were general thematic outlines compiled by federal officials to suggest potential subjects for the photographers working in the field.

11. Ibid., 276.

12. Ibid.

13. Delano, *Photographic Memories,* 94.

14. See Winterry, *Fritz Henle's Rollei.*

15. *WPA Guide to 1930s Arizona,* 434.

16. Ibid.

17. Hyde, *Copper for America,* 164.

18. Cleland, *History of Phelps Dodge,* 258.

19. Ibid.

20. The literature on internment is considerable. For Arizona, see Conrat and Conrat, *Executive Order 9066;* Daniels, *Prisoners without Trial;* Gesensway and Roseman, *Beyond Words;* Gordon and Okihiro, *Impounded;* Higa, *View from Within;* Kuramitsu, "Internment and Identity in Japanese American Art"; Nakayama, *Transforming Barbed Wire;* Nishimoto, *Inside an American Concentration Camp;* Spicer et al., *Impounded People;* and Weglyn, *Years of Infamy.*

21. Poston, known as the Colorado River Center, was located about twenty miles from Parker, on the California/Arizona border. There were also isolation centers at Mayer and Leupp.

22. Eaton, *Beauty behind Barbed Wire,* 74. For more on Eaton, see Van Dommelin, *Allen H. Eaton.*

23. "Arizona's Japanese Citizens," *Arizona Defense News,* published by the Arizona Civilian Defense Coordinating Council, Phoenix, vol. 1, no. 5 (29 December 1941): 3.

24. See Davidov, "'The Color of My Skin, The Shape of My Eyes'"; Higa, "Toyo Miyatake and *Our World*"; Reed, *Japanese Photography in America;* and Robinson, *Elusive Truth.*

25. Peeler, *Illuminating Mind in American Photography,* 321.

26. AA to Nancy Newhall, 1943, in Alinder and Stillman, *AA: L and I,* 144.

27. Ibid.

28. Ibid.

29. Alinder, *Ansel Adams: A Biography,* 236.

30. Archie Miyatake, "Introduction," in Robinson, *Elusive Truth,* 11.

31. Eaton, *Beauty behind Barbed Wire,* 57.

32. Noguchi, *Sculptor's World,* 25. In addition to this and sources cited elsewhere in the notes, for more on Noguchi's Arizona experiences, see Altshuler, *Modern Masters: Isamu Noguchi;* and Hunter, *Isamu Noguchi.*

33. Duus, *Life of Isamu Noguchi,* 168.

34. Noguchi, *Sculptor's World,* 25.

35. Isamu Noguchi, "I Become a Nisei," 1942 MS, in Lyford, "Noguchi," 141.

36. Isamu Noguchi to John Collier, 27 July 1942, in Maeda, "Isamu Noguchi, 5-7-A, Poston, Arizona," 68.

37. Noguchi, *Sculptor's World,* 25.

38. Higa, *View from Within,* 69.

39. Letter to Mr. Fryer, 28 June 1942, from WRA Isamu Noguchi case file, in Higa, *View from Within,* 32.

40. Noguchi, *Sculptor's World,* 25.

41. Isamu Noguchi to Man Ray, 30 May 1942, in Duus, *Life of Isamu Noguchi,* 169.

42. Isamu Noguchi to George Biddle, in Ashton, *Noguchi, East and West*, 70–71.

43. Isamu Noguchi, interview with Paul Cummings, 1973, AAA, Oral History Collection.

44. See Robbins, *Lew Davis*.

45. *Apache Sentinel*, 8 September 1944: 4, in Robinson and Greenhouse, *Art of Archibald J. Motley, Jr.*, 10.

46. Lew Davis, interview with Robert Quinn, 13 January 1979, in *Lew Davis: A Survey of Work*, n.p.

47. Edwin N. Hardy, Colonel, Cavalry, Commanding, to Florence King, 20 February 1943, AAA/WPA/DC-63.

48. The work Motley showed in Arizona was part of a WPA allocation for Fort Huachuca. His paintings, executed between 1934 and 1938, included *Barbecue, Saturday Night, The Picnic, The Liar, Carnival,* and *Arrival at Chickasaw Bayou of the Slaves of President Davis*. These and many of the other works in the exhibition became part of the collection of the Howard University Art Gallery in Washington, D.C., when the base was temporarily deactivated in 1947 (it was reactivated in 1954).

Chapter 8. Conclusion

1. Mark Voris, interview with Sylvia Loomis, 1965, AAA, Oral History Collection.

2. *WPA Guide to 1930s Arizona*, 187.

3. Ibid., 4.

4. Lee "Life on the American Frontier," 41.

SELECTED BIBLIOGRAPHY

Archival Sources

Archives of American Art, Washington, D.C.

Curtis, Philip Campbell. Interview with Sylvia Loomis. 1965. Lange, Dorothea. Interview with Richard K. Doud. 1964.

Delano, Jack. Papers.

Delano, Jack, and Irene Delano, interviews with Richard K. Doud. 1965.

Lee, Russell, and Jean Lee. Interview with Richard K. Doud. 1964.

Noguchi, Isamu. Interview with Paul Cummings. 1973.

Rothstein, Arthur. Interview with Richard K. Doud. 1964.

Sanderson, Phillip. Interview with Sylvia Loomis. 1965.

Seckler, Dorothy G. Interview with Adolph Gottlieb. 1967.

Stryker, Roy Emerson. Interview with Richard K. Doud. 1963–65.

Voris, Mark. Interview with Sylvia Loomis. 1965.

Wardell, Thomas. Interview with Sylvia Loomis. 1965.

Arizona State Library, Archives and Public Records

Hunt, Governor George W. P. Papers. Jay Datus Vertical File.

Arizona State University Libraries. Department of Archives and Special Collections

Curtis, Philip. Collection.

Henninger, Joseph Morgan. Papers.

Wardell, Thomas. Papers.

Library of Congress, Washington, D.C. Manuscript Division

Federal Writers' Project.

Historic American Buildings Survey.

Library of Congress, Washington, D.C. Prints and Photographs Division

Farm Security Administration.

Office of War Information.

National Archives and Records Administration, Washington, D.C., and College Park, Maryland. Still Picture and Textual Records Division
RG 69   Records of the Work Projects Administration.
RG 79   Records of the National Park Service.
RG 83   Records of the Bureau of Agricultural Economics.
RG 121 Records of the Public Building Service.
RG 210 Records of the War Relocation Authority.

Oakland Museum of California
Lange, Dorothea. Collection.

University of California, Berkeley. Bancroft Library.
Regional Oral History Office
"Dorothea Lange: The Making of a Documentary Photographer." Interview by Suzanne B. Reiss. 1968 (conducted 1960–61).
"Paul Schuster Taylor, California Social Scientist." Interview by Suzanne B. Reiss. 1973.

University of California Library, Berkeley
Wallace, Grant. "Maynard Dixon: Painter and Poet of the Far West." Edited by Gene Hailey. Typescript. Abstract from California Art Research, vol. 8, WPA Project 2874, O.P. 65-3-3632, San Francisco, 1937.

Published Sources

Adams, Ansel. *An Autobiography*. With Mary Street Alinder. Boston: Little Brown, 1985.
———. *Born Free and Equal*. New York: U.S. Camera, 1944.
Alinder, James, ed. *Ansel Adams, 1902–1984*. Carmel, CA: Friends of Photography, Untitled Series 37, 1984.
Alinder, Mary Street. *Ansel Adams: A Biography*. New York: Henry Holt, 1996.
Alinder, Mary Street, and Andrea Gray Stillman, eds. *Ansel Adams: Letters and Images, 1916–1984*. Boston: New York Graphic Society, 1988.
Altshuler, Brad. *Modern Masters: Isamu Noguchi*. New York: Abbeville, 1994.
Anderson, James C., ed. *Roy Stryker: The Humane Propagandist*. Louisville: University of Louisville Photographic Archives, 1977.
Anderson, Susan M. *Regionalism: The California View, Watercolors, 1929–1945*. Santa Barbara: Santa Barbara Museum of Art, 1988.
Anreus, Alejandro, Diana L. Linden, and Jonathan Weinberg, eds. *The Social and the Real: Political Art of the 1930s in the Western Hemisphere*. University Park: Pennsylvania State University Press, 2006.
Ansel Adams: New Light: Essays on His Legacy and Legend. San Francisco: Friends of Photography, Untitled Series 55, 1993.

Arizona: A State Guide. New York: Hastings House, 1940.

Armor, John, and Peter Wright. *Manzanar: Photographs by Ansel Adams.* New York: Times Books, 1988.

"Art Center Opens Today." *Arizona Republic,* 15 July 1937.

Ashton, Dore. *Noguchi, East and West.* New York: Alfred A. Knopf, 1992.

Bailey, Paul. *City in the Sun: The Japanese Concentration Camp at Poston, Arizona.* Los Angeles: Westernlore Press, 1971.

Ballinger, James K. *Frederic Remington's Southwest.* Phoenix: Phoenix Art Museum, 1992.

Ballinger, James K., and Andrea D. Rubinstein. *Visitors to Arizona 1846–1980.* Phoenix: Phoenix Art Museum, 1980.

Banfield, Edward C. *Government Project.* Foreword by Rexford Tugwell. Glencoe, IL: Free Press, 1951.

Barnes, Will C. *Arizona Place Names.* 1935. Reprint, Tucson: University of Arizona Press, 1988.

Becker, Heather. *Art for the People: The Rediscovery and Preservation of Progressive- and WPA-Era Murals in the Chicago Public Schools, 1904–1943.* San Francisco: Chronicle Books, 2002.

Beckham, Sue Bridwell. *A Gentle Reconstruction: Depression Post Office Murals and Southern Culture.* Baton Rouge: Louisiana State University Press, 1989.

Bell, William Gardner. "Ross Santee Cowboy Artist: Master of Suggestion and Essentials." *Persimmon Hill* 28 (Spring 2000): 46–56.

Bendavid-Val, Leah. *Propaganda and Dreams: Photographing the 1930s in the USSR and the US.* Zurich: Edition Stemmle, 1999.

Berke, Arnold. *Mary Colter: Architect of the Southwest.* New York: Princeton Architectural Press, 2002.

Berman, Greta. "Self-Knowledge into Form: The Art of Seymour Fogel." *Arts Magazine* 55 (February 1981): 100–104.

Bermingham, Peter. *The New Deal in the Southwest: Arizona and New Mexico.* Tucson: University of Arizona Museum of Art, 1980.

Billington, David P., and Donald C. Jackson. *Big Dams of the New Deal Era: A Confluence of Engineering and Politics.* Norman: University of Oklahoma Press, 2006.

Bindas, Kenneth J. *All of This Music Belongs to the Nation: The WPA's Federal Music Project and American Society.* Knoxville: University of Tennessee Press, 1995.

Bold, Christine. *The WPA Guides: Mapping America.* Jackson: University Press of Mississippi, 1999.

Booth, Peter MacMillan. "Cactizonians: The Civilian Conservation Corps in Pima County, 1933–1942." *Journal of Arizona History* 32 (Autumn 1991): 291–332.

Boyer, Mary G. *Arizona in Literature*. Glendale, CA: Arthur H. Clark Company, 1935.

Brannan, Beverly W., and David Horvath, eds. *A Kentucky Album: Farm Security Administration Photographs, 1935–1943*. Lexington: University Press of Kentucky, 1986.

Briggs, Peter S., and Brian Q. Cannon. *Life and Land: The Farm Security Administration Photographers in Utah, 1936–1941*. Logan, UT: Nora Eccles Harrison Museum of Art, distributed by Utah State University Press, 1988.

Brody, J. J. *Indian Painters and White Patrons*. Albuquerque: University of New Mexico Press, 1971.

———. *Pueblo Indian Painting: Tradition and Modernism in New Mexico, 1900–1930*. Santa Fe: School of American Research Press, 1997.

Brown, Malcolm, and Orin Cassmore. *Migratory Cotton Pickers in Arizona*. Washington, D.C.: United States Government Printing Office for the Works Progress Administration Division of Research, 1939.

Burnside, Wesley M. *Maynard Dixon: Artist of the West*. Provo: Brigham Young University Press, 1974.

Burt, Sarah. "Navajo Nation Council Chamber National Historic Landmark Nomination." Washington, D.C.: National Register of Historic Places, 2002, No. 04001155.

Bustard, Bruce. *A New Deal for the Arts*. Washington, D.C.: National Archives and Records Administration, in association with the University of Washington Press, 1997.

Cahn, Robert, and Robert Glenn Ketchum. *American Photographers and the National Parks*. New York: Viking, 1981.

Cannon, Brian Q. "Casa Grande Valley Farms: Experimenting with the Human and Economic Phase of Agriculture." In Morrissey and Jensen, *Picturing Arizona*, 60—79.

———. *Remaking the Agrarian Dream: New Deal Rural Resettlement in the Mountain West*. Albuquerque: University of New Mexico Press, 1996.

Cardwell, Lawrence. "Salome." *Arizona Highways,* April 1949, 14–17.

———. "These, Too, Are Our People." *Arizona Highways,* May 1948, 18–21.

Carlebach, Michael, and Eugene F. Provenzo Jr. *Farm Security Administration Photographs of Florida*. Gainesville: University Press of Florida, 1993.

Carlisle, John C. *A Simple and Vital Design: The Story of the Indiana Post Office Murals*. Indianapolis: Indiana Historical Society, 1995.

Carlson, Raymond. "Arizona Sketchbook: Ross Santee—Artist-Writer." *Arizona Highways,* January 1939, 14–17, 28.

———. "Report to the Publishers: The Story of Arizona Highways." *Arizona Highways,* July 1963, 2–7, 44–47.

———. "Yesterdays Remembered." *Arizona Highways,* October 1956, 1.

Carr, Carolyn Kinder. *Ohio: A Photographic Portrait, 1935–1941: Farm Security Administration Photographs*. Akron, OH: Akron Art Institute, distributed by Kent State University Press, 1980.

Chadwick, Whitney, Susan Ehrlich, Harry Rand, David S. Rubin, and Dickran Tashjian. *American Dreamer: The Art of Philip C. Curtis*. New York: Hudson Hills Press, in association with the Phoenix Art Museum, 1999.

Chanin, Abe, and Mildred Chanin. *This Land, These Voices: A Different View of Arizona History in the Words of Those Who Lived It*. Flagstaff: Northland Press, 1977.

Christensen, Erwin O. *The Index of American Design*. New York: Macmillan Company; and Washington, D.C: National Gallery of Art, 1950.

Clark, Tony. *Art and Propaganda in the Twentieth Century: The Political Image in the Age of Mass Culture*. New York: Harry N. Abrams, 1997.

Clayton, Virginia Tuttle, Elizabeth Stillinger, Erika Doss, and Deborah Chotner. *Drawing on America's Past: Folk Art, Modernism, and the Index of American Design*. Washington, D.C.: National Gallery of Art, 2002.

Cleland, Roger Glass. *A History of Phelps Dodge, 1834–1950*. New York: Alfred A. Knopf, 1952.

Cohen, Allen, and Ronald L. Filippelli. *Times of Sorrow and Hope: Documenting Everyday Life in Pennsylvania during the Depression and World War II: A Photographic Record*. University Park: Pennsylvania State University Press, 2003.

Collins, William S. *The New Deal in Arizona*. Phoenix: Arizona State Parks Board, 1999.

Conrat, Maisie, and Richard Conrat. *Executive Order 9066: The Internment of 110,000 Japanese Americans*. Los Angeles: California State Historical Society, 1972.

Contreras, Belisario R. *Tradition and Innovation in New Deal Art*. Lewisburg, PA: Bucknell University Press, 1983.

Cooper, Evelyn S. "Etched with Light: A Survey History of Photography in the Territory of Arizona." Ph.D. diss., Arizona State University, 1993.

———. *The Eyes of His Soul: The Visual Legacy of Barry M. Goldwater, Master Photographer*. Tempe: Arizona Historical Foundation, 2003.

Cooper, Thomas Charles. "*Arizona Highways:* From Engineering Pamphlet to Prestige Magazine." M.A. thesis, University of Arizona, 1973.

Cosulich, Bernice. "Old Pueblo Authors and Artists." *Arizona Highways*, January 1944, 32–36

Cripe, Dianne. "New Deal Revisited." *Public Art Review*, 14, no. 1 (Fall-Winter, 2002): 31–33.

Curtis, James. *Mind's Eye, Mind's Truth: FSA Photography Reconsidered*. Philadelphia: Temple University Press, 1989.

Curtis, Philip C. "The Phoenix Art Center." In *Art for the Millions: Essays from the 1930s by Artists and Administrators of the WPA Federal Art Project,* edited by Francis V. O'Connor, 221–23. Greenwich, CT: New York Graphic Society, 1973.

Cutler, Phoebe. *The Public Landscape of the New Deal.* New Haven: Yale University Press, 1985.

Daniel, Pete, Merry A. Foresta, Maren Stange, and Sally Stein. *Official Images: New Deal Photography.* Washington, D.C.: Smithsonian Institution Press, 1987.

Daniels, Roger. *Prisoners without Trial: Japanese Americans in World War II.* New York: Hill and Wang, 1993.

Davidov, Judith Fryer. "'The Color of My Skin, The Shape of My Eyes': Photography of the Japanese-American Internment by Dorothea Lange, Ansel Adams, and Toyo Miyatake." *Yale Journal of Criticism* 9 (Fall 1996): 223–44.

——. "The Only Gentile among the Jews: Dorothea Lange's Documentary Photography." In *Women's Camera Work: Self/Body/Other in American Visual Culture,* 215—93. Durham: Duke University Press, 2008.

Davidson, Lisa Pfueller, and Martin J. Perschler, "The Historic American Buildings Survey during the New Deal Era: Documenting 'a Complete Resume of the Builders' Art.'" *CRM: The Journal of Heritage Stewardship* 1, no. 1 (Fall 2003): 49–73.

Delano, Jack. *Photographic Memories.* Washington, D.C.: Smithsonian Institution Press, 1997.

D'Emilio, Sandra, and Suzan Campbell. *Visions and Visionaries: The Art and Artists of the Santa Fe Railway.* Salt Lake City: Peregrine Smith Books, 1991.

Dixon, Maynard. "Arizona in 1900." *Arizona Highways,* February 1942, 16–19, 40.

Doss, Erika. "Between Modernity and 'the Real Thing': Maynard Dixon's Mural for the Bureau of Indian Affairs." *American Art* 18 (Fall 2004): 8–31.

Doty, C. Stewart. *Acadian Hard Times: The Farm Security Administration in Maine's St. John Valley.* Orono: University of Maine Press, 1991.

Dunn, Dorothy. *American Indian Painting of the Southwest and Plains Areas.* Albuquerque: University of Mexico Press, 1968.

Duus, Masayo. *The Life of Isamu Noguchi: Journey without Borders.* Translated by Peter Duus. Princeton: Princeton University Press, 2004.

Dyer, Robert C. "Ansel Adams: Photographer, Environmentalist, Humorist." *Arizona Highways,* January 1991, 4–11.

Eaton, Allen H. *Beauty behind Barbed Wire: The Arts of the Japanese in Our War Relocation Camps.* Foreword by Eleanor Roosevelt. New York: Harper and Brothers, 1952.

Eli, Joyce. "Dorothea Lange and Paul Taylor: Chroniclers and Conscience of a Decade." *The Californians* 3 (March/April 1985): 10–22.

Emry Kopta: The Sculptor—The Man (1884–1953). Rancho Palos Verde, CA: Emry and Anna Kopta Foundation, 1982.

Ensenberger, Peter. "Barry Goldwater on Photography." *Arizona Highways,* May 1988, 13–17.

Etulain, Richard W., and Glenda Riley, eds. *The Hollywood West: Lives of Film Legends Who Shaped It*. Golden, CO: Fulcrum Publishing, 2001.

———. *Re-Imagining the Modern American West: A Century of Fiction, History, and Art*. Tucson: University of Arizona Press, 1996.

Fahlman, Betsy. "Constructing an Image of the Depression: Aesthetic Visions and New Deal Photography in Arizona." In Morrisey and Jensen, *Picturing Arizona,* 2–21.

———. "Cotton Culture: Dorothea Lange in Arizona." *Southeastern College Art Conference Review* 13 (1996): 32–41.

———. *The Cowboy's Dream: The Mythic Life and Art of Lon Megargee*. Wickenburg, AZ: Desert Caballeros Western Museum, 2002.

Far from Main Street: Three Photographers in Depression-Era New Mexico; Russell Lee, John Collier, Jr., and Jack Delano. Santa Fe: Museum of New Mexico Press, 1994.

Faris, James C. *Navajo and Photography: A Critical History of the Representation of an American People*. Albuquerque: University of New Mexico Press, 1996.

Farmer, Frances. "Art Controversy Falls upon Safford Valley." *Arizona Daily Star,* 14 January 1940.

"Federal Sponsored Community Art Centers." WPA Technical Series, Art Circular No. 1 (8 October 1937): 1.

Findlay, James A., and Margaret Bing. *The WPA: An Exhibition of Works Progress Administration (WPA) Literature and Art from the Collections of the Bienes Center for the Literary Arts*. Fort Lauderdale: Bienes Center for the Literary Arts, 1998.

Finnegan, Cara. *Picturing Poverty: Print Culture and FSA Photographs*. Washington, D.C.: Smithsonian Institution Press, 2003.

Fleischhauer, Carl, and Beverly W. Brannan, eds. *Documenting America, 1935–1943*. Berkeley: University of California Press, in association with the Library of Congress, 1988.

Flynn, Kathryn A. *The New Deal: A 75th Anniversary Celebration*. With Richard Polese. Salt Lake City: Gibbs Smith, 2008.

———. *Treasures on New Mexico Trails: Discover New Deal Art and Architecture*. Santa Fe: Sunstone Press, 1995.

Fogel, Jared Allen. "Seymour Fogel (1911–1984): A Portrait of the Artist." In *Seymour Fogel (1911–1984): Paintings and Drawings from the 1930s and 1940s,* n.p. Chicago: Thomas McCormick, 1997.

Fogel, Jared Allen, and Robert L. Stevens. "The Safford, Arizona, Murals of Seymour Fogel: A Study in Artistic Controversy." *Social Education* 60 (September 1996): 287–91.

Ford, Moselle Alden. "Ross Santee: Author and Artist of the Southwest." M.A. thesis, University of Texas at El Paso, 1966.

Forster, Elizabeth W., and Laura Gilpin. Martha A. Sandweiss, ed. *Denizens of the Desert: A Tale in Word and Picture of Life amongst the Navaho Indians.* Albuquerque: University of New Mexico Press, 1988.

Ganzel, Bill. *Dust Bowl Descent.* Lincoln: University of Nebraska Press, 1984.

Gawthrop, Louis C. "Images of the Common Good." *Public Administration Review* 53 (November-December 1993): 508–15.

Gesensway, Deborah, and Mindy Roseman. *Beyond Words: Images from America's Concentration Camps.* Ithaca: Cornell University Press, 1987.

Gibbs, Linda Jones, with an essay by Deborah Brown Raisiel. *Escape to Reality: The Western World of Maynard Dixon.* Provo: Brigham Young Museum of Art, 2000.

Gill, John Purifoy. *Post Masters: Arkansas Post Office Art in the New Deal.* State University: Arkansas State University, 2002.

Gilpin, Laura. *The Enduring Navaho.* Austin: University of Texas Press, 1968.

Goetzmann, William H., and William N. Goetzmann. *The West of the Imagination.* New York: W. W. Norton, 1986.

Goldberg, Robert Alan. *Barry Goldwater.* New Haven: Yale University Press, 1995.

Goldwater, Barry M. *Delightful Journey down the Green and Colorado Rivers.* Tempe: Arizona Historical Foundation, 1970.

———. *People and Places.* New York: Random House, 1967.

Gordon, Linda, and Gary Y. Okihiro, eds. *Impounded: Dorothea Lange and the Censored Images of Japanese American Internment.* New York: W. W. Norton, 2006.

Graff, Nancy Price. *Looking Back at Vermont: Farm Security Administration Photographs, 1936–1942.* Middlebury, VT: Middlebury College Museum of Art, 2002.

Gray, Mary Lakritz. *A Guide to Chicago's Murals.* Chicago: University of Chicago Press, 2001.

Gray, Michael R. *New Deal Medicine: The Rural Health Programs of the Farm Security Administration.* Baltimore: Johns Hopkins University Press, 1999.

Gregory, James N. *American Exodus: The Dust Bowl Migration and Okie Culture in California.* New York: Oxford University Press, 1989.

Grundberg, Andy. "FSA Color Photography: A Forgotten Experiment." *Portfolio* 4 (July-August 1983): 52–57.

Guimond, James. *American Photography and the American Dream.* Chapel Hill: University of North Carolina Press, 1991.

Haas, Karen E., and Rebecca A. Senf. *Ansel Adams in the Lane Collection*. Boston: Museum of Fine Arts, 2005.

Hagerty, Donald J. *Canyon de Chelly: 100 Years of Painting and Photography*. Salt Lake City: Gibbs-Smith Publisher, 1996.

———. *Desert Dreams: The Art and Life of Maynard Dixon*. Salt Lake City: Gibbs-Smith Publisher, 1998.

Hall, Daniel A. "Federal Art Patronage of Art in Arizona, 1933–43." M.A. thesis, Arizona State University, 1974.

———. "A WPA Art Center in Phoenix: 1937-40." In *Art in Action: American Art Centers and the New Deal*, edited by John Franklin White, 114–30. Metuchen, NJ: The Scarecrow Press, 1987.

Hammond, Anne. *Ansel Adams: Divine Performance*. New Haven: Yale University Press, 2002.

Handy, Ellen. "Farm Security Administration Color Photographs." *Arts Magazine* 58 (January 1984): 18.

Harris, Jonathan. *Federal Art and National Culture: The Politics of Identity in New Deal America*. New York: Cambridge University Press, 1995.

Hastings, Scott E., Jr., and Elsie R. Hastings. *Up in the Morning Early: Vermont Farm Families in the Thirties*. Hanover, NH: University Press of New England, 1992.

Hemingway, Andrew. *Artists on the Left: American Artists and the Communist Movement, 1926–1956*. New Haven: Yale University Press, 2002.

Hendrickson, Paul. *Bound for Glory: America in Color, 1939–43*. New York: Harry N. Abrams, 2004.

Heyman, Therese Thau. *Celebrating a Collection: The Work of Dorothea Lange, Documentary Photographer*. Oakland, CA: Oakland Museum, 1978.

———, ed. *Seeing Straight: The f.64 Revolution in Photography*. Oakland: Oakland Museum, 1992.

Heyman, Therese Thau, Sandra Phillips, and John Szarkowski. *Dorothea Lange: American Photographs*. San Francisco: San Francisco Museum of Modern Art and Chronicle Books, 1994.

Higa, Karen M. "Toyo Miyatake and *Our World*." In *Only Skin Deep: Changing Visions of the American Self*, by Coco Fusco and Brian Wallis, 335–43. New York: International Center of Photography and Harry N. Abrams, 2003.

———. *The View from Within: Japanese American Art from the Internment Camps, 1942–1945*. Los Angeles: Japanese American National Museum, UCLA Wight Art Gallery, and UCLA Asian American Studies Center, 1994.

Hight, Elton Thomas. "Philip Campbell Curtis (1907-): A Study of His Life and Painting." M.A. thesis, Arizona State University, 1969.

Hills, Patricia. *Social Concern and Urban Realism: American Painting of the 1930s*. Boston: Boston University Art Gallery, 1983.

Historic America: Buildings, Structures, and Sites. Washington, D.C.: Library of Congress, 1983.

Hoefer, Jacqueline. *A More Abundant Life: New Deal Artists and Public Art in New Mexico.* Santa Fe: Sunstone Press, 2003.

Hoffman, Abraham. *Unwanted Mexican Americans in the Depression: Repatriation Pressures, 1929–1939.* Tucson: University of Arizona Press, 1974.

Holt, M. G. "Arizona through the Eyes of One Who Knows It." *Arizona Highways,* March 1934, 21.

Howard, Kathleen L., and Diana F. Pardue. *Inventing the Southwest: The Fred Harvey Company and Native American Art.* Flagstaff: Northland Publishing, 1996.

Hunter, Sam. *Isamu Noguchi.* New York: Abbeville, 1978.

Hurley, F. Jack. *Portrait of a Decade: Roy Stryker and the Development of Documentary Photography in the Thirties.* Baton Rouge: Louisiana State University Press, 1972.

———. *Russell Lee, Photographer.* Dobbs Ferry, NY: Morgan and Morgan, 1978.

Hurst, Tricia. "Emry Kopta (1884–1953): Each Respected the Other." *Southwest Art* 11 (April 1982): 84–91.

Hyde, Charles K. *Copper for America: The United States Copper Industry from Colonial Times to the 1990s.* Tucson: University of Arizona Press, 1998.

Iverson, Peter. *Barry Goldwater: Native Arizonan.* Norman: University of Oklahoma Press, 1997.

———. *Diné: A History of the Navajos.* Albuquerque: University of New Mexico Press, 2002.

Jackson, Guy L. "Arizona Pageant of Progress." *Arizona Highways,* September 1944, 17–24.

James, George Wharton. *Arizona: The Wonderland.* Boston: Page, 1917.

Jensen, Kirsten. "'It Was Just a Job': Making the Prosaic Symbolic in Russell Lee's 1940 Photographs of Arizona Migrant Camp and Cooperative Farm Women." *Journal of Arizona History* 44 (Spring 2003): 25–44.

Johnson, Brooks. *Mountaineers to Main Streets: The Old Dominion as Seen through the Farm Security Administration Photographs.* Norfolk, VA: Chrysler Museum, 1985.

Johnson, G. Wesley, Jr., ed. *Phoenix in the Twentieth Century: Essays in Community History.* Norman: University of Oklahoma Press, 1993.

Jones, Stephanie. "American Indian Painting and Visual Rhetorics for Social and Aesthetic Change, 1916–1943." M.Phil., Birkbeck College, University of London, 2008.

Karaim, Reed. "Of Trading Posts, Hogans, and Navajo Tacos." *Preservation* 57 (March/April 2005): 60–65.

Keane, Melissa. "Cotton and Figs: The Great Depression in the Casa Grande Valley." *Journal of Arizona History* 32 (Autumn 1991): 267–90.

Keller, Judith. *In Focus: Dorothea Lange.* Los Angeles: J. Paul Getty Museum, 2002.

Keller, Ulrich. *The Highway as Habitat: A Roy Stryker Documentation, 1943–1955.* Santa Barbara: University Art Museum, 1986.

Kirkpatrick, Nancy C. "Ross Santee, Arizona Writer and Illustrator: A Bibliography." Tucson: University of Arizona Graduate Library School, 1972.

Kovinick, Phil, and Marian Yoshiki-Kovinick. *An Encyclopedia of Women Artists of the American West.* Austin: University of Texas Press, 1998.

Kozol, Wendy. "Madonnas of the Fields: Photography, Gender, and 1930s Farm Relief." *Genders* 2 (Summer 1988): 1–23.

Kuramitsu, Kristine C. "Internment and Identity in Japanese American Art." *American Quarterly* 47 (December 1995): 619–58.

Lamar, Jack. "Arizona's Department of Library and Archives." *Arizona Highways,* March 1940, 12–15, 37–38.

Langa, Helen. *Radical Art: Printmaking and the Left in 1930s New York.* Berkeley: University of California Press, 2004.

Lange, Dorothea, and Paul Schuster Taylor. *An American Exodus: A Record of Human Erosion.* New York: Reynal and Hitchcock, 1939.

Larson, Gary O. *The Reluctant Patron: The United States Government and the Arts, 1943–1965.* Philadelphia: University of Pennsylvania Press, 1983.

Lee, Russell. "Life on the American Frontier—1941 Version, Pie Town, N.M." *U.S. Camera* 4 (October 1941): 39–54, 88–89.

Leibowitz, Rachel. "Constructing the Navajo Capital: Landscape, Power, and Representation at Window Rock." Ph.D. diss., University of Illinois at Urbana-Champaign, 2007.

Leighninger, Robert, Jr. *Long-Range Public Investment: The Forgotten Legacy of the New Deal.* Columbia: University of South Carolina Press, 2007.

Leonard, Stephen J. *Trials and Triumphs: A Colorado Portrait of the Great Depression with FSA Photographs.* Niwot, CO: University Press of Colorado, 1993.

LeSeur, Geta. *Not All Okies Are White: The Lives of Black Cotton Pickers in Arizona.* Columbia: University of Missouri Press, 2000.

Lew Davis: A Survey of Work from 1936 to 1978. Scottsdale: Scottsdale Center for the Arts, 1979.

Loftis, Anne. "Paul Taylor Finds a Photographer." In *Witness to the Struggle: Imaging the 1930s California Labor Movement,* 115–40. Reno: University of Nevada Press, 1998.

Look, David W., and Carol L. Perrault. *The Interior Building: Its Architecture and Its Art.* Washington, D.C.: United States Department of the Interior, 1986.

Lorentz, Pare, and Paul S. Taylor. "Dorothea Lange: Camera with a Purpose." In *U.S. Camera 1941, Vol. 1, America,* edited by T. J. Maloney, 93–116, 229. New York: Duell, Sloan, and Pierce, 1941.

Loscher, Tricia. "Kate Thomson Cory: Artist and Ethnographer of Arizona." M.A. thesis, Arizona State University, 2000.

———. "Kate Thomson Cory: Artist in Hopiland." *Journal of Arizona History* 43, no. 1 (Spring 2002): 1–40.

Lowitt, Richard. *The New Deal and the West.* Bloomington: University of Indiana Press, 1984.

Lozowick, Louis. *William Gropper.* Philadelphia: Art Alliance Press, 1983.

Luckingham, Bradford. *Minorities in Phoenix: A Profile of Mexican American, Chinese American, and African American Community, 1860–1992.* Tucson: University of Arizona Press, 1994.

———. *Phoenix: The History of a Southwestern Metropolis.* Tucson: University of Arizona Press, 1989.

———. "The Promotion of Phoenix." In *Phoenix in the Twentieth Century: Essays in Community History,* edited by G. Wesley Johnson, Jr., 83–91. Norman: University of Oklahoma Press, 1993.

———. *The Urban Southwest: A Profile History of Albuquerque, El Paso, Phoenix, Tucson.* El Paso: University of Texas at El Paso, Texas Western Press, 1982.

Luey, Beth, and Noel J. Stowe, eds. *Arizona at Seventy-Five: The Next Twenty-Five Years.* Tempe: Arizona State University Public History Program and the Arizona Historical Society, 1987.

Lyford, Amy. "Noguchi, Sculptural Abstraction, and the Politics of Japanese-American Internment." *Art Bulletin* 85 (March 2003): 137–51.

Maack, Richard. "The 'Lost' Photographs of Ansel Adams." *Arizona Highways,* April 2005, 6–17.

Maeda, Robert J. "Commentary: Isamu Noguchi: A Defining Moment in My Life." *Amerasia Journal* 20 (1994): 57–58.

———. "Isamu Noguchi: 5-7-A, Poston, Arizona." *Amerasia Journal* 20 (1994): 60–76.

Mangione, Jerre. *The Dream and the Deal: The Federal Writers' Project, 1935–1943.* Boston: Little, Brown, 1972.

Marling, Karal Ann. *Wall to Wall America: A Cultural History of Post-Office Murals in the Great Depression.* Minneapolis: University of Minnesota Press, 1982.

Marx, Leo. *The Machine in the Garden.* New York: Oxford University Press, 1964.

Maxwell, Margaret F. *A Passion for Freedom: The Life of Sharlot Hall.* Tucson: University of Arizona Press, 1982.

McDannell, Colleen. *Picturing Faith: Photography and the Great Depression.* New Haven: Yale University Press, 2004.

McDonald, William Francis. *Federal Relief Administration and the Arts: The Origins and Administrative History of the Arts Projects of the Works Progress Administration.* Columbus: Ohio State University Press, 1969.

McElvaine, Robert S., ed. *Encyclopedia of the Great Depression.* 2 vols. New York: Macmillan Reference USA, The Gale Group, 2004.

———. *The Great Depression: America, 1929–1941.* New York: Times Books, 1984.

McEuen, Melissa A. *Seeing America: Women Photographers between the Wars.* Lexington: University Press of Kentucky, 2000.

McKinzie, Richard D. *The New Deal for Artists.* Princeton: Princeton University Press, 1973.

McLerran, Jennifer. "Inventing 'Indian Art': New Indian Policy and the Native Artist as 'Natural' Resource." Ph.D. diss. University of Washington, 1999.

McWilliams, Carey. *Ill Fares the Land: Migrants and Migratory Labor in the United States.* 1942. Reprint, New York: Arno, 1976.

Mecklenberg, Virginia. *The Public as Patron: A History of the Treasury Department Mural Program, Illustrated with Paintings from the Collection of the University of Maryland Art Gallery.* College Park: University of Maryland, 1979.

Meeks, Eric V. *Border Citizens: The Making of Indians, Mexicans, and Anglos in Arizona.* Austin: University of Texas Press, 2007.

Melosh, Barbara. *Engendering Culture: Manhood and Womanhood in New Deal Public Art and Theater.* Washington, D.C.: Smithsonian Institution Press, 1991.

Melton, Brad, and Dean Smith, eds. *Arizona Goes to War: The Home Front and the Front Lines during World War II.* Tucson: University of Arizona Press, 2003.

Meltzer, Milton. *Dorothea Lange: A Photographer's Life.* New York: Farrar, Straus and Giroux, 1978.

Milner, Clyde A., II, Carol A. O'Connor, and Martha A. Sandweiss. *The Oxford History of the American West.* New York: Oxford University Press, 1994.

Moore, Robert J. *The Civilian Conservation Corps in Arizona's Rim Country: Working in the Woods.* Reno: University of Nevada Press, 2006.

Moore, Sarah J. "No Woman's Land: Arizona Adventurers." In *Independent Spirits: Women Painters of the American West, 1890–1945,* edited by Patricia Trenton, 130–51. Los Angeles: Autry Museum of Western Heritage, in association with Berkeley: University of California Press, 1995.

Morrissey, Katherine G. "Migrant Labor Children in Depression-Era Arizona." In Morrissey and Jensen, *Picturing Arizona,* 22–41.

Morrissey, Katherine G., and Kirsten Jensen, eds. *Picturing Arizona: The Photographic Record of the 1930s.* Tucson: University of Arizona Press, 2005.

Murals by American Painters and Photographers. New York: Museum of Modern Art, 1932.

Murphy, Mary. *Hope in Hard Times: New Deal Photographs of Montana, 1936–1942.* Helena: Montana Historical Society Press, 2003.

Murphy, Nina L. *The History of Women's Physical Education at Arizona State University, 1885–1969.* Tempe: Arizona State University, Bureau of Publications, 1969.

Murray, John A. *Cinema Southwest: An Illustrated Guide to the Movies and Their Locations.* Flagstaff: Northland Publishing, 2000.

———. *Mythmakers of the West: Shaping America's Imagination.* Flagstaff: Northland Publishing, 2001.

Myers, Joan. *Pie Town Woman.* Albuquerque: University of New Mexico Press, 2001.

Nakayama, Thomas, ed. *Transforming Barbed Wire: The Incarceration of Japanese Americans in Arizona during World War II.* Phoenix: Arizona Humanities Council, 1997.

Nash, Gerald D. *The American West Transformed: The Impact of the Second World War.* Bloomington: Indiana University Press, 1985.

———. *The Federal Landscape: An Economic History of the Twentieth Century.* Tucson: University of Arizona Press, 1999.

Natanson, Nicholas. *The Black Image in the New Deal: The Politics of FSA Photography.* Knoxville: University of Tennessee Press, 1992.

Nature in Architecture: The Work of Sim Bruce Richards. San Diego: San Diego Natural History Museum, 1984.

Nelson, Christine. "Indian Art in Washington: Native American Murals in the Department of the Interior Building." *American Indian Art Magazine* 20 (Spring 1995): 70–83.

New Deal Art: California. Santa Clara: de Saisset Art Gallery and Museum, University of Santa Clara, 1976.

Newhall, Beaumont. *Focus: Memoirs of a Life in Photography.* Boston: Little, Brown, 1993.

Newhall, Nancy. *Ansel Adams: The Eloquent Light.* Millerton, NY: Aperture, 1980.

"New Resettlement Plans: Resettlement Administration Selects Arizona for Historic Trials in Rural Housing and Cooperation." *Arizona Producer,* 1 March 1937, 1, 31.

Nishimoto, Richard S. *Inside an American Concentration Camp: Japanese American Resistance at Poston, Arizona.* Tucson: University of Arizona Press, 1995.

Noble, May. "Arizona Artists." *Arizona Teacher and Home Journal,* 11 February 1923: 7–10.

Noguchi, Isamu. *A Sculptor's World.* New York: Harper and Row, 1968.

———. "Trouble among Japanese Americans." *New Republic,* 1 February 1943, 142–43.

Norwood, Vera, and Janice Monk, eds. *The Desert Is No Lady: Southwestern Landscapes in Women's Writing and Art.* New Haven: Yale University Press, 1987.

Nucci, Sarah Louise. "Kate Thomson Cory: An Independent Victorian Woman in Arizona." M.A. thesis, Arizona State University, 2001.

Nunn, Tey Marianna. *Sin Nombre: Hispana and Hispano Artists of the New Deal Era.* Albuquerque: University of New Mexico Press, 2001.

Nyerges, Alexander Lee. *In Praise of Nature: Ansel Adams and Photographers of the American West.* Dayton, OH: Dayton Art Institute, 1999.

O'Connor, Sandra Day, and H. Alan Day. *Lazy B: Growing Up on a Cattle Ranch in the American Southwest.* New York: Random House, 2002.

Ohrn, Karin Becker. *Dorothea Lange and the Documentary Tradition.* Baton Rouge: Louisiana State University Press, 1980.

———. "What You See Is What You Get: Dorothea Lange and Ansel Adams at Manzanar." *Journalism History* 4 (Spring 1977): 14–22, 32.

O'Kane, Walter Collins. "Emry Kopta: Sculptor of Indians," and "The Story of a Fountain." *Arizona Highways,* August 1937, 4–5, 34–39.

Okrent, Daniel. *The Way We Were: New England Then, New England Now,* New York: Grove Weidenfeld, 1989.

Olson, James S. *Historical Dictionary of the Great Depression, 1929–1940.* Westport, CT: Greenwood Press, 2001.

———, ed. *Historical Dictionary of the New Deal: From Inauguration to Preparation for War.* Westport, CT: Greenwood Press, 1985.

O'Neal, Hank. *A Vision Shared: A Classic Portrait of America and Its People, 1935–1943.* New York: St. Martin's Press: 1976.

Otero, Linda R. "Refusing to Be 'Undocumented': Chicana/os in Tucson during the Depression Years." In Morrissey and Jensen, *Picturing Arizona,* 42–59.

Pace, Michael. "Emery Kolb and the Fred Harvey Company." *Journal of Arizona History* 24 (Winter 1983): 339–62.

Parisi, Philip. *The Texas Post Office Murals: Art for the People.* College Station: Texas A and M Press, 2004.

Park, Marlene, and Gerald Markowitz. *Democratic Vistas: Post Offices and Public Art in the New Deal.* Philadelphia: Temple University Press, 1984.

———. *New Deal for Art: The Government Art Projects of the 1930s with Examples from New York City and State.* Hamilton, NY: Gallery Association of New York State, 1977.

Parman, Donald L. *Indians and the American West in the Twentieth Century.* Bloomington: Indiana University Press, 1994.

———. *The Navajos and the New Deal.* New Haven: Yale University Press, 1976.

Partridge, Elizabeth, ed. *Dorothea Lange: A Visual Life*. Washington, D.C.: Smithsonian Institution Press, 1994.

Patterson, Ann, and Mark Vinson. *Landmark Buildings: Arizona's Architectural Heritage*. Phoenix: Arizona Highways (Arizona Department of Transportation), 2004.

"Paul Schuster Taylor." In *Photography within the Humanities,* by Eugenia Parry Janis and Wendy MacNeil, 26–41. Danbury, NH: Addison House Publishers, 1977.

Peatross, C. Ford., ed. *Historic America: Buildings, Structures and Sites Recorded by the Historic American Buildings Survey and the Historic American Engineering Record*. Washington, D.C.: Library of Congress, 1983.

Peeler, David P. *Hope among Us Yet: Social Criticism and Social Solace in Depression America*. Athens: University of Georgia Press, 1987.

———. *The Illuminating Mind in American Photography: Stieglitz, Strand, Weston, Adams*. Rochester, NY: University of Rochester Press, 2001.

Pells, Richard H. *Radical Visions and American Dreams: Culture and Social Thought in the Depression Years*. New York: Harper and Row, 1973.

Penkower, Monty Noam. *The Federal Writers' Project: A Study in Government Patronage of the Arts*. Urbana: University of Illinois Press, 1977.

Peterson, Charles E. "The Historic American Buildings Survey: Its Beginnings." In Peatross, *Historic America: Buildings,* 7—21.

Phillips, Sandra S. "Ansel Adams and Dorothea Lange: A Friendship of Differences." In *Ansel Adams: New Light, Essays on His Legacy and Legend,* 51–61. Untitled Series 55. San Francisco: Friends of Photography, 1993.

Plattner, Steven W. *Roy Stryker, U. S. A., 1943–1950: The Standard Oil (New Jersey) Photography Project*. Austin: University of Texas Press, 1983.

Powell, Lawrence Clark. *Arizona: A Bicentennial History*. New York: W. W. Norton; and Nashville: American Association for State and Local History, 1976.

———. "How He Pictured the West [Ross Santee]." *Westways* 65 (March 1973): 46–50, 84–84.

———. *Southwest Classics: The Creative Literature of the Arid Lands, Essays on the Books and Their Writers*. Los Angeles: Ward Ritchie Press, 1974.

Prucha, Frances Paul. *The Great Father: The United States Government and the American Indians*. Lincoln: University of Nebraska Press, 1986.

Puckett, John Rogers. *Five Photo-Textual Documentaries from the Great Depression*. Ann Arbor, Michigan: UMI Research Press, 1984.

Pyne, Stephen J. *How the Grand Canyon Became Grand: A Short History*. New York: Penguin, 1998.

Raeburn, John. *A Staggering Revolution: A Cultural History of Thirties Photography*. Urbana: University of Illinois Press, 2006.

Recording a Vanishing Legacy: The Historic American Buildings Survey in New Mexico, 1933–Today. Santa Fe: Museum of New Mexico Press, 2001.

Reed, Dennis. *Japanese Photography in America.* Los Angeles: George J. Doizaki Gallery, Japanese American Cultural and Community Center, 1985.

Reid, Robert L. *Back Home Again: Indiana in the Farm Security Administration Photographs, 1935–1943.* Bloomington: Indiana University Press, 1987.

———. *Picturing Minnesota, 1936–1943: Photographs from the Farm Security Administration.* St. Paul: Minnesota Historical Society Press, 1989.

———. *Picturing Texas: The FSA/OWI Photographers in the Lone Star State.* Austin: Texas State Historical Association, 1994.

Reid, Robert L., and Larry A. Viskochil. *Chicago and Downstate: Illinois as Seen by the Farm Security Administration Photographers, 1936–1943.* Urbana and Chicago: Chicago Historical Society and University of Illinois Press, 1989.

Reinsdorfer, Kathryn, "Arizona History through Art." *American Art Review* 12 (March-April 2000): 194–205.

Reisner, Marc. *Cadillac Desert: The West and Its Disappearing Water.* New York: Penguin Books, 1993.

Robbins, Carolyn C. "A Century of Women Artists," *American Art Review,* 13, no. 1 (January-February 2001): 182–91.

———. "The Hardrock Miner in Arizona: William D. White and Lew Davis." M.A. thesis, Arizona State University, 1986.

———. *Lew Davis: "The Negro in America's Wars" and Other Major Paintings.* Scottsdale: Scottsdale Center for the Arts, 1990.

Robinson, Gerald H. *Elusive Truth: Four Photographers at Manzanar.* Introduction by Archie Miyatake. Nevada City, CA: Caul Mautz Publishing, 2002.

Robinson, Jontyle Theresa, and Wendy Greenhouse. *The Art of Archibald J. Motley, Jr.* Chicago: Chicago Historical Society, 1991.

Rothman, Hal K., ed. *The Culture of Tourism, the Tourism of Culture: Selling the Past to the Present in the American Southwest.* Albuquerque: University of New Mexico Press, 2003.

Rothstein, Arthur. *Arthur Rothstein: Words and Pictures.* New York: Amphoto, 1979.

———. *Documentary Photography.* Boston: Focal Press, 1986.

Rowe, Jeremy. *Photographers in Arizona, 1850–1920: A History and Directory.* Nevada City, CA: Carl Mautz Publishing, 1997.

Russell, Herbert K. *A Southern Illinois Album: Farm Security Administration Photographs, 1936–1943.* Carbondale: Southern Illinois University Press, 1990.

Sandweiss, Martha A. *Laura Gilpin: An Enduring Grace*. Fort Worth, TX: Amon Carter Museum, 1986.

Santee, Ross. "Advice Is All Right If You Don't Take Too Much of It." *American Magazine,* June 1928, 36–9, 156–59.

———. "The West I Remember." *Arizona Highways,* October 1956, 10–23.

Schindler-Carter, Petra. *Vintage Snapshots: The Fabrication of a Nation in the W. P. A. American Guide Series*. New York: Peter Lang Publishing, 1999.

Schulz, Constance B. *Bust to Boom: Documentary Photographs of Kansas, 1936–1949*. Lawrence: University Press of Kansas, 1996.

———, ed. *Michigan Remembered: Photographs from the Farm Security Administration and the Office of War Information, 1936–1943*. Detroit: Wayne State University Press, 2001.

———, ed. *A South Carolina Album, 1936–1948: Documentary Photography in the Palmetto State from the Farm Security Administration, Office of War Information, and Standard Oil of New Jersey*. Columbia: University of South Carolina Press, 1992.

Schwantes, Carlos A. *Vision and Enterprise: Exploring the History of the Phelps Dodge Corporation*. Tucson: University of Arizona Press; and Phoenix: Phelps Dodge Corporation, 2000.

Searcy, Paula Marie. "Ansel Adams and *Arizona Highways:* A Mutually Beneficial Relationship." *Arizona Highways,* June 2000, 8–9.

Several, Michael. "Photographic Memories: Miyatake at Manzanar." *Public Art Review* 7 (Spring/Summer 1996): 22–24.

Shadegg, Stephen. "Arizona on Treasure Island." *Arizona Highways,* June 1939, 4–7.

Sheridan, Thomas E. *Arizona: A History*. Tucson: University of Arizona Press, 1995.

———. *Los Tucsonenses: The Mexican Community in Tucson, 1854–1941*. Tucson: University of Arizona Press, 1986.

Sherwood, Robert Emmet. *The Petrified Forest*. New York: Scribner, 1935.

Shindo, Charles J. *Dust Bowl Migrants in the American Imagination*. Lawrence: University of Kansas Press, 1997.

Short, C. W., and R. Stanley-Brown. *Public Buildings: Architecture under the Public Works Administration, 1933–1939*. Introduction by Richard Guy Wilson. 2 vols. 1939. Reprint, New York: DaCapo Press, 1986.

Simpson, Pamela H. "Pioneer Mother Monuments, 1914–1930: Images of Western Expansion." *Southeastern College Art Conference Review* 13 (2003): 435–43.

Smith, J. Russell, and M. Ogden Phillips, *North America*. Westport, CT: Greenwood Press, 1968.

Smith, Page. *Democracy on Trial: The Japanese American Evacuation and Relocation in World War II*. New York: Simon and Schuster, 1995.

Snively, Tamara Jane. "The Sculpture of Raymond Phillips Sanderson." M.A. thesis, Arizona State University, 1973.

Sonnichsen, Charles Leland. *Tucson: The Life and Times of an American City.* Norman: University of Oklahoma Press, 1982.

Spaulding, Jonathan. *Ansel Adams and the American Landscape: A Biography.* Berkeley: University of California Press, 1995.

Spicer, Edward, Asael T. Hansen, Katherine Louomala, and Marvin K. Oppler. *Impounded People: Japanese Americans in the Relocation Centers.* 1946. Reprint, Tucson: University of Arizona Press, 1969.

Stange, Maren. *Symbols of Ideal Life: Social Documentary Photography in America, 1890–1950.* New York: Cambridge University Press, 1989.

Starr, Kevin. *Endangered Dreams: The Great Depression in California.* New York: Oxford University Press, 1996.

Stein, Sally. "FSA Color: The Forgotten Experiment." *Modern Photography,* January 1979, 90–98, 162–64, 166.

———. "Passing Likeness: Dorothea Lange's *Migrant Mother* and the Paradox of Iconicity." In *Only Skin Deep: Changing Visions of the American Self,* by Coco Fusco and Brian Wallis, 345–55. New York: International Center of Photography and Harry N. Abrams, 2003.

Steinbeck, John. *The Grapes of Wrath.* New York: Viking Press, 1939.

Stevens, Joseph E. *Hoover Dam: An American Adventure.* Norman: University of Oklahoma Press, 1988.

Stewart, Rick. *Lone Star Regionalism: The Dallas Nine and Their Circle.* Dallas: Dallas Museum of Art, 1985.

Stewart, Todd. *Placing Memory: A Photographic Exploration of Japanese American Internment.* Norman: University of Oklahoma Press, 2008.

Stillman, Andrea G., ed. *The Grand Canyon and the Southwest: Ansel Adams.* Introduction by William A. Turnage. Boston: Little, Brown, 2000.

Stillman, Andrea G., and William A. Turnage, eds. *Ansel Adams: Our National Parks.* Boston: Little, Brown, 1992.

Stoeckle, John D., and George Abbott White. *Plain Pictures of Plain Doctoring: Vernacular Expression in New Deal Medicine and Photography.* Cambridge, MA: MIT Press, 1985.

Stories from Life: The Photography of Horace Bristol. Athens: Georgia Museum of Art, University of Georgia, 1995.

Stott, Annette. "Prairie Madonnas and Pioneer Women: Images of Emigrant Women in the Art of the Old West." *Prospects* 21 (1996): 299–325.

Stott, William. *Documentary Expression and Thirties America.* New York: Oxford University Press, 1973.

Stragnell, Robert, and Jim Willoughby. "Pioneer Women: Arizona History through Art." *American Art Review* 10 (March-April 1998): 154–57.

Street, Richard Steven. "Paul S. Taylor and the Origins of Documentary

Photography in California, 1927–1934." *History of Photography* 7 (October-December 1983): 293–304.

———. *Photographing Farmworkers in California*. Stanford: Stanford University Press, 2004.

Stryker, Roy E., and Nancy Wood. *In This Proud Land: America 1935–1943 as Seen in the FSA Photographs*. Greenwich, CT: New York Graphic Society, 1973.

Suran, William C. *The Kolb Brothers of Grand Canyon*. Grand Canyon: Grand Canyon Natural History Association, 1991.

Swenson, James R. "Dorothea Lange's Portrait of Utah's Great Depression." *Utah Historical Quarterly* 70 (Winter 2002): 39–62.

Szarkowski, John. *Ansel Adams at 100*. Foreword by Sandra S. Phillips. Boston: Little Brown, in association with the San Francisco Museum of Modern Art, 2001.

Szarkowski, John, J. B. Colson, and Linda Peterson. *Russell Lee Photographs: Images from the Russell Lee Photograph Collection at the Center for American History*. Austin: University of Texas Press, 2007.

Taylor, Paul Schuster. "Again the Covered Wagon." *Survey Graphic* 24 (July 1935): 348–51.

———. "Mexicans North of the Rio Grande." *Survey Graphic* 19 (May 1931): 135–40, 197, 200–202.

———. "Migratory Labor in the United States," *Monthly Labor Review* (March 1937), published by the Bureau of Labor Statistics, United States Department of Labor, Serial No. R.530.

———. *On the Ground in the Thirties*. Preface by Clark Kerr. Salt Lake City: Peregrine Smith Books, 1983.

Taylor, Paul Schuster, and Dorothea Lange. *An American Exodus: A Record of Human Erosion*. Rev. ed. New Haven: Yale University Press, 1969.

Threads of Culture: Photography in New Mexico, 1939–1943: Russell Lee, John Collier, Jr., Jack Delano: The Pinewood Collection of FSA Photographs. Santa Fe: Museum of Fine Arts, Museum of New Mexico, 1993.

The Thunderbird Remembered: Maynard Dixon, the Man and the Artist. Los Angeles: Gene Autry Western Heritage Museum, in association with the University of Washington Press, 1994.

Topping, Gary. "Arizona Highways: A Half-Century of Southwestern Journalism." *Journal of the West* 19 (April 1980): 71–80.

Trimble, Marshall. *Arizona: A Cavalcade of History*. Tucson: Treasure Chest Publications, 1989.

———. *Arizona 2000: A Yearbook for the Millennium*. Flagstaff: Northland, 1998.

Truettner, William H., ed. *The West as America: Reinterpreting Images of the Frontier, 1820–1920*. Washington, D.C.: National Museum of American Art, 1991.

Tsujimoto, Karen. *Dorothea Lange: Archive of an Artist*. Oakland: Oakland Museum of California, 1995.

Two Views of Manzanar: An Exhibition of Photographs by Ansel Adams/Toyo Miyatake. Los Angeles: Frederick S. Wight Art Gallery, University of California, 1978.

Valle, James E. *The Iron Horse at War*. Berkeley: Howell-North Books, 1977.

Van Dommelin, David B. *Allen H. Eaton: Dean of American Crafts*. Pittsburgh: Local History Company, 2004.

Vigneault, Marissa B. "The Hidden Life of William Gropper's *Construction of a Dam*." Master's Research Paper, American University, 2001.

Vilander, Barbara. *Hoover Dam: The Photographs of Ben Glaha*. Tucson: University of Arizona Press, 1999.

Wagoner, Jay J. *Arizona's Heritage*. Salt Lake City: Peregrine Smith, 1977.

Walczak, Dawne Louise. "Philip C. Curtis, American Postwar Realism: The Random Ritual Procession." M.A. thesis, Arizona State University, 1985.

Ware, Susan. *Holding Their Own: American Women in the 1930s*. Boston: Twayne, 1982.

Watkins, T. H. *The Hungry Years: A Narrative History of the Great Depression in America*. New York: Henry Holt and Company, An Owl Book, 1999.

————. *Righteous Pilgrim: The Life and Times of Harold L. Ickes, 1874–1952*. New York: Henry Holt, 1990.

Weadock, Jack F. "A Dedication to the Memory of Ross Santee, 1889–1965." *Arizona and the West* 7 (Autumn 1965): 183–86.

Weglyn, Michi. *Years of Infamy: The Untold Story of America's Concentration Camps*. New York: William Morrow, 1976.

Weigle, Marta. "Finding the 'True America': Ethnic Tourism in New Mexico during the New Deal." *Folklife Annual* (1988–89): 58–73.

————. *Women of New Mexico: Depression Era Images*. Santa Fe, NM: Ancient City Press, 1993.

————, ed. *New Mexicans in Cameo and Camera: New Deal Documentation of Twentieth Century Lives*. Albuquerque: University of New Mexico Press, 1985.

Weigle, Marta, and Barbara A. Babcock, eds. *The Great Southwest of the Fred Harvey Company and the Santa Fe Railway*. Phoenix: Heard Museum, 1996.

Weisiger, Marsha L. *Land of Plenty: Oklahomans in the Cotton Fields of Arizona, 1933–1942*. Norman: University of Oklahoma Press, 1995.

————. "Mythic Fields of Plenty: The Plight of Depression-Era Oklahoma Migrants in Arizona." *Journal of Arizona History* 32 (Autumn 1991): 241–66.

The West and Walter Bimson: Paintings, Watercolors, Drawings and Sculpture Collected by Mr. Walter Reed Bimson. Tucson: University of Arizona Museum of Art, 1971.

Westerlund, John S. *Arizona's War Town: Flagstaff, Navajo Ordnance Depot, and World War II.* Tucson: University of Arizona Press, 2003.

Westerns of the Red Rock Country: 43 Movies Filmed in Sedona. Sedona: Bradshaw Color Studies, 1991.

Westphal, Ruth Lilly, and Janet Blake Dominick, eds. *American Scene Painting, California, 1930s and 1940s.* Irvine, CA: Westphal Publishing, 1991.

Wilson, Charis, and Edward Weston, *California and the West.* 1940. Reprint, Millerton, NY: Aperture, 1978.

Wilson, Chris. *The Myth of Santa Fe: Creating Modern Regional Tradition.* Albuquerque: University of New Mexico Press, 1997.

Wilson, Michael G., and Dennis Reed. *Pictorialism in California: Photographs 1900–1940.* Malibu: J. Paul Getty Museum; and San Marino: Henry E. Huntington Library, 1994.

Wilson, Richard Guy, "American Modernism in the West: Hoover Dam." In *Images of an American Land: Vernacular Architecture in the Western United States,* edited by Thomas Carter, 291–314. Albuquerque: University of New Mexico Press, 1997.

Winkler, Allan M. *The Politics of Propaganda: The Office of War Information, 1942–1945.* New Haven: Yale University Press, 1978.

Winterry, Vivienne Tallal. *Fritz Henle's Rollei.* New York: Hastings House, 1950.

Wollenberg, Charles. "Introduction." In *John Steinbeck, The Harvest Gypsies.* Berkeley: Heyday Books, 1988.

———. *Photographing the Second Gold Rush: Dorothea Lange and the Bay Area at War.* Berkeley: Heyday Books, 1995.

Wood, Nancy C. *Heartland New Mexico: Photographs from the Farm Security Administration, 1935–1943.* Albuquerque: University of New Mexico Press, 1989.

The WPA Guide to 1930s Arizona: Compiled by the Workers of the Writers' Program of the Work Projects Administration in the State of Arizona. Foreword by Stewart L. Udall. Tucson: University of Arizona Press. 1989.

Wright, Nancy Kirkpatrick. "Kate Thomson Cory: Camera and Paintbrush." *Cactus and Pine* 9 (August 1997): 1–18.

Wright, Peter, and John Armor. *The Mural Project: Photography by Ansel Adams.* Santa Barbara, CA: Reverie Press, 1989.

Wroth, William, ed. *Russell Lee's FSA Photographs of Chamisal and Peñasco, New Mexico.* Santa Fe: Ancient City Press; and Colorado Springs: Taylor Museum of the Colorado Springs Fine Arts Center, 1985.

Young, Nancy Beck, William D. Pederson, and Bryon W. Daynes, eds. *Franklin D. Roosevelt and the Shaping of American Political Culture.* Armonk, NY: M. E. Sharpe, 2001.

Zielinski, John M. *Unknown Iowa: Farm Security Photos, 1936–1941: A Classic Portrait of Iowa and Its People.* Kalona, Iowa: Photo-Art Gallery Publications, 1977.

FIGURE CREDITS

1.1 Chart of major New Deal Agencies. Drawn by Susan Selkirk.

2.1 Arthur Rothstein, Arizona-New Mexico State Line. Library of Congress Prints and Photographs Division, Farm Security Administration—Office of War Information Collection; LC-USF34-024230-D.

2.2 Dorothea Lange, Sign near Saint David. Library of Congress Prints and Photographs Division, Farm Security Administration—Office of War Information Collection; LC-USF34-017264-E.

2.3 Russell Lee, Lineman on telephone pole. Library of Congress Prints and Photographs Division, Farm Security Administration—Office of War Information Collection; LC-USF33-012683-M5.

2.4 Russell Lee, Tourist court, Phoenix. Library of Congress Prints and Photographs Division, Farm Security Administration—Office of War Information Collection; LC-USF33-012670-M4.

2.5 Hoover Dam, *Arizona Highways,* June 1939. Photograph published with permission of *Arizona Highways.*

2.6 Lon Megargee and Charles Percy Austin, Mural at the Century of Progress International Exposition. Fred Wilson Collection, Heard Museum Archives, Phoenix, Arizona.

2.7 Russell Lee, Roadside tourist attraction, Maricopa County. Library of Congress Prints and Photographs Division, Farm Security Administration—Office of War Information Collection; LC-USF33-012670-M3.

2.8 Russell Lee, Zoo and Museum, Apache Junction. Library of Congress Prints and Photographs Division, Farm Security Administration—Office of War Information Collection; LC-USF33-012674-M5.

2.9 Russell Lee, Cactus light standard, Phoenix. Library of Congress Prints and Photographs Division, Farm Security Administration—Office of War Information Collection; LC-USF34-036182-D.

3.1 Exterior, Phoenix Federal Art Center, 710 East Adams Street. National Archives and Records Administration; 69-AS-01-07.

3.2 Interior, Phoenix Federal Art Center. Philip C. Curtis Collection, Arizona Collection, Department of Archives and Special Collections, Arizona State University Libraries.

3.3 Baumgartner, Wilson, Tenney, Davis, Sanderson, and Richards. Philip C. Curtis Collection, Arizona Collection, Department of Archives and Special Collections, Arizona State University Libraries.

3.4 Lew Davis, *Underground,* oil painting for the Federal Art Project, unlocated. Philip C. Curtis Collection, Arizona Collection, Department of Archives and Special Collections, Arizona State University Libraries.

3.5 Cover, *Arizona: A State Guide.* New York: Hastings House, 1940. Courtesy of the Bienes Center for the Literary Arts, Broward County Libraries Division, Fort Lauderdale, Florida.

3.6 Ross Santee, 1940, from *The WPA Guide to 1930s Arizona,* by the Workers of the Writers' Program of the Work Projects Administration in the State of Arizona, copyright 1989, The Arizona Board of Regents. Photograph courtesy of Daniel H. Ball.

3.7 Elizabeth Johnson, 1942, Brand from Lazy B Ranch. Image courtesy of the Board of Trustees, National Gallery of Art, Washington, D.C.

3.8 Russell Lee, Shells of old buildings, Tombstone. Shot for the Farm Security Administration. Courtesy of the Roy Stryker Collection, Special Collections, University of Louisville, 78.9.895; Library of Congress number: LC-USF34-036375-D.

4.1 Joseph Morgan Henninger, *Spanish Influence in Arizona,* 1934, oil on canvas. Arizona State University, reproduced with permission of the Arizona Board of Regents; photograph from the Arizona State Library, Archives and Public Records, History and Archives Division, Phoenix; 98-3609 or 98-9832.

4.2 Joseph Morgan Henninger, *Industrial Development in Arizona,* 1934, oil on canvas. Arizona State University; reproduced with permission of the Arizona Board of Regents; Tim Trumble photograph, copyprint by Daniel H. Ball.

4.3 Emry Kopta, *Kachina Fountain,* 1934. Courtesy of Museum of Northern Arizona Photo Archives; MS-240-2-976.

4.4 Lon Megargee, *Agriculture,* 1934, oil on canvas. Arizona Capitol Museum, Arizona State Library, Archives and Public Records; History and Archives Division, Phoenix; photograph courtesy of Daniel H. Ball.

4.5 Raymond Phillips Sanderson, *Miners' Monument,* 1935, Bisbee. FSA Photograph by Russell Lee, 1940. Library of Congress Prints and Photographs Division, Farm Security Administration-Office of War Information Collection; LC-USF33-012697-M5.

4.6 Raymond Phillips Sanderson, *Miner,* 1939. Arizona State University, Libraries, Department of Archives and Special Collections, Philip Curtis Collection.

4.7 Sim Bruce Richards, *Desert Mining Community,* 1937, pencil and ink on paper. Courtesy of Janet Richards.

4.8 Lon Megargee, Phoenix Post Office competition entry, 1937. National Archives and Records Administration; 121-MS-12-C-PAMC-3.

4.9   Lew Davis, Phoenix Post Office competition entry, 1937. National Archives and Records Administration; 121-MS-PAMC-02C.

4.10 Lew Davis, Phoenix Post Office competition entry, 1937. National Archives and Records Administration; 121-MS-PAMC-02D.

4.11 Lew Davis, Phoenix Post Office competition entry, 1937. National Archives and Records Administration; 121-MS-PAMC-02B.

4.12 Lew Davis, Phoenix Post Office competition entry, 1937. National Archives and Records Administration; 121-MS-PAMC-02A.

4.13 Oscar Berninghaus, *Communication during the Period of Exploration,* 1937–38, Phoenix, oil on canvas. National Archives and Records Administration; 121-PS-1916.

4.14 Oscar Berninghaus, *Pioneer Communication,* 1937–38, Phoenix, oil on canvas. National Archives and Records Administration; 121-PS-1915.

4.15 Laverne Nelson Black, *Historical Background,* 1937–38, Phoenix, oil on canvas. National Archives and Records Administration; 121-PS-2006.

4.16 Laverne Nelson Black, *The Progress of the Pioneer,* 1937–38, Phoenix, oil on canvas. National Archives and Records Administration; 121-PS-2005.

4.17 Seymour Fogel, 48 States Competition entry for Safford Post Office, 1939. National Archives and Records Administration; 121-PS-7784.

4.18 Seymour Fogel, *The History of the Gila Valley: Migration,* 1939–42, Safford, tempera on gesso and plaster, Post Office, Safford. National Archives and Records Administration; 121-GA-18-FOGEL (1)-PS 7784.

4.19 Sim Bruce Richards, Modern dance murals, 1939, Women's Activity Building, Arizona State University. Courtesy of Janet Richards. Demolished.

4.20 John Porter Leeper, *Women in Sports and the Arts,* 1939, oil on canvas, Women's Activity Building, Arizona State University. Arizona State University, Libraries, Department of Archives and Special Collections, Philip Curtis Collection. Unlocated.

4.21 Robert Kittredge, *Apache Chiefs Geronimo and Vittorio,* 1939, Springerville. National Archives and Records Administration; 121-CMS-05D-22.

4.22 Robert Kittredge, *Arizona Logging,* 1940, Post Office, Flagstaff, plaster relief. National Archives and Records Administration; 1212-CMS-05D-21.

4.23 Jay Datus, *Arizona Pageant of Progress,* 1937–38. Arizona State Library, Archives and Public Records, History and Archives Division, Phoenix; 99-9994.

4.24 Gerald Nailor at work on *The History and Progress of the Navajo Nation,* Navajo Nation Council Chamber, Window Rock, 1943. Photograph by Milton Snow. Records of the Bureau of Indian Affairs, National Archives and Records Administration; 75-NG-4-NC-2-9.

5.1   Russell Lee, Municipal golf course, Phoenix, May 1940. Library of Congress Prints and Photographs Division—Farm Security

Administration—Office of War Information Collection; LC-USF34-036157-D.

5.2   Russell Lee, Salesman demonstrating an electric refrigerator to members of the United Producers' and Consumers' Cooperative of Phoenix. Library of Congress Prints and Photographs Division—Farm Security Administration—Office of War Information Collection; LC-USF34-036192-D.

5.3   Russell Lee, Agua Fria Farm Security Administration Camp, chart. May 1940. Library of Congress Prints and Photographs Division, Farm Security Administration—Office of War Information Collection; LC-USF34-036148-D.

5.4   Russell Lee, Agua Fria Farm Security Administration Camp, view from water tower, May 1940. Library of Congress Prints and Photographs Division, Farm Security Administration—Office of War Information Collection; LC-USF33-012655-M2.

5.5   Russell Lee, Migratory laborer and wife, Agua Fria FSA Camp, May 1940. Library of Congress Prints and Photographs Division, Farm Security Administration—Office of War Information Collection; LC-USF33-012666-M5.

5.6   Russell Lee, Migrant agricultural worker, Agua Fria FSA Camp, May 1940. Library of Congress Prints and Photographs Division, Farm Security Administration—Office of War Information Collection; LC-USF34-035978-D.

5.7. Russell Lee, Operation at Cairns General Hospital, Eleven Mile Corner, February 1942. Library of Congress Prints and Photographs Division, Farm Security Administration—Office of War Information Collection; LC-USF33-013245-M1.

5.8   Russell Lee, Jitterbug contest, FSA Camp, Yuma, March 1942. Library of Congress Prints and Photographs Division, Farm Security Administration—Office of War Information Collection; LC-USF34-072187-D.

5.9   Russell Lee, Casa Grande Valley Farms, wife of a member, May 1940. Library of Congress Prints and Photographs Division, Farm Security Administration—Office of War Information Collection; LC-USF34-036367-D.

5.10 Russell Lee, Chandler Farms, trench silo, May 1940. Library of Congress Prints and Photographs Division, Farm Security Administration—Office of War Information Collection; LC-USF34-036176-D.

5.11 Russell Lee, Chandler Farms, apartment house, May 1940. Library of Congress Prints and Photographs Division, Farm Security Administration—Office of War Information Collection; LC-USF34-036094-D.

5.12 Russell Lee, Bisbee, May 1940. Library of Congress Prints and Photographs Division, Farm Security Administration—Office of War Information Collection; LC-USF34-036370-D.

5.13 Russell Lee, Sacramento Pit, Bisbee, May 1940. Library of Congress Prints and Photographs Division, Farm Security Administration—Office of War Information Collection; LC-USF34-036441-D.

5.14 Russell Lee, Home of a merchant, Concho, September 1940. Library of Congress Prints and Photographs Division, Farm Security Administration—Office of War Information Collection; LC-USF34-037799-D.

5.15 Russell Lee, Members of the last remaining Mormon family, Concho, October 1940. Library of Congress Prints and Photographs Division, Farm Security Administration—Office of War Information Collection; LC-USF34-037948-D.

5.16 Russell Lee, Taliesin, May 1940. Library of Congress Prints and Photographs Division, Farm Security Administration—Office of War Information Collection; LC-USF34-036161-D.

5.17 Russell Lee, WPA work, Safford, May 1940. Library of Congress Prints and Photographs Division, Farm Security Administration—Office of War Information Collection; LC-USF34-036417-D.

5.18 Russell Lee, Madonna of the Trail, Springerville, April 1940. Library of Congress Prints and Photographs Division, Farm Security Administration-Office of War Information Collection; LC-USF34-035965-D.

5.19 Russell Lee, Marriage mill, Salome, February 1942. Library of Congress Prints and Photographs Division, Farm Security Administration—Office of War Information Collection; LC-USF33-013244-M1.

5.20 Dorothea Lange, Highway 87 near Coolidge, migratory cotton picker, November 1940. National Archives and Records Administration, Bureau of Agricultural Economics; 83-G-44211.

5.21 Dorothea Lange, Cortaro Farms, Pinal County, November 1940. National Archives and Records Administration, Bureau of Agricultural Economics; 83-G-44337.

5.22 Dorothea Lange, Truckload of cotton pickers, Pinal County, November 1940. National Archives and Records Administration, Bureau of Agricultural Economics; 83-G-44093.

5.23 Dorothea Lange, Cotton picker, Maricopa County, November 1940. National Archives and Records Administration, Bureau of Agricultural Economics; 83-G-41840.

5.24 Dorothea Lange, *Migratory Cotton Picker, Eloy, Arizona*, 1940, gelatin silver print. Virginia Museum of Fine Arts, Richmond, acc. no. 89.28, photo no. 46975; © The Dorothea Lange Collection, Oakland Museum of California, City of Oakland; gift of Paul S. Taylor.

5.25 Dorothea Lange, on Highway 87, Chandler, November 1940. National Archives and Records Administration, Bureau of Agricultural Economics; 83-G-44358.

5.26 Dorothea Lange, near Coolidge, young girl, November 1940. National Archives and Records Administration, Bureau of Agricultural Economics; 83-G-44368.

5.27 Dorothea Lange, Children in a democracy, Pinal County, November 1940. National Archives and Records Administration, Bureau of Agricultural Economics; 83-G-41825.

5.28 Dorothea Lange, Children of drought refugee family, Chandler, May 1937. Library of Congress Prints and Photographs Division, Farm Security Administration—Office of War Information Collection; LC-USF34-016791-C.

5.29 Dorothea Lange, *Zanjero*, Pinal County, November 1940. National Archives and Records Administration, Bureau of Agricultural Economics; 83-G-44021.

5.30. Dorothea Lange, Weighing cotton, Pinal County, November 1940. National Archives and Records Administration, Bureau of Agricultural Economics; 83-G-44334.

5.31 Dorothea Lange, Yaqui Indian cotton picker, Pinal County, November 1940. National Archives and Records Administration, Bureau of Agricultural Economics; 83-G-41832.

5.32 Dorothea Lange, Yaqui Indian *Jacal*, Pinal County, November 1940. National Archives and Records Administration, Bureau of Agricultural Economics; 83-G-44020.

6.1 Russell Lee, Copper smelter, Douglas, May 1940. Library of Congress Prints and Photographs Division, Farm Security Administration—Office of War Information Collection; LC-USF34-036436-D.

6.2 Ansel Adams, Grand Canyon National Park, 1941. National Archives and Records Administration. Department of the Interior, Mural Project; 79-AAF-9.

6.3 Russell Lee, Grand Canyon of the Colorado River, October 1940. Library of Congress Prints and Photographs Division, Farm Security Administration—Office of War Information Collection; LC-USF34-037856-D.

6.4 Ansel Adams, White House Ruins, Canyon de Chelly, 1941. National Archives and Records Administration. Department of the Interior, Mural Project; 79-AAC-1.

6.5 Ansel Adams, Navajo woman and infant, Canyon de Chelly, 1941. National Archives and Records Administration. Department of the Interior, Mural Project; 79-AAK-1.

6.6 Ansel Adams, Walpi, 1941. National Archives and Records Administration. Department of the Interior, Mural Project; 79-AAS-1.

6.7 Russell Lee, Roosevelt Dam, Gila County, May 1940. Library of Congress Prints and Photographs Division, Farm Security Administration-Office of War Information Collection; LC-USF33-012654-M4.

6.8 Ansel Adams, Hoover Dam, 1941. National Archives and Records Administration. Department of the Interior, Mural Project; 79-AAB-6.

6.9 Ben Glaha, Workman with water bag. Library of Congress Prints and Photographs Division Lot 7365, LC-USZ-89645.

6.10 Maynard Dixon, *Tired Men*, 1934, oil on canvas. Private collection, copyright 2009; image courtesy of the Gerald Peters Gallery, Santa Fe, New Mexico.

6.11 Maynard Dixon, *High Scalers*, 1934, oil on board. Special Collections, University of Nevada-Reno Library.

6.12 William Gropper, *Construction of the Dam*, 1938–39. Smithsonian American Art Museum, Washington, D.C; transfer from the U.S. Department of the Interior, National Park Service, 1965.18.11A-C.

7.1 Jack Delano, Train load of military tanks, March 1943. Library of Congress Prints and Photographs Division, Farm Security Administration—Office of War Information Collection; LC-USW3-021355-E.

7.2 Jack Delano, Young Indian laborer, Winslow, March 1943. Library of Congress Prints and Photographs Division, Farm Security Administration—Office of War Information Collection; LC-USW3-021222-E.

7.3 Fritz Henle, Open-pit copper mine, Phelps Dodge Mining Corporation, Morenci, December 1942. Library of Congress Prints and Photographs Division, Farm Security Administration—Office of War Information Collection; LC-USW3-027813-E.

7.4 Fritz Henle, Electric shovel, open-pit copper mine, Morenci, December 1942. Library of Congress Prints and Photographs Division, Farm Security Administration—Office of War Information Collection; LC-USW3-027777-E.

7.5 Fritz Henle, Phelps Dodge Mining Corporation workers, Morenci, December 1942. Library of Congress Prints and Photographs Division, Farm Security Administration—Office of War Information Collection; LC-USW3- 027819-E.

7.6 Russell Lee, Morenci copper mine mill. Library of Congress Prints and Photographs Division, Farm Security Administration—Office of War Information Collection; LC-USF34-036489-D.

7.7 Toyo Miyatake, *Garden of Native Cactus*, Gila River, c. 1944–45. Courtesy of the Toyo Miyatake Studio, San Gabriel, Calif.

7.8 Isamu Noguchi, Plans for Poston Cemetery, blueprint, 1942. © 2008, The Isamu Noguchi Foundation and Garden Museum, New York/Artists Rights Society [ARS], New York.

7.9   Lew Davis, *The Founding of Fort Huachuca,* 1943, oil on board. Fort Huachuca Museum, U.S. Department of the Army, Sierra Vista.

7.10 Lew Davis, *The Negro in America's Wars,* 1944, oil on board. Howard University Gallery of Art, Washington, D.C.

7.11 Art Workshop, Fort Huachuca. Fort Huachuca Museum, U.S. Department of the Army, Sierra Vista.

7.12 Lew Davis, *History Will Judge Us by Our Deeds*, 1943, silkscreen poster. Courtesy of the Arizona Historical Society/Tempe.

8.1   Dorothea Lange, Saturday afternoon, Eloy, November 1940. National Archives and Records Administration. Bureau of Agricultural Economics; 83-G-41855.

8.2   Fritz Henle, Guard, Phelps Dodge copper mine, Morenci. December 1942. Library of Congress Prints and Photographs Division, Farm Security Administration—Office of War Information Collection; LC-USW3-027775-E.

8.3   Russell Lee, A member of the Chandler Farms FSA with his wife and child. Library of Congress Prints and Photographs Division, Farm Security Administration—Office of War Information Collection; LC-USF34-36075-D.

INDEX

The Aborigine (Megargee), 44–45

Adams, Ansel, 6, 7, 21, 71, 110, 111–117, 119–120, 124, 125, 126, 127, 138, 139, 163 n1, 163 n8; photographs by: Canyon de Chelly, 115, 116; Grand Canyon, 113; Hoover Dam, 119; Walpi, 117 *Born Free and Equal*, 138

African Americans, 2, 7, 106, 143–148, 163 n62, 166 n44, 166 n48

Agriculture (Megargee), ii, iv, 45–46

Agua Fria Farm Security Administration Camp, 74–78

airplane travel, 14–15

Albuquerque, 20

American Economic Life (Tugwell), 71

An American Exodus (Lange and Taylor), 95

American Guide series, 33

American Institute of Architects, 37

Apache, 58, 60, 62, 64–65, 66, 143

Apache Chiefs Geronimo and Vittorio (Kittredge), 62, 64–65

Apache Scouts (Davis), 143

Apache Junction, 18–19

Arizona, 17

Arizona: A State Guide, 4, 14, 18, 32, 33–35, 38, 43, 84, 85, 91, 96, 109–110, 119, 122–123, 133–134, 154, 159 n67

Arizona art history, 157 n21, 163 n1

Arizona Artists' Guild, 22

Arizona Civilian Defense Coordinating Council, 138

Arizona Defense News, 138

Arizona Department of Library and Archives, 5, 66–67

Arizona Farm Labor Service, 96–97

Arizona Highway Commission, 13

Arizona Highways, 13–15, 31, 32, 33, 116, 156 n9

Arizona Logging (Kittredge), 65

Arizona Museum of History (now the Phoenix Museum of History), 22

Arizona Pageant of Progress (Datus), 66–67

Arizona Republican, 11

Arizona State Capitol, 5, 16, 66–67

Arizona State Fair, 21

Arizona, state symbols of, 4–5, 14–19, 33, 35, 42, 51, 52, 66–67, 152, 153–154

Arizona State Teachers College, 5, 42–44, 62–63; B.B. Moeur Activity Building, 62–63. *See also* Joseph Morgan Henninger, Emry Kopta, John Porter Leeper, Sim Bruce Richards

Arizona State University. *See* Arizona State Teachers College

Army, 143–148

Asian Americans. *See* Japanese Americans

Atchison, Topeka, and Santa Fe Railway, 14, 21, 130, 131–132, 156 n11

Austin, Charles Percy, 16–17

automobile travel, 13–14, 33

Baumgartner, Creston, 26, 28

Baxter, 83, 84

B.B. Moeur Activity Building, 62–63

Beauty behind Barbed Wire (Eaton), 139, 165 n22

Bermingham, Peter, 31

Berninghaus, Oscar, 5, 49, 52–53, 56; murals by: *Communication during the Period of Exploration*, 52–53, 56; *Pioneer Communication*, 53, 56

Biddle, Francis, 143

Bimson, Walter, 24

Bisbee, 5, 45, 47–48, 72, 84, 85, 110, 133, 135

Black, Laverne Nelson, 5, 49, 52, 54–55, 57, 160 n17; murals by: *Historical Background*, 55, 57; *The Progress of the Pioneer*, 55, 57

borders, 8, 12

Borg, Carl Oscar, 26

Born Free and Equal (Adams), 138

Boulder City, 120

Boulder Dam. *See* Hoover Dam

branding irons, 37

Bright Angel Lodge, 13

Bristol, Horace, 162 n16

Buffalo Bill Cody's Wild West shows, 16

Bureau of Agricultural Economics, 5, 6, 12, 92–108, 149

Bureau of Indian Affairs (BIA), 4, 7, 67, 140–141, 142

Bureau of Reclamation, 4, 6, 7, 96, 118, 119, 120, 164 n20

Burton Cairns General Hospital, 77, 79

cacti, 18–19

Cahill, Holger, 26, 29

California (culture compared with Arizona's), 20–21, 24, 94

California Impressionism, 21

Camelback Farms (Glendale, Baxter, Phoenix Homesteads), 72, 80, 83–84

Cameron, 114

Candelaria, Juan, 87

Canyon de Chelly, 68, 111, 114–115, 116

Carlson, Raymond, 14, 31–32

Casa Grande, 137

Casa Grande Valley Farms, 11, 72, 80, 82, 162 n19

Century of Progress International Exposition (Chicago), 16–17

Chandler, 101, 104

Chandler Farms, 72, 80, 82–83, 150, 152

The Chasm of the Colorado (Moran), 6

Cherokee, 49, 161 n42

Chicana/os. *See* Hispanic

child labor, 100, 102–103

Children in a Democracy, 103

children's art, 27

Chinle, 114

Civilian Exclusion Order (Executive Order 9066), 137

Civil Works Administration, 4, 5, 38, 68

Cochise, 143

Cochise County Courthouse, 45, 47–48

Coconino County, 65

Collier, John, 67, 116, 140, 141, 143

Colorado River, 8, 119, 120, 130

Colorado River Relocation Center (Poston), 137, 140–143, 165 n21

Colter, Mary Jane, 13, 20, 156 n11

Colton, Harold, 22

Colton, Mary-Russell Ferrell, 22

Communication during the Period of Exploration (Berninghaus), 52–53, 56

Coolidge, 95, 102

Concho, 2, 72, 85–87

Construction of the Dam (Gropper), 122, 124–125

copper mining, 12, 16, 29, 33, 45, 47–48, 72, 84–86, 96, 109–110, 132–137, 149–150, 162 n35

Cortaro Farms (Pinal County), 97, 106, 107

Cory, Kate, 39, 164 n20

cotton, 12, 96–102

Courbet, Gustave, 99

cowboy, 16, 32, 34–35

Cowboy (Santee), 32

Curtis, Edward S., 92, 116

Curtis, Philip C., 4, 25–29, 31, 48, 157 n11

A Dash for the Timber (Remington), 17

Datus, Jay, 5, 66–67; mural by: *Arizona Pageant of Progress*, 66–67

Daughters of the American Revolution, 89

Davis, Lew, 7, 20, 22, 26, 28, 29, 30, 50–55, 143–148, 158 n36, 166 n44; murals by: *Apache Scouts*, 143; *The Founding of Fort Huachuca*, 143, 144; *The Negro in America's Wars*, 144–145; Phoenix Post Office competition entry, 52–55; *The Surrender of Geronimo*, 143, 146; painting by: *Underground*, 30; poster by: *History Will Judge Us by Our Deeds*, 146–147

Death Valley, 114

Delano, Jack, 7, 128–132, 164 n4; photographs by: Train load of military tanks on the Atchison, Topeka, and Santa Fe Railway, 131; Young Indian laborer working at the Atchison, Topeka, and Santa Fe Railway yard, Winslow, 132

Department of the Interior, 6, 7, 37, 67, 70, 111–117, 119, 122, 126, 140, 163 n10

Desert Mining Community (Richards), 49

Desert View Watch Tower (Colter), 13

Dixon, Maynard, 6, 20, 26, 92, 93, 120, 122–123, 164 n21; paintings by: *High Scalers*, 122–123; *Tired Men*, 120, 122

documentary photography, 2, 71–108, 125–127, 138

Douglas, 84, 110

Dows, Olin, 41

dude ranches, 13, 33, 35

Dunn, Dorothy, 20, 68

Eaton, Allen, 139, 141, 165 n22

Eleven Mile Corner FSA Camp, 77, 79

Eloy, 96, 100, 103, 105, 149, 150

El Paso, 137

Evans, Jessie Benton, 26

Evans, Walker, 126

Farm Security Administration (FSA), 1, 2, 3, 4, 5, 6, 7, 11, 12, 71–91, 93, 95, 106, 108, 109, 110, 112, 113, 116, 118, 125, 126, 128, 129, 130, 135, 138, 146, 155 n2, 155–156 n4

Federal Art Center (Phoenix), 4, 21–22, 23–31, 37, 48, 62; Arizona Artists, 158 n35

Federal Art Center (Raleigh, North Carolina), 25

Federal Art Project (FAP), 23–31, 36, 41, 129, 152; Arizona artists, 158 n35; craft project, 159 n74

Federal Emergency Relief Administration (FERA), 29

Federal Music Project, 4, 39–40, 159 n81

Federal Theatre Project, 39

Federal Writers' Project, 4, 24, 31–35, 138, 158 n52

Flagstaff, 2, 5, 22, 62, 65, 131

Flagstaff Post Office, 5, 62, 65. *See also* Robert Kittredge

Flute Ceremony, 43–44

Fogel, Seymour, 5, 58–61, 64, 160 n18; mural by: *History of the Gila Valley*, 60–61; Safford Post Office competition entry, 59

Ford, John, 17, 77, 162 n16

"The Forgotten Man" (Dixon), 93

Fort Huachuca, 2, 7, 143–148, 166 n44, 166 n48. *See also* Lew Davis, Archibald J. Motley, Jr., Elizabeth Olds, Dox Thrash, Charles White, and Hale Woodruff

Fort Lowell, 38

Fortune Magazine, 132, 163 n1

48 States Competition, 5, 58–61; f.64 group, 120, 127

The Founding of Fort Huachuca (Davis), 143, 144

Fred Harvey Company, 14, 20, 156 n11

Ganado, 43

Geronimo, 59, 62, 64–65, 143, 146

Gila County, 118

Gila River Relocation Center, 137, 139, 140

Gilpin, Laura, 116

Glaha, Ben, 6, 120–121, 122, 124, 164 n19

Glendale, 83, 84

Globe, 31, 32, 84, 109

Goldwater, Barry, 116

golf, 73–74

Graham, Martha, 62–63, 160 n36

Graham County Chamber of Commerce, 59

Grand Canyon, 6, 8, 13, 14, 21, 34–35, 41, 111, 113–114, 127

The Grand Canyon of the Yellowstone (Moran), 6

Grand Coulee Dam, 122

The Grapes of Wrath (Steinbeck), 77, 94, 162 n16, 162 n46

Grey, Zane, 17

Gropper, William, 6, 122–125, 164 n26; mural by: *Construction of the Dam*, 122, 124–125

Guggenheim Foundation, 122, 143, 163 n1

Hall, Dick Wick, 91

Hall, Sharlot, 38

Halseth, Odd, 24

Harlem Dancers (Olds), 148

Hayden, Carl T., 30, 49–50, 60, 158 n44

Hayden, F.V., 6

Heard, Dwight, 22

Heard, Maie, 22, 25, 26, 157 n18

Heard Museum, 22, 36

Henle, Fritz, 7, 128, 132–137, 149, 151, 165 n14; photographs by: Morenci, 133, 134, 135, 151

Henninger, Joseph Morgan, 42–43, 159 n3; murals by: *Industrial Development in Arizona*, 43; *Spanish Influence in Arizona*, 42–43

High Scalers (Dixon), 122–123

Highway Commission, 13

highways, 13–14

Hine, Lewis, 71

Hispanic, 2, 12, 20, 21, 42, 72, 85–87, 103–106, 163 n59, 163 n60, 155 n1; artists, 155 n1

Historical Background (Black), 55, 57

Historic American Buildings Survey (HABS), 2, 4, 37–38, 159 n77

Historical Section. *See* Farm Security Administration

History and Progress of the Navajo Nation (Nailor), 67–70

History of the Gila Valley (Fogel), 60–61

History Will Judge Us by Our Deeds (Davis), 146–147

Hollywood. *See* movies

Hoover Dam, 6, 8, 14, 15, 111, 114, 117–125, 164 n18, 164 n19, 164 n20. *See also* Ansel Adams, Kate Cory, Maynard Dixon, Ben Glaha, and William Gropper

Hoovervilles, 12

Hopi, 20–21, 43–44, 53, 92, 111, 117, 161 n42

Hopi Flute Player (Kopta), 43–44

Hotel Alvarado (Albuquerque), 20

Hotel Westward Ho (Phoenix), 16, 18–19

Howard University Art Gallery, 148, 166 n48
Hubbell Trading Post (Ganado), 43
Hunt, George W.P., 20, 51

Ickes, Harold, 111, 163 n10
Image of Freedom, 126
Index of American Design (IAD), 4, 36–37, 129,
    159 n70
Indian Arts and Crafts Board, 67
Indian Building, 20
Indian Detours, 20, 59
Indian New Deal, 67, 116, 161 n40, 161 n41,
    161 n42, 161 n43
Indian Reorganization Act, 67
Indian School (Phoenix), 161 n42
Indian School (Santa Fe), 20, 68
Industrial Development in Arizona (Henninger), 43
internment camps, 7, 137–143, 165 n20, 165 n21,
    165 n22
irrigation, 8, 33, 45, 73, 96, 104–105

jacal, 107–108
Jackson, Helen Hunt, 21
Japanese Americans, 2, 7, 12, 132, 137–143, 165 n20,
    165 n21, 165 n22, 165 n24, 165 n32
Jerome, 22
Johnson, Elizabeth, 37

Kabotie, Fred, 161 n42
Kachina Fountain (Kopta), 43–44
Kayenta, 114
Kittredge, Robert, 5, 61, 62, 64–65; sculpture by:
    Apache Chiefs Geronimo and Vittorio, 62,
    64–65; Arizona Logging, 65
Kopta, Emry, 43–44, 160 n6; sculpture by: Hopi
    Flute Player, 43–44; Kachina Fountain,
    43–44

Lange, Dorothea, 1, 5, 6, 8, 10, 12, 71, 72, 77, 80,
    92–108, 120, 126, 127, 134, 138, 139, 149, 150,
    161 n6; photographs by: Chandler, 101,
    104; Coolidge, 95, 102; Cortaro Farms, 97;
    Eloy, 100, 103, 105, 106, 107, 150; Maricopa
    County, 99; Pinal County, 97, 98, 103, 105,
    106, 107; Saint David, 10
Lange, Martin, 120
Latter Day Saints, Church of. See Mormon
Lawrence, Jacob, 145
Lazy B Ranch, 37, 159 n75

Lee, Doris Emrick, 72, 73
Lee, Jean Smith, 73
Lee, Russell, 5, 6, 11, 12, 13, 18–19, 38–39, 47, 71,
    72–91, 92,108, 110, 113–114, 118, 127, 135–136,
    138, 150, 152, 154, 161 n1, 161 n6;
    photographs by: Agua Fria Farm Security
    Administration Camp, 76, 78; Apache
    Junction, 19; Bisbee, 47, 85, 86; Casa Grande
    Valley Farms, 11, 82; Chandler Farms,
    83, 84, 152; Concho, 86, 87; Douglas, 110;
    Eleven Mile Corner, 79; Grand Canyon, 114;
    Maricopa County, 18; Morenci, 136; Phoenix,
    13, 19, 39, 74, 75; Roosevelt Dam, 118; Safford,
    89; Salome, 91; Springerville, 90; Taliesin, 88;
    Tombstone, 38–39; Yuma, 81
Leeper, John Porter, 26, 62–63; mural by:
    Women in Sports and the Arts, 62–63
Leimbach, August, 88–90, 162 n38, 162 n39
Lescher and Mahoney, 48–49, 62
Leupp, 165 n21
Levy, Julien, 111
Library of Congress, 3, 37
The Livelihood and Religious Rites of the Navajo
    Indians (Shirley), 67
Look Magazine, 130
Lorentz, Pare, 162 n44
Los Angeles, 21, 29, 43, 62, 138, 140

Madonna of the Trail, 88–90, 162 n38, 162 n39
Man Ray, 142
Manifest Destiny, 6, 89, 124
Manzanar, 137, 138, 139
Maricopa County, 18, 74, 99
marriage mills, 91
Marx, Leo, 124
Mayer, 165 n21
Mayers, Murray, and Phillip, 67
Megargee, Lon, ii, iv, 16–17, 20, 41, 43, 44–46,
    49–51, 156 n13; murals by: Phoenix Post
    Office competition entry, 50–51; paintings
    by: The Aborigine, 44–45; Agriculture, ii, iv,
    45–46; A Spanish Padre, 45
Men and Horses (Santee), 32
Merritt, Ralph P., 139
Mesa, 16
Mesa Verde National Park, 114
Mexican. See Hispanic
Mexican Americans. See Hispanic
Mexico City, 27

Miami, 110

Migrant Mother (Lange), 71

Migration of the Negro (Lawrence), 145

migratory labor, 6, 8, 10, 71–108, 149, 163 n59

Millet, Jean-François, 99

Miner (Sanderson), 48

Miners' Monument (Sanderson), 45, 47–48

Mission Revival, 20, 21

Miyatake, Toyo, 7, 138–140, 141, 142, 165 n24;
    photograph by: Garden of Native Cactus,
    Gila River, 140

Moe, Henry Allen, 143

Monument Valley, 17, 114

Moran, Thomas, 6, 156 n6, 156 n14; paintings by:
    The Grand Canyon of the Yellowstone, 6;
    The Chasm of the Colorado, 6

Morenci, 133–137, 149–151

Mormon, 16, 58–59, 72, 87

Motley, Archibald, J., Jr., 146, 148, 166 n48

movies, 16, 17, 18, 21, 32, 35, 55, 77

Mural Project (Adams), 7, 111–117, 119–120

murals, 2, 3, 4–5, 41–70, 111, 146

Museum of Fine Arts (Santa Fe), 20

Museum of Modern Art, 28, 83, 111, 126

Museum of Northern Arizona (Flagstaff), 22

Nailor, Gerald, 5, 67–70, 161 n42, 161 n43; mural
    by: *History and Progress of the Navajo
    Nation*, 67–70

National Park Service, 7, 37, 112

National Youth Administration, 79, 129

Native Americans, 2, 12, 14, 16, 18–19, 20–21,
    33, 34–35, 36, 38–39, 42, 43–45, 49, 50–51,
    52–56, 58–61, 62, 64 65, 66, 67–70, 92,
    93, 96, 106–108, 111, 114, 116–117, 131–132,
    137, 143–144, 161 n40, 161 n41, 161 n42, 161
    n43; Apache, 58, 60, 62, 64–65, 66, 143;
    Cherokee, 49, 161 n2; Hopi, 20–21, 43–44,
    53, 92, 111, 117, 161 n42; Navajo, 5, 20, 43,
    67–70, 92, 111, 116–117, 131–132, 161 n43;
    Yaqui, 12, 106–108

Navajo, 5, 20, 43, 67–70, 92, 111, 116–117, 131–132,
    161 n43

Navajo Nation Council Chamber, 5, 67–70, 161n
    43

The Negro in America's Wars (Davis), 144–145

Nevada, 8, 119, 120

New, Lloyd Kiva, 161 n42

New Deal art, 155 n3

New Mexico (culture compared with Arizona's),
    20–21, 24, 58–60, 157 n20

Newhall, Beaumont, 114, 126

Newhall, Nancy, 114

Noguchi, Isamu, 7, 140–143, 165 n32; works by:
    Plans for Poston Cemetery, 142

Norton, Louise, 28

O'Connor, Sandra Day, 37, 159 n75

Office of Indian Affairs. *See* Bureau of Indian
    Affairs Office of War Information (OWI),
    2, 3, 4, 7, 71, 109, 116, 128–137, 149, 164 n2

Old Tucson, 17

Olds, Elizabeth, 148

Oraibi, 161 n42

O'Sullivan, Timothy, 114

Painted Desert, 14

Parker, 137

Payne, Edgar, 26

Pearl Harbor, 128, 137, 140

The Petrified Forest (Sherwood), 11

Phelps Dodge Mining Corporation, 72, 85, 133,
    135, 137, 151, 162 n35

Phoenix, 4, 5, 11, 12, 13, 16, 18–19, 21–22, 24, 25–30,
    39, 42, 43, 45, 48–57, 66–67, 73–74, 83, 84

Phoenix College, 29–31, 62

Phoenix Fine Arts Association, 22, 25–26

Phoenix Homesteads, 83

Phoenix Post Office, 5, 48–57, 62. *See also* Oscar
    Berninghaus, Laverne Nelson Black, Lew
    Davis, Lon Megargee

photo-murals, 111, 163 n9

Pinal County, 11, 97, 98, 103, 105, 106, 107

Pioneer Communication (Berninghaus), 53, 56

The Plough That Broke the Plains (Lorenz),
    162 n44

Post Office murals, 4, 5, 48–65, 156 n5

Poston. *See* Colorado River Relocation Center

Powell, John Wesley, 6

Powell, Lawrence Clark, 14

Prescott, 38, 39

Progress of the American Negro (White), 148

The Progress of the Pioneer (Black), 55, 57

propaganda, 126, 128–129, 164 n2

public health, 77, 79, 100, 162 n17

Public Works Administration, 39, 66, 67, 74

Public Works of Art Project (PWAP), 5, 23, 39,
    41–48, 93, 120

railroad, 2, 14, 109, 129–132. *See also* Atchison, Topeka, and Santa Fe Railway
Ramona (Jackson), 21
Reclamation Act, 118
Remington, Frederic, 16–17, 156 n14
Resettlement Administration (RA), 71, 73, 93, 94
Richards, Sim Bruce, 28, 49, 62–63, 160 n9, 160 n36, 160 n37; Phoenix Post Office competition entry: *Desert Mining Community*, 49; mural by: modern dance, 62–63
Riis, Jacob, 71
Rivera, Diego, 58, 73
Roosevelt, Franklin Delano, 1, 12, 30, 33, 41, 71, 137, 151
Roosevelt Dam, 51, 118
Rothstein, Arthur, 8, 9, 10, 130; photograph by: Arizona-New Mexico state line, 9
Route 66, 8, 94
Rowan, Edward B., 50, 59–60

Sacramento Pit, 85–86
Safford, 5, 58–61, 64, 70, 88–89, 143
Safford Post Office, 5, 58–61, 70. *See also* Seymour Fogel
Saguaro National Monument, 111
Saint David, 10
Salome, 89, 91
Salome Sun, 91
San Xavier del Bac, 2, 16, 38, 42
Sanderson, Raymond Phillips, 22, 26, 28, 45, 47–48, 160 n7; sculpture by: *Miner*, 48; *Miners' Monument*, 45, 47–48
Santa Fe, 20, 24
Santa Fe Railway. *See* Atchison, Topeka, and Santa Fe Railway
Santee, Ross, 4, 24, 31–35, 158 n51, 159 n69; books by: *Cowboy*, 32; *Men and Horses*, 32
Scottsdale, 87–88
Sedona, 62
Shahn, Ben, 73
Sharlot Hall Museum, 38
Sheeler, Charles, 163 n1
Sheep industry, 85, 87
Sheets, Millard, 26
Sherwood, Robert Emmet, 11
Shirley, Charles K., 67, 68; sculpture by: *The Livelihood and Religious Rites of the Navajo Indians*, 67
shooting scripts, 165 n10

Sierra Club, 6
Sierra Vista, 143–148
Smoki Museum, 38–39
Smoki People, 38–39
Snow, Milton ("Jack"), 68–69
Social Security Building (Washington, D.C.), 61
Sonnichsen, Charles Leland, 12
Spanish. *See* Hispanic
Spanish colonial era, 16, 20, 38, 42–43, 45, 48–49, 50, 52–53, 60, 66, 68
Spanish Influence in Arizona (Henninger), 42–43
A Spanish Padre (Megargee), 45
Springerville, 5, 62, 64–65, 70, 88–90, 162 n38, 162 n39
Springerville Post Office, 5, 62, 64–65. *See also* Robert Kittredge
Stagecoach, 17
Stegner, Wallace, 126
Steinbeck, John, 94, 162 n16, 162 n46
Stieglitz, Alfred, 126
Strand, Paul, 129
Stryker, Roy, 71, 73, 83, 88, 93, 106, 127, 128, 130, 161 n2
Sun City, 77
The Surrender of Geronimo (Davis), 143, 146
Swing, David Carrick, 29–31, 62

Taliesin, 49, 72, 87–88
Taos, 20, 24, 52, 54
Taos Society of Artists, 20
Tate, Homer, 88–89
Taylor, Paul Schuster, 93, 94, 95
Taylor Grazing Act, 2
Tempe. *See* Arizona State Teachers College
Tenney, Burdell, 26, 28
Thrash, Dox, 148
Tired Men (Dixon), 120, 122
Tombstone, 38–39
tourism, 6, 8, 10, 12–14, 16, 20–21, 33, 35, 38, 67, 72, 84, 88, 94, 106, 156 n11
Treasury Department of Painting and Sculpture (later the Section of Fine Arts), 41, 50
Treasury Relief Art Project (TRAP), 29
trench silo, 82–83
Tsinnajinnie, Andy van, 68
Tuba City, 92
Tucson, 1, 11, 12, 16, 17, 20, 22, 23, 24, 38, 39
Tucson Fine Arts Association, 22, 24
Tugwell, Rexford, 71

tungsten mining, 132
Tuzigoot, 38

Underground (Davis), 29–30, 51
United Producers' and Consumers' Cooperative
     (Phoenix), 74–75
United States Capitol, 6
University of Arizona, 23
U.S.S. Arizona, 128

Valley National Bank, 24
Valley of the Sun, 13
Vittorio, 62, 64–65
Voris, Mark H., 23–26, 30, 31, 152–153
Vroman, Adam Clark, 116

Walpi, 111, 114, 117
War Relocation Authority, 4, 7, 137–143
Watkins, H.P., 59
Wayne, John, 17
Webb, Del, 77, 153
westerns. *See* movies
Weston, Edward, 126, 127, 162 n36, 163 n1
Wheeler Expedition, 114
White, Charles, 148
White House Ruins, Canyon de Chelly, 114–115

Wilson, Fred, 16
Wilson, Kathleen, 26, 28
Winslow, 132
Window Rock, 5, 67–70, 161 n42
Women in Sports and the Arts (Leeper), 62–63
Women's Club of Phoenix, 21
Woodruff, Hale, 148
Works Progress Administration/Work Projects
     Administration (WPA), 3, 23, 27, 29, 31, 41,
     48, 62, 88, 111, 152
World War II, 1, 2, 7, 14, 40, 74, 77, 124, 128–148,
     150–151, 153
The WPA Guide to 1930s Arizona. See *Arizona:
     A State Guide*
Wright, Frank Lloyd, 26, 49, 62, 72, 87–88, 143
Writers' Project. *See* Federal Writers' Project

Yaqui, 12, 106–108
Yellowstone National Park, 6
Yosemite National Park, 6, 112
Yuma, 79–81, 91

zanjero, 104–105, 163 n60
Zion National Park, 114
Zorro, 21

ABOUT THE AUTHOR

Betsy Fahlman is a professor of art history at Arizona State University. A special-ist in American art of the first half of the twentieth century, her broad research interests include American modernism, women, industrial archeology, and the art history of Arizona. She received her MA and PhD degrees from the University of Delaware and has taught at ASU since 1988. She is the author of *The Cowboy's Dream: The Mythic Life and Art of Lon Megargee* (2002), a book about Arizona's original cowboy artist. She has published widely in the field, and major works include *Chimneys and Towers: Charles Demuth's Late Paintings of Lancaster* (2007), *James Graham & Sons: A Century and a Half in the Art Business* (2007), *Guy Pène du Bois: Painter of Modern Life* (2004), and *John Ferguson Weir: The Labor of Art* (1997).